The Art and Science of **Aging Well**

A

Physician's Guide
to a Healthy Body,
Mind, and Spirit

THE ART AND SCIENCE OF Aging Well

Mark E. Williams, M.D.

SPEAKING
TIGER
ACADEMIC

SPEAKING TIGER PUBLISHING PVT. LTD.
4381/4 Ansari Road, Daryaganj
New Delhi 110002
India
www.speakingtigerbooks.com

First South Asia Edition Published by Speaking Tiger 2016

This edition is published solely for distribution in South Asia by arrangement with the University of North Carolina Press, Chapel Hill, North Carolina, 27514 USA
www.uncpress.unc.edu

ISBN: 978-93-86050-78-6

To my wife, Jane,

and our sons, John

and James

Contents

Illustrations

"Begin at the beginning," the King said, very gravely,
"and go on till you come to the end: then stop."
— Lewis Carroll, *Alice's Adventures in Wonderland*

You only live once, but if you do it right, once is enough.
— Mae West

Preface

We are often led to believe that aging is something that simply happens. You might lose your memory, or you might stay sharp. You might remain strong, or you might wither and weaken. You might enjoy yourself, or you might be miserable. But while many things are indeed beyond our control in life, the truth is that we have considerable choice in determining the quality of our own old age.

My aim in writing this book is to offer a more accurate, realistic, and helpful portrait of human aging than what you have likely encountered in the mass media, in the workplace, in our broader culture, and perhaps in your own inner thoughts and fears. What we are up against is ageism—the mistaken belief that all old people are the same and that they are falling apart. Buying into this destructive myth causes personal, social, economic, and health care tragedies. The relentless focus on preserving our youth devalues the personal and social significance of old age and robs us of many of the diverse pleasures that aging can bring.

This book does not advocate for a certain type of old age, and it does not propose a "new norm" of aging. Rather, it endeavors to provide practical and philosophical insights that I hope will help you face down ageism, find opportunities for personal growth, and approach your own aging with optimism and perhaps even joy. Through observations of the diversity of experiences that come with aging, this book celebrates our intrinsic value as human beings—a value that does not diminish with the passage of time.

I came to write this book because I have seen way too many people shortchange themselves of the old age they deserve. For nearly four decades I have been a practicing physician in the field of geriatrics, the care of elderly people—indeed, I am part of one of the first cohorts of American doctors formally trained in that medical specialty when it emerged in the late 1970s. My patients, who average eighty-three years of age, come to me for help and guidance as they navigate the physical and emotional changes that accompany growing old. I have had the privilege of knowing many inspiring older people who take life by the horns, continuing to work, play, create, and smile until their last days. But I have also seen far too many people—misinformed about aging and about the incredible opportunities around them—limiting themselves unnecessarily simply because of their age. This needless loss of human potential and productivity is staggering. I conceived of this book as an effort to help more people overcome society's biases and enjoy full, productive lives—all the way to the very end.

Before we begin, curious readers may want to get to know me a bit better. I grew up in the rural South in a very small hometown community where people spoke to each other on the street and sat on the front porch or took long walks after supper. As a child I pored over the perception puzzles in my favorite magazine, *Highlights for Children*, and voraciously consumed the entire canon of Arthur Conan Doyle's Sherlock Holmes stories. I discovered at a young age the enchantment of performing magic, a hobby I have continued to foster to this day. Looking back, I realize that throughout my childhood passions ran a common thread: a fascination with mystery and the distinction between how things appear to be and how they actually are.

I found myself dwelling in this appearance-versus-reality distinction again when I gained a liberal arts education and then went on to pursue medical training. As a young medical student I began to feel an uneasiness, that something was not quite right. The mid-1970s had seen major scientific and medical advances with great promise to relieve human suffering, but the application of this knowledge was often ineffective, especially in the treatment of elderly people. I saw far too many instances where old people were not being treated as people.

A two-year stint as a Robert Wood Johnson Clinical Scholar crystallized my sense of social responsibility and solidified my resolve to improve medical care for older people. My research interest focused on understanding the epidemiology of dependency: Why did some people go into nursing homes while others with similar diseases did not? Is there a subset of skills we all need to maintain our independence? I created an original testing protocol that timed individuals as they performed twenty-seven simple manual tasks chosen to reflect the skills we need to live independently. For example, subjects would use a teaspoon to transfer dried kidney beans from one bowl to another to simulate eating. Other tasks involved opening various locks and latches. To summarize over twenty years of my research life, the total time it takes an individual to perform these basic tasks is intimately associated with that person's future need for nursing home care. Individuals who take an excessive amount of time are at high risk to enter long-term care, whereas those who are quick and efficient are at low risk regardless of the diseases on their medical problem list.

After beginning that research adventure I decided—with the full support of my loving wife, to whom I am eternally grateful—to pursue a career in geriatric medicine. I thus became one of the first physicians in America to receive formal fellowship training in this area. At the time the decision was a bold one, and more than once I heard instructors, colleagues, and friends questioning my judgment. "What is a person like you going to do in geriatric medicine?" Interestingly, several of my most vocal skeptics have since migrated into geriatrics careers.

Within a decade I was offered the best job in the country: developing the geriatric medicine program at my alma mater, the University of North Carolina. Another extraordinary stroke of good fortune placed my new office adjacent to Dr. Mack Lipkin Sr., one of the giants of clinical medicine who had retired to North Carolina to continue his teaching and writing. We established a close friendship, shared clinical perspectives, and had many conversations and tuna fish sandwiches. I was stunned when Dr. Lipkin asked me to be his personal physician. Our relationship deepened, and I was honored to share the personal insights and perceptions of a wise, sensible, and articulate physician. Over time I came to know the aging process intimately by witnessing it in Dr. Lipkin, in my hundreds of other geriatric patients, and in myself.

The years since have been busy and productive. As I grow personally and professionally, I learn a great deal from my patients. My dedication to improving the care of older people has expanded beyond my teaching responsibilities and active medical practice, and the idea began to coalesce for a multimedia approach to provide a comprehensive look at growing old. The chief components are this book and eventually a major documentary video series.

The five secrets presented here represent my personal and professional experiences that have been informed and enriched by a variety of sources over the decades. Because I am primarily a clinician, much of the material in this book comes from my clinical experience. You will also find it heavily sprinkled with insights from other branches of human knowledge, as well as my own personal reflections. One cannot separate the mind from the body, and in looking at aging I find biology, psychology, history, culture, and spirituality to be intricately interwoven.

This book is not meant to be the last word on aging. It is a personal view with all my biases, blind spots, and limitations, and it will not surprise me if others do not always share my opinions. There are many ways to accomplish the goal of aging well, and there are numerous books on aging and health. I am reminded of the ancient parable of men examining an elephant in a dark room. Each man felt a part of the elephant and came away convinced that he had real knowledge of the beast. One man felt the legs and concluded that an elephant was like a column; another felt the ears and was convinced that the elephant was like a broad leaf, and so on. Those who heard the men were befuddled by the diversity of descriptions and the passionate conviction of each observer. Ultimately what was needed was to turn on the lights and view the elephant directly, rather than attempt to reconcile the disparate points of view. I hope this book can provide at least a little illumination to help you face directly the mysterious elephant that is human aging.

This book is not conceived to show you how to stop or reverse the aging process. It does not promise eternal youth or advocate antiaging strategies. Rather, it presents various perspectives on how our minds, bodies, and emotions change with the passage of time and offers some concrete actions each of us can take to lead healthier and happier lives. The perspective of biological change looks at our systems from a scientific point of view to unravel how (and sometimes why) aging changes our bodies and brains over time. An equally important perspective is how we interpret and deal with these changes and what adaptive strategies best ensure our success. At the heart of this book is a sincere desire to help you develop the perspective and tools to remain happy, productive, and creative despite the inevitable changes we all face.

For the first time in human history, most of us can expect to live well into our eighties. Because human longevity has increased so rapidly—the average life expectancy at birth has nearly doubled over the past one hundred years!—most of our experiences and beliefs about aging and elderly people are far out-of-date. We are literally living in the past. Counter to many of the stereotypes and assumptions that have persisted from these earlier days, it is clear now that there is considerable interplay between our biological aging, our specific life circumstances, our attitudes and beliefs, and the lifestyle choices that we make. Ultimately, each of us is the beneficiary of our investments in aging well, and to a large extent we will reap what we have sown. Who among us does not deserve to harvest the very best?

This book has been a selfish pleasure for me to write, and my hope is that it will stimulate your thinking about aging and health. The more complete our understanding of aging, the better prepared we will be to address the daily challenges inherent with growing older. We each have two eyes that do not see the same things in exactly the same way; it is because of each eye's slightly different perspective that our brains can perceive depth. By presenting a point of view on aging that may be slightly different from yours, I hope that we can together create a greater depth of perception on aging and the end of life. In the words of Robert Browning (1812–89), in the first verse of his poem "Rabbi Ben Ezra":

> Grow old along with me!
> The best is yet to be,
> The last of life, for which the first was made:
> Our times are in His hand
> Who saith "A whole I planned,
> Youth shows but half; trust God: see all, nor be afraid!"

At times our own light goes out and is rekindled by a spark from another person. Each of us has cause to think with deep gratitude of those who have lighted the flame within us.
— Albert Schweitzer

Piglet noticed that even though he had a Very Small Heart, it could hold a rather large amount of Gratitude.
— A. A. Milne, *Winnie-the-Pooh*

Acknowledgments

Although this book is attributed to a single author, it is really a gift from a number of individuals. My thanks to them is hardly adequate. My perspective has been shaped by interacting with elderly people and their families; sharing principles of aging and geriatric medicine with medical students, medical residents, and colleagues; reading and rereading books and scientific articles; giving oral and written presentations to local, regional, national, and international audiences; and reflecting on my own aging with friends and family.

Special thanks must go to the late Idries Shah, whose books opened my awareness to our inner and outer worlds. His profound inspiration is reflected throughout this book. I also must acknowledge the significant influence of Simone de Beauvoir and her monumental work *The Coming of Age.* On rereading various versions of my manuscript I realized how much her thinking and scholarship have affected my perspectives and attitudes on aging. Many of her original themes and observations are woven throughout this book.

An anonymous gentleman from my hometown deserves very special mention for his advice to me in my mid-teens when he told me to wake up, not to aim too low, and to always strive to use whatever potential I had to the greatest extent. To an insecure adolescent boy that unsolicited guidance had a profound positive effect and was one of the first conscious shocks that I remember.

I especially wish to acknowledge Nortin Hadler, M.D., my brilliant mentor and my first internal medicine attending physician when I was an inexperienced third-year medical student. He had a lot to do with my choice of geriatric medicine as a career. Without his guidance my life course would have been profoundly different.

I also thank the late T. Franklin Williams, M.D., my geriatric fellowship director and friend who devoted time and attention to show me firsthand the ways of the skilled and experienced geriatrician. His humane values and compassionate perceptions have had a considerable influence on my approach to aging and elderly patients. My first clinical experience with him was seeing a homeless elderly man in the geriatric clinic. Before starting the interview Dr. Williams asked him if he was hungry. The man said that he had not eaten in days. Frank immediately left the clinic and bought a hot meal, which the man devoured. Only after he was finished did the clinical evaluation continue. With Dr. Williams's assistance and support, I was able to attend a three-week seminar in Salzburg, Austria, in 1983 that addressed issues of aging, health, and productivity. The seminar with thirty-two international leaders of aging was led by Dr. Robert Butler, founding director of the National Institute on Aging of the National Institutes of Health; Dr. James Birren, a pioneer in gerontology; Dr. Alvar Svanborg, gerontology adviser to the World Health Organization and a leader in Swedish geriatric medicine; and Dr. Betty Friedan, cofounder of the National Organization for Women. This was another life-changing experience for me, filled with many powerful insights.

Dr. Nancy Connelly, a colleague at the UNC Program on Aging, deserves recognition for helping me in the late 1980s to formulate the section on death and dying for a possible documentary film series.

I owe special debts of gratitude to Jane Williams, Windy Forch, Carolyn Engelhard, and Drs. Kerr White and Edward Weissman, who read and endured early versions of the manuscript and encouraged me with numerous helpful suggestions. I especially thank Mary Patricia Marshall, my ninety-three-year-old reader, for her discerning edits. I also acknowledge the extremely perceptive copyediting of Trish Watson. Her skillful attention to the manuscript improved both technical accuracy and literary continuity.

Anne Frances Johnson deserves special mention for her brilliant editing, provocative questions, and thoughtful suggestions. Her insightful perspective clarified and streamlined the flow of ideas.

Finally, this book would not be possible without the enthusiastic encouragement of my wife, Jane, and my sons, John and James. Their love and support form the core of my personal and professional life.

Prologue A Parable and a Framework for Aging Well

There is an ancient Sufi parable of the horse, carriage, driver, and master. Their trip represents not a leisurely excursion but the journey to fulfill one's destiny. In the ideal circumstance the master is making steady progress toward the goal in a well-maintained carriage being driven by an experienced driver and pulled by a strong, well-trained horse. In reality, however, it too often happens that the driver is drunk in a public bar, having abandoned his responsibilities. Rejecting the idea that he is a servant of a higher master, he wastes his time, money, and energy and neglects the horse and carriage. As a result, the horse is untrained, starving, and weak. The carriage has fallen into disrepair. The master, knowing his carriage is unfit for travel, is stuck where he stands.

This parable is a powerful allegory of the need to balance and maintain the mind, body, and emotions in order to complete our personal journeys. The carriage symbolizes our physical body, with its instinctive, sensory, and motor components; the horse represents our emotions, with our energies, feelings, fears, and desires; the driver signifies our intellect, with its ability to observe, think, compare, and concentrate. The master is our soul, the essence of who we really are. Only when everything is in balance and in good working order can we find and pursue our personal destiny.

The neglectful driver's state of drunkenness illustrates our self-deception through illusions, daydreams, fantasies, indulgences, and frustrations. With an intellect fed only by our sensory inputs, our past suffering, our prior conditioning, and a mechanical reaction to daily events, we fall prey to the seductive illusion that we are in control of ourselves and our destiny when in fact we are stuck inside the metaphorical tavern. In this state we fail to realize that outside we have a body that we need to maintain and emotions that we need to manage. As a result, our mind, body, and emotions are not even close to having a harmonious relationship with one another, and we waste precious time, energy, and potential.

To break free of this cycle, we must first appreciate our reality: the driver must wake up and see his state for what it is. Aging secret 1 reflects this step. Whatever our condition throughout life, coming face to face with the fact that we are growing old often provides an attention-getting shock and the sudden realization that, with limited time on this Earth, now is the time to get out of the tavern and on the road to fulfill our destiny. It is our intellect that must leave the comfort of habit and begin to rebuild our body and manage our emotions. Trying to restore balance by starting with the horse or the carriage will not work because our bodies and emotions react to stimuli and cannot accomplish meaningful activity on their own. Having faced the truth of his state, the driver realizes he must learn how to repair and maintain the carriage by challenging his body and revive the horse by nurturing and disciplining his emotional self. He also realizes that he has some work to do on himself by becoming a more informed, skilled, humane, and humble driver. Aging secrets 2, 3, and 4 address this process of self-examination and proper maintenance of our physical, mental, and emotional health.

Once the preliminary work has been done, the driver realizes that each of the parts needs renewed interconnection. The horse must be carefully harnessed to the carriage and fitted with a bridle and reins. When everything is in its proper order, the driver can take the reins, mount the carriage, and go on some short practice rides to await the master's directions. Only then will the master appear and occupy the carriage. The driver must be patient, alert, and receptive to the master's guidance before they can proceed on their journey. This is the essence of aging secret 5.

For me, this parable is an apt reflection of the crossroads that aging represents. Although many of us do not live to our full potential at every stage of life, we can—with proper preparation, care, and maintenance—have considerable control over our aging. An awakening begins when we recognize that at a fundamental level there is more to life than the mechanical struggles to maximize comfort or pleasure and to minimize pain or distress. Realizing that we can objectively observe our personal situation, we can then begin to take corrective action. Perseverance, the triumph of willpower, becomes vital as we establish and maintain a more positive and realistic approach to our aging. According to a Buddhist saying, "If we are facing in the right direction, all we have to do is keep on walking."

How can we know if we are facing in the right direction or making progress? One way is to keep our failures from causing self-pity. Robert F. Kennedy said in his 1966 Day of Affirmation address, "Only those who dare to fail greatly can ever achieve greatly." *Real* effort and *real* action are needed, not half-hearted action and effort. None of the secrets for aging well will work without continuing effort. There are no shortcuts. The basketball player who fails to practice and casually tosses the ball toward the basket is not likely to score. The gardener must dig, remove weeds, water, and keep up the process for the entire gardening season in order to enjoy the bounty at season's end.

This work is yours and yours alone. "Always remember that you are absolutely unique. Just like everyone else" (attributed to Margaret Mead). We are each distinctive creatures, and in my experience we only grow more unique as we age. If we are ever to fulfill our destiny, it will have to come out of our own experience and perseverance, not those of someone else. By discovering our own deepest sense of living within the time that is given us, we can discover what best cultivates a blossoming of our humanity and dedicate ourselves to that.

The initial work on our intellect, body, and emotions is very different from the work of restoring an appropriate balance among them. The connections we develop within ourselves are like those bonding the horse, carriage, driver, and master. The harness attaching the horse to the carriage is a firm, direct attachment. The carriage will always follow the horse as our bodies always respond to our emotions. Try to think of an emotion without a corresponding physical feeling or reaction. There are none. The driver communicates with the horse through the reins, a more subtle communication than a harness. The horse must be trained to respond to the reins to move forward, stop, or change direction. The horse cannot appreciate or understand the thoughts of the driver but can respond to guidance from the reins. Finally, the driver must be awake and attentive to the invisible medium of the master's voice and completely loyal to following the master's direction. The journey to fulfill our destiny usually contains unforeseen detours and diversions. The driver cannot say to himself, "Now that the journey has begun I can take over because I think I know where we are going." The driver is obliged to be humble, attentive, and diligent as he executes his responsibilities in service to the master.

Strong patterns of habit tend to keep us in a comfortable state of intoxication. We need to become aware of our habits and the power they have over our consciousness, and we must learn how to reduce their influence on our actions, reactions, and behaviors. An irony is that we really give up nothing of value through this awakening. What we lose is self-deception, fear, and suffering.

By starting to notice how we react to and interact with the outside world, we can begin a process of uncritical self-observation. Through this process we can recognize and modify the habits that keep our intellect drunk in the tavern and develop a new reverence for our intellect, body, and emotions. Our driver may now experience a new level above ground, sitting on the carriage box. We might have flashes of intuition and feel a deeper sense of connectedness with other people and with the world around us. We grow into a better sense of what we need to do and how best to do it. Things then begin to feel more balanced and productive. We have more energy and vitality. This book offers some of the tools to help you move this process forward.

In some versions of the parable the driver must slowly begin the journey while awaiting the guidance of the master. That presence of the master cannot be forced or demanded. Like appreciating a shooting star or finding a sand dollar on the beach, there will be no preamble with warning shots or trumpets to announce the master's presence. We must simply be patient, attentive, and vigilant and know how, where, and when to look and listen. With diligent self-observation and careful maintenance of the horse, carriage, and driver, our intuitions deepen, and finally we appreciate the master's presence in the carriage. Only now does the driver realize that the master has always been there, patiently awaiting the opportunity to communicate the appropriate route.

Now is the time to start our journey.

There is no cause for fear. It is imagination, blocking you as a wooden bolt holds the door. Burn that bar.
— Rumi

Don't judge each day by the harvest you reap but by the seeds that you plant.
— Robert Louis Stevenson

Aging Secret 1 Appreciate Your Reality

Most of us spend a large portion of our lives seeing older people as "other." We were all at some point children, so we remember to a certain extent what that was like. As we reach adulthood and journey through middle age, we discover our interests, find an occupation, carve out our niche in the world, and perhaps build a family of our own. Along the way we create identities for ourselves that stem from our roles in the family, workplace, or community. But although we all encounter older people throughout our lives and may have the opportunity to watch loved ones grow into old age, the view of older people as a group different from oneself often remains stubbornly persistent.

The truth is that old age is not some distant place or group of "others" but an integral part of who we are now. The body we reside in today is also our future dwelling place in old age. And at any age we are all people—equally valuable, capable, and worthy. The essence of aging secret 1 is to face the truth that we are likely to grow old and to begin to consider what this means to each of us. In the analogy of the horse, carriage, driver, and master introduced in the prologue to this book, the first step is for the driver to emerge from the tavern and critically examine his own state and that of his horse and carriage. With this examination I hope you will see—perhaps with some relief—that your later years do not have to be marked by deterioration and fear. In many ways, old age can be more a culmination of life than a prelude to death.

Of course, although aging is an intimate, personal process, it does not occur in a vacuum. The larger demographic trends of one's society and the way in which aged people are perceived and treated greatly influence the experience of growing old. Today the United States, in common with other nations, is undergoing a social revolution—one rooted not in a new ideology but in our changing population patterns. For the first time in history, infants in fortunate nations like ours can expect to live well into their eighties. This demographic revolution increases pressure on resources as it also creates further social change and new opportunities for older people. Many of our deep-seated cultural stereotypes do not describe accurately the "new wave" of elderly people or their potential contributions to society. The next few chapters aim to create a more realistic picture of aging by taking a critical look at the roles, understanding, and perceptions of aging and older people in our society today and in the past.

The central conflict of aging is between you today and you in the future. Who are you becoming? How will you look? What will you be able to do physically and mentally? What goals and projects will you pursue? How will you handle crises? The end of life? From the beginning of history people have asked these questions and have searched for ways to approach the later years with grace—productively, creatively, and with satisfaction. Each of us influences the answers to these questions through the choices we make in earlier years. If you avoid premature death, you are ultimately obliged to live in old age whether you develop a satisfactory image of yourself or not. You have a choice in the attitude you take about your own aging—and that attitude will be a critical factor in your success. The first order of business is to appreciate your reality and develop an understanding of what you can expect as you grow old. Then you can examine for yourself the rich potential of your later years.

> **He who loves practice without theory is like the sailor who boards ship without a rudder and compass and never knows where he may cast.**
> **— Leonardo da Vinci**

> **We must be willing to let go of the life we've planned to have the life that is waiting for us.**
> **— E. M. Forster**

Chapter 1 **You'll Probably Grow Old**

For the first time in human history many of us can realistically expect to live into old age. A baby born today in most parts of America, Europe, and the Pacific Rim has a better than 50 percent chance of living beyond the age of eighty. In Monaco, the country with the most impressive longevity, the average life expectancy at birth is over eighty-nine! If you are already eighty you have a 50 percent chance of reaching ninety. To put these startling statistics in context, consider the fact that during the Bronze Age (about 3000 B.C.) the average life expectancy at birth was eighteen. By the days of the Roman Empire it had risen to about thirty-five. In early twentieth-century America it was only forty-seven. This means it took humankind two millennia to increase average life expectancy by twelve years (from thirty-five to forty-seven). In the last one hundred years the average life expectancy at birth has nearly doubled from forty-seven to eighty.

Our increased longevity has dramatic implications at numerous levels—the individual, the family, the community, and society. Between 1900 and 2012 the percentage of Americans over age sixty-five more than tripled, from 4 percent (3.1 million) to over 13 percent (43.1 million). According to census projections, this population will almost double to reach nearly 80 million by 2040. Moreover, these are not idle speculations—all of the people who will be "old" in the year 2040 are alive today!

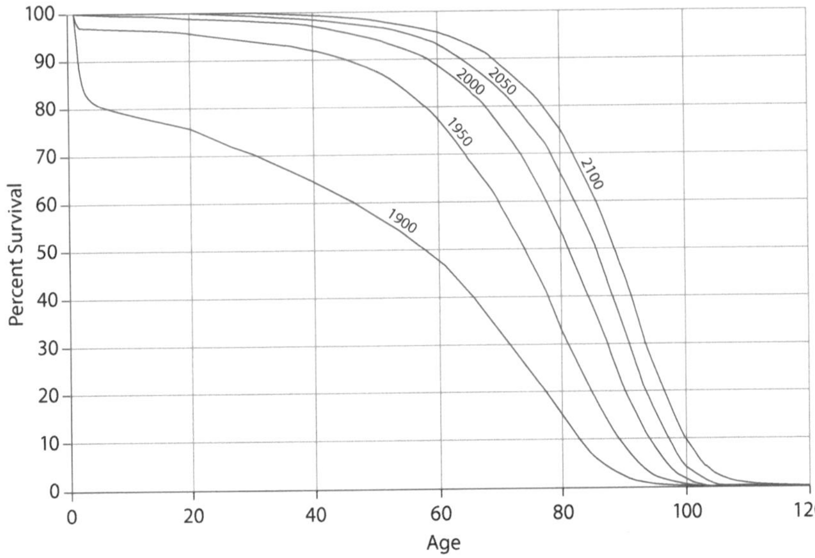

Illustration 1. Estimated survival curves for the U.S. population in 1900, 1950, 2000, 2050, and 2100. These curves show how longevity has increased over the years—a trend that is expected to continue in the future. (Social Security Administration, "Life Tables for the United States Social Security Area 1900–2100," fig. 5, http://www.ssa.gov/oact/NOTES/as120/LifeTables_Body.html)

WHAT DETERMINES LONGEVITY?

Though of course it is impossible to know how long a particular individual will live, we can learn a great deal from studies at the population level. Life course epidemiology is the study of the factors that influence our longevity. Recent research in this field has convincingly shown that the major causes of death—those accounting for about 70 percent of deaths—relate directly to one's environment, such as having clean air and water, a stable supply of healthy food, and a safe place to rest at the end of the day. This observation appears to be consistent across cultures. The other 30 percent of our mortality hazard relates mainly to our genetics and health-adverse behaviors for specific diseases, such as heart disease.

Which environmental factors are associated with longer life-spans, and which may contribute to premature death? One key feature is socioeconomic status and, more specifically, the income gap between the wealthiest and the poorest members of a society, sometimes called the Robin Hood index. Technically, the Robin Hood index is the proportion of money needed to be transferred from the rich to the poor to achieve equality. However, it is not just the difference between the wealthiest and the poorest that seems to matter but how rich or poor you are relative to others in your specific community. This effect may stem from a sense of "social standing" related to job options, possessions, feelings of inadequacy, and a variety of personal and social factors.

Education also clearly plays a role in determining your socioeconomic status and thus also influences longevity. Another critical factor is job satisfaction. If your boss is a tyrant and your work environment is stressful, your longevity is compromised no matter how much money you make. For example, several studies document that being laid off or experiencing loss of job security is associated with earlier death, often from heart disease.

Living with a loving partner extends longevity. Caring for a pet also confers a salutary effect. On the other hand, activities such as smoking can accelerate aging of the skin, heart, lungs, blood vessels, and bone and can cause cancer, resulting in premature death. A great many environmental factors also affect quality of life but do not necessarily affect longevity. For example, excessive noise affects the ears, and ultraviolet light ages the eyes and skin. The following chapters explore the ways we can influence our environment for the benefit of both our longevity and our quality of life.

WHAT DOES "REDUCING YOUR RISK" REALLY MEAN?

In addition to identifying broad associations between life-span and environmental factors, epidemiology can also help us connect specific causes of death with their associated risk factors. The technical term for these studies is "proximate cause epidemiology." Let's take cardiovascular disease (also called heart disease) as an example. As the number one cause of death worldwide, cardiovascular disease has been extensively studied. Its well-recognized risk factors include age, hypertension, diabetes mellitus, high cholesterol, smoking, and family history, among many others. What you may find surprising is that modifying these risk factors (at least those that are under one's control) may reduce a person's likelihood of dying from heart disease, though probably not by very much. More telling, modifying these risk factors has little or no effect on mortality. In other words, we may be able to change the likely cause of our death without meaningfully lengthening our lives. Consider which matters more to you: what your death certificate will ultimately list as your primary cause of death, or the ability to have a meaningful life as long as it lasts.

A lot of risk factor modification is much ado about the trivial. If we carefully examine the mountains of scientific evidence, it becomes clear that the impacts are typically on the order of absolute reductions in deaths of 0.5 to 2 percent. In other words, fifty to two hundred people need to be treated over extended periods of time (a decade or so) to prevent one premature death (that otherwise would not have occurred). Realistically, an intervention such as aggressively treating high blood pressure might reduce an otherwise normal individual's risk of a bad outcome such as a stroke or heart attack from 5 percent to 3 percent, a 2 percent reduction over five to ten years.

It is easy to be confused about risk factor modification by what we read or hear in the media. *Absolute risk reduction*, the difference between our baseline risk and the reduced risk with the intervention, is what really matters. But clinical studies and the media frequently trumpet *relative risk reduction*, which is the percentage your risk has been reduced. In the example above for treating hypertension, the relative risk reduction would be a 40 percent drop in the risk from 5 percent to 3 percent. Which sounds more convincing, "We can reduce your risk of a stroke or heart attack by 40 percent" or "We can lower your *absolute* risk of a stroke or heart attack by 2 percent (or one in fifty)"? These statements are mathematically equivalent.

YOU STILL CAN'T LIVE FOREVER

Despite recent gains in longevity, the death rate has held steady at one per person (it has remained remarkably constant for millennia). Although you are likely to attain old age, living indefinitely is not an option. The implication of our inevitable mortality is that the *nature* of life's journey becomes more important than its length. And the good news is that a wealth of scientific evidence shows that we can significantly influence the quality and possibly the rate of our aging.

The target of modern preventive health care is to extend longevity by reducing premature death, which certainly seems reasonable in very young populations with many decades of remaining life. However, defining "premature death" becomes increasingly problematic the older we become and ultimately misses the point because the death rate is still one per person. It is my view that at some stage of life the target of prevention needs to shift from maximizing longevity to maintaining function and minimizing dependency. As we live longer and better, we should focus on those factors that threaten our independence, such as problems of vision, hearing, mobility, and memory. As a geriatrician I tell my very elderly patients that my goal is to keep each of them smiling and happy for as long as possible. So far, no one has voiced a different objective.

■ WHAT DOES OLD AGE MEAN TODAY?

Old age, once the privilege of the very few, has become the modern destiny for most of us. This is a monumental achievement of the twentieth century that ranks with placing a man on the moon, advances in telecommunication, splitting the atom, and unraveling our DNA. But where is the celebration? No one seems to appreciate the truly historic human accomplishment of unprecedented life expectancy.

Our rapid demographic changes have left most of us living in the past in our generally negative attitudes about aging and elderly people. The same outmoded beliefs are embedded in many of our social programs. In our youth-oriented culture, most of us still view old people as physically decrepit or in rapid and inevitable decline. Mentally they are viewed as forgetful or childish, with little ability to learn and adapt. Socially and economically they often are considered a burden. With such stereotypes, where is the expectation and encouragement for the continuing capacity of elderly people to enrich their own lives and to enrich society?

Chronological age has virtually lost its meaning as a useful index of individual capacity. Today's aging Americans are typically far from decrepit. Less than 25 percent of them experience any significant disability and less than 5 percent are in nursing homes. Intellectually, when they take advantage of new opportunities to learn and grow, they thrive. With suitable occupation they work with zest and competence well beyond the traditional age of retirement. Many have an emotional maturity and the kind of wisdom that come only with age and having experienced life in all of its phases.

To be sure, many old people have special needs for health care and other supports. But these cannot be provided competently without abandoning the old stereotypes and without a broader public understanding of today's elderly population and its relationship to the rest of society. A humane society respects the special character inherent in every stage of life and in every person. We need to take a closer personal look at growing old, and we need to redefine the meaning of later life in our society. This vital redefinition requires public discussion that takes advantage of historical and cross-cultural perspectives, as well as research on aging in the biological and social sciences. This discussion begins with each of us as we face our own aging and consider the future we want to create.

Myths which are believed in tend to become true.
— George Orwell

It is a capital mistake to theorize before one has data.
— Sir Arthur Conan Doyle

Chapter 2 Eight Aging Myths You Don't Have to Fall For

A well-known parable describes a university professor who went on a pilgrimage to visit a famous Zen master. While the master quietly served tea, the professor talked about Zen. The master poured the visitor's cup to the brim, and then kept pouring. The professor watched the overflowing cup until he could no longer restrain himself. "It's overfull! No more will go in!" the professor blurted. "You are like this cup," the master replied. "How can I show you Zen unless you first empty your cup?" In the same way, we need to empty ourselves of myths and misinformation on aging so that we can appreciate the reality of our situation. Let's examine some of the more destructive aging myths so that we can more accurately plan for and embrace the aging process.

■ MYTH 1: ALL OLDER PEOPLE ARE BASICALLY THE SAME, AND THEY ARE FALLING APART

This myth stems from a view of older people as "other" and is reinforced through caricature depictions such as those you might find in television commercials. In reality, as we age we actually become more unique and differentiated, more individualized, and less like one another. None of us ages in exactly the same way, and each of us ages at a different rate. Anyone who has attended a class reunion can verify that some classmates seem to have aged very little over the elapsed time while others seem to have grown considerably older. So we may see one elderly person with bright eyes and sagging muscles and another with creaking joints and an active mind.

The physical changes that accompany aging depend on a cluster of interrelated biological circumstances rather than a single dominant factor. Aging represents interactions among our unique genetic endowment, environmental factors that are largely outside our control, and factors that result from the choices we make. These choices may accelerate or retard the progression of physical change. For example, cigarette smoking appears to speed up aging of the lungs, heart, and blood vessels, in addition to substantially increasing the risk of cancer. Getting regular exercise, on the other hand, can slow the aging process by stimulating the body's ability to repair itself.

On the whole, people today are not only living longer but aging better. Longitudinal studies from the United States, Sweden, and other countries show continued improvements in the health status of people sixty-five and older. The results show, for example, that a seventy-five-year-old person in 1990 was roughly the biological equivalent of a sixty-five-year-old in 1960. Such findings also confirm the remarkable biological diversity and heterogeneity of aging.

■ MYTH 2: LOSING WEIGHT WILL EXTEND YOUR LIFE

Very few of us are satisfied with our weight. We search for the latest miracle diet and see the barrage of weight loss headlines on magazines in the grocery checkout aisle and on the Internet. They tell us we can lose weight and flatten our abdomens or tighten our buns in less than six weeks. Although these messages are often cloaked in health claims, the root of our obsession with weight loss stems more from our perceptions of what society deems beautiful or attractive. In terms of health and longevity, it turns out that having ten or twenty extra pounds can actually be protective. A number of longitudinal studies back this up, including the Framingham Heart Study, the 90+ Study, and the National Health and Nutrition Examination Survey III sponsored by the National Center for Health Statistics of the U.S. Centers for Disease Control and Prevention.

The scientific determination of body heft is a measure called the body mass index (BMI). Adolphe Quetelet devised the BMI, a simple measure derived by dividing body weight in kilograms by the square of the height in meters, in the early nineteenth century as a statistical

Weight	(lb)	125	130	135	140	145	150	155	160	165	170	175	180	185	190	195	200	205	210	215	220	225
	(kg)	56.8	59.1	61.4	63.6	65.9	68.2	70.5	72.7	75.0	77.3	79.5	81.8	84.1	86.4	88.6	90.9	93.2	95.5	97.7	100.0	102.3
Height																						
(in)	(cm)																					
58	147.3	26	27	28	29	30	31	32	34	35	36	37	38	39	40	41	42	43	44	45	46	47
59	149.9	25	26	27	28	29	30	31	32	33	34	35	36	37	38	39	40	41	43	44	45	46
60	152.4	24	25	26	27	28	29	30	31	32	33	34	35	36	37	38	39	40	41	42	43	44
61	154.9	24	25	26	27	27	28	29	30	31	32	33	34	35	36	37	38	39	40	41	42	43
62	157.5	23	24	25	26	27	27	28	29	30	31	32	33	34	35	36	37	38	38	39	40	41
63	160.0	22	23	24	25	26	27	28	28	29	30	31	32	33	34	35	36	36	37	38	39	40
64	162.6	22	22	23	24	25	26	27	28	28	29	30	31	32	33	34	34	35	36	37	38	39
65	165.1	21	22	23	23	24	25	26	27	28	28	29	30	31	32	33	33	34	35	36	37	38
66	167.6	20	21	22	23	23	24	25	26	27	27	28	29	30	31	32	32	33	34	35	36	36
67	170.2	20	20	21	22	23	24	24	25	26	27	27	28	29	30	31	31	32	33	34	35	35
68	172.7	19	20	21	21	22	23	24	24	25	26	27	27	28	29	30	30	31	32	33	34	34
69	175.3	18	19	20	21	21	22	23	24	24	25	26	27	27	28	29	30	30	31	32	33	33
70	177.8	18	19	19	20	21	22	22	23	24	24	25	26	27	27	28	29	29	30	31	32	32
71	180.3	17	18	19	20	20	21	22	22	23	24	24	25	26	27	27	28	29	29	30	31	31
72	182.9	17	18	18	19	20	20	21	22	22	23	24	24	25	26	27	27	28	29	29	30	31
73	185.4	17	17	18	19	19	20	20	21	22	22	23	24	24	25	26	26	27	28	28	29	30
74	188.0	16	17	17	18	19	19	20	21	21	22	23	23	24	24	25	26	26	27	28	28	29
75	190.5	16	16	17	18	18	19	19	20	21	21	22	23	23	24	24	25	26	26	27	28	28
76	193.0	15	16	16	17	18	18	19	20	20	21	21	22	23	23	24	24	25	26	26	27	27

Illustration 2. Chart to calculate body mass index from height and weight. (Adapted from National Institutes of Health, http://www.nhlbi.nih.gov/health/educational/lose_wt/BMI/bmi_tbl.htm)

measure to compare body weight across populations. Underweight is defined as a BMI under 18.5, and obesity is a BMI over 30. Morbid obesity is a BMI over 40.

The relationship between BMI and mortality is essentially a shallow U-shape, as shown in illustration 3. Persons on the extremes of body weight have much higher mortality rates than those in the middle, where the curve is almost flat. Morbid obesity (BMI over forty) is a life-limiting condition. The epidemic of childhood obesity is of concern because it indicates inactivity and increases the likelihood of developing some chronic diseases, which both shortens life-span and decreases quality of life. The higher death rates at the extreme low end of the weight curve are likely explained by serious illnesses, such as malignancy (either diagnosed or undiagnosed), or eating disorders, such as anorexia nervosa.

The middle ranges of the curve reveal some interesting nuances. Numerous studies from around the world consistently show that individuals thinner than normal have higher mortality rates than moderately obese individuals even when the studies control for underlying

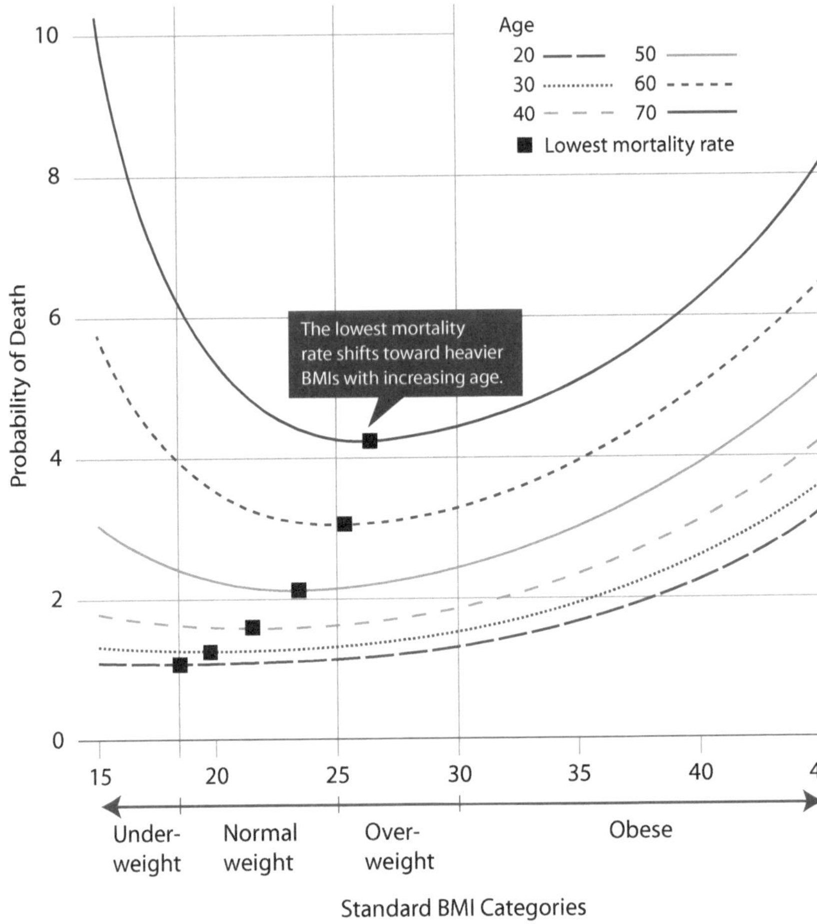

Illustration 3. Standardized mortality by body mass index and age. (Reprinted by permission from Macmillan Publishers Ltd.: *Nature* 497 [May 23, 2013]: 428–30)

illness, smoking, and other factors. In addition, those who are slightly (10 to 15 percent) overweight are less likely to have osteoporosis, which contributes to the risk of hip fractures. Risk for lung cancer also may be reduced for this group. Researchers from the U.S. Centers for Disease Control and Prevention concluded in 2005 that body weight may not be a risk factor for coronary artery disease except at the highest weights. These data are consistent with a number of large epidemiological studies that have not found a connection between obesity and heart disease.

In addition, the act of losing weight can actually reduce your longevity. In one study of fifty- to seventy-year-old Americans, those who had lost weight within the last two years were more likely to die than those who had not lost weight. The trend was consistent among normal-weight, overweight, and obese people. Another study showed that people whose weight had dropped by 15 percent or more at any point during their lifetime had an increased risk of death compared with people in the same BMI category who had not lost weight (or had lost less than 5 percent of their maximum body weight). This increase is due primarily to heart disease and means that in a very real sense dieting may be hazardous to your health. As a geriatrician I worry when one of my patients starts to lose weight, and I make every effort to try to reverse that trend while looking for an illness that is not otherwise manifest.

The major exceptions to my "don't worry about dieting" mantra are individuals on the steep side of the "U" with a BMI over thirty-five, who may benefit from modest weight loss. I also recommend weight loss for those with significant obesity who also have diabetes mellitus, hypertension, or painful osteoarthritis of the hips or knees. In these conditions losing 5 to 10 percent of body weight can often significantly reduce the number of medications needed to control the diseases and, in the case of osteoarthritis, can improve function and reduce pain.

It seems paradoxical that we appear to be having an obesity epidemic in the midst of a period of historically unprecedented longevity. This raises an interesting question: Who determines what an ideal body weight is? Is it based on science or social desires? After all, the lusty, full-figured bodies of women painted by Peter Paul Rubens, the Flemish baroque painter of the seventeenth century, seem to border on morbid obesity by modern standards. Why should we base our self-image on today's thin, lean, muscular, tanned stereotypes of Madison Avenue and Hollywood glamour models? As far as I am concerned, as long as you stay away from the arms of the "U" you are fine.

■ MYTH 3: WE BECOME MORE FORGETFUL AND SENILE AS WE AGE

Sir Thomas Beecham (1879–1961), British conductor and founder of both the London Philharmonic Orchestra and the Royal Philharmonic Orchestra, once saw a stately lady in the lobby of a Manchester hotel. He could not quite remember where he had seen her but did remember that she had a famous brother. He tried to finesse the situation by asking her how her brother was doing and if he was still employed. The woman replied, "He is doing well and is still King."

Each of us has concerns about our memory, and these concerns seem to increase as we get older. We buy into the classical (and modern) stereotype of an old person as someone who becomes progressively more forgetful and childish. What makes things worse is that as we age, our contemporary society seems less forgiving of mistakes. We internalize those social values, and if we forget where we placed our car keys, a process of self-doubt begins: "Is this the beginning of Alzheimer's disease?" To me a law of the universe is that we attract what we fear, so our preoccupations can distract us to the point that we forget something else: "Now what did I come in here to get?" A vicious circle can develop.

Most minor forgetfulness is completely normal and inconsequential. Well over half of individuals over eighty-five have completely normal cognitive function. This is not to trivialize the devastating effects of such dementing illnesses as Alzheimer's disease. The key point is that such conditions are *diseases* that affect memory and other cognitive domains. They do not represent normal aging. Furthermore, they may be preventable or forestalled with active mental activity earlier in life.

Consider a remarkable scientific study known as the Nun Study, a fifteen-year longitudinal study of 678 Catholic sisters 75 to 107 years of age who were members of the School Sisters of Notre Dame congregation. Each nun had annual cognitive, physical, and functional evaluations during old age, and postmortem examinations were performed on the participants' brains. Each had written an autobiographical essay in her twenties when taking her vows. These essays provided researchers with linguistic and stylistic information to compare with later cognitive outcomes. Interestingly, the nuns who filled their sentences with more ideas subsequently had much lower rates of Alzheimer's disease than did those with very simple sentence construction. The study was particularly unique because many typical lifestyle factors, such as nutrition, environment, and access to health care, were virtually identical for the nuns. One of the implications of this study is that learning, creativity, and mental activity in youth can likely help reduce your chance of acquiring a dementing illness later in life.

■ MYTH 4: LEARNING AND CREATIVITY DECLINE AS WE AGE (YOU CAN'T TEACH AN OLD DOG NEW TRICKS)

This destructive myth is related to the previous myth of inevitable cognitive decline. One of my patients is a 103-year-old former Foreign Service worker who is writing a book on international diplomacy. For the past five years he has worked on it every morning for a couple of hours, pecking away on his portable Smith Corona manual typewriter. Has aging negatively affected his learning and creativity? If it has, I cannot see it. Except for his advanced age and his perseverance as a writer, he really is not atypical.

Assuming that learning and creativity inevitably decline with aging is not only inaccurate and pessimistic but potentially dangerous. Creative and active projects are crucial to aging well and experiencing a vital longevity. Creativity is the working side of our imagination. It has elements of action, participation, and the use of talent. None of this is limited by normal aging. To be sure, elements of our creativity change over our lives. But these changes are enriching, not eroding. To quote Aristotle's *Nicomachean Ethics*, "Learning is an ornament in prosperity, a refuge in adversity, and a provision in old age."

Psychological health in older age is correlated with lifelong learning. Leonardo da Vinci remarked in his *Notebooks*, "Learning acquired in youth arrests the evil of old age; and if you understand that old age has wisdom for its food, you will so conduct yourself in youth that your old age will not lack for nourishment." The continuation of learning capacity throughout life is strongly influenced by interest, activity, motivation, and health. By cultivating interests when we are young and staying active and productive as we age, we can indeed continue to find enrichment and creative expression in our later years.

■ MYTH 5: AGING IS IMMUTABLE; THERE IS NOTHING WE CAN DO ABOUT IT

Many of us assume that our aging has been hardwired through our genes and that our longevity ultimately depends on how wisely we chose our parents and grandparents. On first glance the evidence seems compelling: identical twins have more concordant life-spans than do fraternal twins, and it is easy to find kindreds with impressive longevity. In fact, researchers have made careers of studying families with strikingly long lives. The challenge is that our genes interact with our activities, our lifestyle, and our environment, and having a genetic predisposition is not the same as having our genes determine our longevity. For example, even if I had a pedigree of extraordinary longevity, I would be foolish to brandish a seven-iron on a golf course in a thunderstorm. Looking more closely at the evidence, it turns out that genes are more important in determining our likelihood of developing certain life-shortening diseases than they are in determining our likelihood of living a long time.

A study of over 13,000 Swedish twins provides compelling evidence that only 30 percent of our longevity could relate to our genes. In fact, the typical longevity difference of the twins was about fifteen years. Thus, 70 percent of our aging is within our control. Moreover, only about half of the cognitive changes observed in the study were related to heredity. In the Nun Study discussed earlier there were two biological sisters who were each over ninety. The mentally active sister had no cognitive impairment, while her less intellectually active younger sister developed dementia. The message of these and other landmark studies of aging and cognitive function is that mental activity sometimes can trump genetic predisposition.

We should be concerned not so much with our genes as with how those genes are expressed—and that, by and large, is determined by our environment and activities throughout life. In some ways your genetic endowment is like a ski lift that gets you safely to the peak of reproductive efficiency. Then it is your choice how to travel down the slope. The journey can be exciting, risky, and short, or it can be well paced and leisurely. Lifestyle choices really do matter. You can let your genetic code mechanically play itself out, or you can take charge to modify some of your genetic software through lifestyle choices. This is good news because it means that your quality of life in old age is largely within your control.

■ MYTH 6: OLDER PEOPLE ARE A SOCIAL AND ECONOMIC BURDEN

This destructive myth is unjust and unwarranted on many levels. Part of the problem is that many of us have an overly narrow view of productivity in terms of the old manufacturing line perspective: as long as we are on the production line, we are contributing to society, but when we step off the line, we become a drain on resources. In an industrial society human value often becomes measured only in terms of immediate productivity and profit.

This mind-set is narrow and baseless. Consider unpaid work, such as volunteering, raising children, caring for an ill relative, or managing a household. Are these activities unproductive and an economic burden on our society, or do these activities not only reduce costs to the larger society but also contribute to societal welfare? As we age, the likelihood increases that we will retire from paid activities. Do we then become a societal burden with no other ways to meaningfully contribute to society? Since we do not keep national statistics on the activities of older people (or others who are not employed in the traditional sense), the numbers we collect and report do not reflect their vital contributions to human productivity. We urgently need to develop broader and more inclusive productivity measures.

Another problem with viewing old people as a burden is that aging involves our future selves. Old people are not a disenfranchised minority; they are ourselves in the future. This fact means that people with negative views of aging and elderly people have sealed their own fate. As Walt Kelly's comic strip character Pogo remarked on Earth Day in 1971, "We have met the enemy and he is us."

Based on our other myths and misperceptions, we erroneously assume that aging will increase our disability and dependency. As a result, we are presupposed to think that increases in life expectancy will disproportionately magnify costs of health care and social support. But where is the evidence for this assumption? Countries such as Japan are aging more rapidly than the United States, and they are not going bankrupt from the increased "graying" of their population. Health care costs depend far more on the mechanisms of care delivery than on the demographics of a population.

Older people are not profligate consumers of health care. To be sure, elderly people take more prescription drugs, see doctors more often, and require more hospitalizations than do younger people. But these factors do not imply that most of our health care expenditures are aimed at the elderly population. Throughout the history of health care a person's last illness has always been the most expensive, regardless of age.

The key point is that aging does not simply draw out the latter stages of dependency and incapacity. Rather, it is that our social systems have not provided adequate opportunities for individual contributions and self-expression.

■ MYTH 7: OLDER PEOPLE ARE NOT INTERESTED IN SEX

Sexual activity does not have to decline with aging. When sexual activity declines, the reason often has less to do with performance capacity than with imagination and expectation. It is true that arousal and stimulation take longer the older we get. Erectile dysfunction does increase in men with advancing age, but not as much as has been widely believed. There is no evidence that aging has any significant negative effects on women's sexual capacity or pleasure.

The evidence from a recent survey of U.S. adults speaks for itself. In the survey, about a quarter of men and a third of women aged eighteen to thirty-one report being very happy with their sex life. That percentage jumps to nearly 50 for those over age sixty-five. Moreover, 50 percent in this group continued to be sexually active, and almost 40 percent wanted to have sex more frequently. Three-quarters of the sexually active men and 70 percent of the sexually active women said they were as satisfied as or more satisfied than when they were in their forties. Perhaps we readjust our expectations, become less inhibited, and feel more relaxed and confident as we age.

Sexual activity is also positively related to longevity. In scientific studies married men live approximately eight years longer than men who never married, and married women live three years longer than women who never married. The difference seems to be related to reduced rates of cardiovascular disease and cancer. In another study men who had more than two orgasms a week were much less likely (nearly 50 percent) to die over the follow-up period than were men having fewer than one orgasm a month. For women sexual satisfaction is positively correlated with longevity. All of this evidence suggests that sexual activity and satisfaction do not have to decline as we age, and the more we enjoy it, the greater the benefits to our health and longevity. Perhaps the real secret is being in a stable and loving relationship.

■ MYTH 8: GROWING OLD MEANS LIVING IN AN INSTITUTION IN A STATE OF DEPENDENCY

The reality is not this pessimistic: no more than 25 percent of people will stay in a nursing home at any time in their lives, including short visits for rehabilitation. In 2012 just 3.5 percent of U.S. seniors lived in nursing homes. Like each of our aging myths, half-truths and misconceptions cloud the reality. In practice older people today live in a great variety of circumstances. Many live independently in their own homes. Some have occasional or full-time help from nurses or other support providers. Some live in group homes with other older adults to share resources and enjoy companionship; others live with their adult children or other younger relatives. Assisted living facilities have rapidly become popular, as have a variety of facilities providing specialized care, for example, for those with dementia.

Our assumptions about how older people live again stem from the misguided tendency to lump all elderly people together and the failure to appreciate older people as a heterogeneous group (myth 1). Subgroups require careful definition and special attention; for example, women, who constitute a large majority of older adults, may have different needs and experiences than men. The "very old-old" (age ninety and beyond) are the fastest-growing subgroup and also have a unique set of needs and experiences. Those who are dependent or disabled are an important subgroup but are not the majority of elderly people. Honest exploration of old age must also acknowledge a chasm between rich and poor because societal, literary, and historical biases tend to hide this, and it can have a huge impact on a person's options and quality of life.

We all have to confront the fact that we will likely decline physically in some ways as we age. But the degree and impact of these changes are strongly determined by how an individual responds to those changes. Often the changes of the body mean less than the attitude adopted toward these changes. Clearly, the changes that occur affect men and women differently, as women significantly outlive men. But to men aging may not be so physically harsh. White hair and wrinkles do not necessarily conflict with manly ideals. Men seem to have social advantages, while women have biological advantages.

In general, disease limits a person's function more than age does. Aging is a process of growth and not a set of ideas, factors, or changes to which we resign ourselves. If someone is experiencing continued personal growth despite physical changes, is he or she really in decline? It depends on your perspective. Consider a ripple produced by throwing a stone in the water. The height of its wave decreases as the circle expands. Do you identify with the ripple in the water, with its wave decreasing in amplitude over time, or do you identify with the expanding circle of consciousness that takes time to develop?

The charm of history and its enigmatic lesson consist in the fact that, from age to age, nothing changes and yet everything is completely different.

— Aldous Huxley

Now King David was old and stricken in years; and they covered him with clothes, but he gat no heat. Wherefore his servants said unto him, Let there be sought for my lord the king a young virgin: and let her stand before the king, and let her cherish him, and let her lie in thy bosom, that my lord the king may get heat.

— 1 Kings 1:1–2

Chapter 3 Views of Aging through Human History

Interest in aging and the well-being of elderly people is evident throughout recorded history. Although in past centuries the average life expectancy from birth was dramatically shorter, there have always been people who live into old age. This achievement is simply much more common today. Reviewing perspectives on aging from a variety of cultures and times in human history reveals a nearly universal quest for the causes of aging and techniques to live a long and healthy life.

As mentioned in Chapter 1, societal influences profoundly affect our longevity and quality of life. How an individual or society treats older people is inextricably linked with medical knowledge, available technology, religious doctrine, health beliefs, and socioeconomic forces. In earlier times the social standing of individuals reaching old age often depended on their value to the group; their strength, skill, or knowledge; and available resources and religious beliefs. The Khoikhoi (which means "real people"), for example, a hunting and gathering tribe in southwestern Africa, had a tribal council that consisted of the headmen of all the clans. Elders of the various clans played a valuable role by serving as clan representatives to unify the clans and settle disputes among them.

Generally speaking, societies with plentiful resources have tended to treat older people well, but in some cultures when times were difficult older members were neglected or even sacrificed. In some societies, older people have been highly respected and enjoyed strong legal protections as a result of widely held beliefs in an afterlife and in a departed spirit's ability to intervene in the affairs of the living. A quick tour of views of aging in different cultures and times helps us position our current views on aging (and our modern aging myths) within the larger context of how people have dealt with the reality of human aging throughout history.

ANCIENT EGYPT

From the age of the pyramids (around 3000 B.C.) Egyptian society had highly developed family life and religious beliefs in an afterlife. Sons were expected to care for elderly parents, especially the father, and to maintain their tombs. Living to 110 years was considered the reward for a balanced and virtuous life. Aging was associated with illness, and health beliefs centered on cleansing the body with ritual sweating, vomiting, and bowel cleansing. The customary greeting was "How do you sweat?"

The Edwin Smith surgical papyrus, written in 2800–2700 B.C., is one of the oldest existing medical documents. It contains the earliest known written remedy for aging, titled "The Book for Transforming an Old Man into a Youth of Twenty." This book has a recipe for a special ointment and directions for its use: "It is a remover of wrinkles from the head. When the flesh is smeared therewith it becomes a beautifier of the skin, remover of blemishes, of all disfigurements, of all signs of age, of all weaknesses which are in the flesh." In the margin is a note written in informal Coptic script by the scribe drawing the hieroglyphs: "Found effective myriad times."

Illustration 4 shows the image of a bent human figure resting on a staff. This is the Egyptian hieroglyph indicating "old age" or "to grow old." It is the earliest known artistic depiction of an old person. This papyrus tells us unmistakably that since the beginning of recorded history people have tried to minimize or avoid aging because of the diminishment of vitality and strength. The ambivalence regarding growing old is clear and echoes throughout history. We fear growing old. Though it is the alternative of death, to some aging itself is even more threatening.

Another ancient Egyptian medical document, the Ebers Papyrus (ca. 1550 B.C.), contains the earliest known attempt to explain the manifestations of aging. It describes urinary difficulties such as frequent urination and obstruction, cardiac pain, palpitations, deafness,

Illustration 4.
Egyptian hieroglyph for "old age" or "to grow old." (Adapted from the Edwin Smith surgical papyrus, http://oi.uchicago.edu/sites/oi.uchicago.edu/files/uploads/shared/docs/oip4.pdf, page 103, line 9)

eye diseases, and malignancy. To the Egyptians, "debility through senile decay" was caused by "purulency of the heart." This theory that some unknown process affects the heart and causes aging is reflected in other ancient cultures.

■ ANCIENT INDIA

The advanced pre-Aryan culture around 2500–1500 B.C. had public sanitation, wells, and sewers. The Aryan invasion around 1500 B.C. resulted in the decline of this public health infrastructure but established Ayurvedic medicine, which persists to this day. Ayurvedic, meaning "science of life," emphasizes mental and physical hygiene through diet, exercise, meditations, and medications.

Much ancient Indian thought is summarized in the *Sushruta Samhita* (A.D. 400), a medical text written by a surgeon and teacher of Ayurveda. The text deals with surgery, rejuvenation, and prolongation of life, as well as the goal of preparing the spirit for death. In the worldview represented by this text, illness and aging result from disharmony. Diagnosing an illness involves divination and observation. Four types of disease were recognized: trauma, bodily (internal imbalance), mental (excessive emotions), and natural (aging and physical deprivation).

ANCIENT CHINA

Older people in ancient China were generally well respected and treated with reverence. From about 2900 B.C. health was based on Tao, "the way," which focuses on the balance of nature's duality as represented by yin and yang. Following Tao meant living in moderation, equanimity, and proper conduct. The emphasis was on preventing illness through the balance of earth, air, fire, water, and metal by means of specific exercises, diets, and living in accord with the seasons.

The *Yellow Emperor's Classic of Internal Medicine* (200 B.C.) describes illness as imbalance and health and longevity as balance as called for by Tao. Some common treatments to restore balance have persisted into modernity and include acupuncture, herbal remedies, and dietary modification. Some aging processes such as reduced hearing were considered to be diseases. To the ancient Chinese the ideal was for life to end in very old age without sensory or mental impairment.

ANCIENT GREECE

The ancient Greeks generally abhorred aging, as it represented a decline from highly prized youth and vigor. However, older warriors, elder philosophers, and statesmen were typically well treated. Ironically, the Spartans, who valued the physical ideal most, also were those who most respected the wisdom of elderly citizens. In the seventh century B.C. they set up the Gerousia, a counsel of twenty-eight men and two kings who were all over age sixty, to control the city-state and manage community affairs.

In the sixth century, Pythagoras popularized the idea that four elements (earth, fire, air, water) with corresponding qualities (dry, hot, cold, wet) and seasons (autumn, summer, spring, winter) formed the foundation for the four bodily humors: blood, phlegm, yellow bile, and black bile. The essence of the theory was that the four humors were balanced in health, whereas an imbalance would produce a change in temperament or illness. Later, Theophrastus (who succeeded Aristotle in the Peripatetic School of philosophy) linked personality to the humors: those with excess blood were sanguine, those with an abundance of phlegm were phlegmatic, too much yellow bile produced a choleric personality, and those with too much black bile were melancholic.

In about the fourth century B.C. Hippocrates developed a theory of aging, positing that each individual has a finite quantity of innate heat or vital force. Each person uses this force at a unique rate, and the heat can be replenished but not fully to the previous level. Thus, the reserve diminishes until death, and the manifestations of aging are the result of this loss. The loss of innate heat was looked upon not as the result of supernatural influences or a process that can be halted but, rather, as the natural and normal course of things. Hippocrates felt that one must assist nature rather than work against it, and his advice for longevity was moderation and the maintenance of daily activities.

About a century later Aristotle (384–322 B.C.) expounded (in his typically interminable detail) a theory of aging and death in his book *On Youth and Old Age, on Life and Death, and on Respiration.* His theory builds on Hippocrates's view of heat as an essential quality of life. According to Aristotle, everything that lives has a soul, whose seat is in the heart, and cannot exist without natural heat. The soul is combined at birth with innate heat and requires heat to survive in the body. Life consists of maintaining this heat in its relationship to the soul. Aristotle likened the innate heat to a fire, which is maintained and provided with fuel. Just as a fire can run out of fuel or be put out, innate heat also could be extinguished or exhausted. Continuing to produce the heat requires fuel, and as the fuel is used up, the flame diminishes as in old age. A feeble flame is extinguished more easily than the strong flame of youth. Left undisturbed, the flame goes out as the fuel is exhausted, and the person dies of old age.

■ ANCIENT ROME

The ancient Romans were aware of the many lines of thought on aging and death held elsewhere in the world. Cicero (106–43 B.C.) acknowledged in *De Senectute* (*On Old Age*), "As I give thought to the matter, I find four causes for the apparent misery of old age: first, it withdraws us from active accomplishments; second, it renders the body less powerful; third, it deprives us of almost all forms of enjoyment; fourth, it stands not far from death." But he also saw older people as a source of great wisdom and believed that a stable old age was based on a stable youth.

The height of ancient contributions to conceptions of aging and health was reached with Galen, a Roman physician who lived around A.D. 200. In essence Galen reconciled the theory of the four humors (Pythagoras) with the idea of inner heat (Hippocrates and Aristotle), as well as monotheism and notions of the spirit. In Galen's view the body is the instrument of the soul. The soul is maintained in the body by heat, which is in turn derived from the humors. Over the course of life we gradually dehydrate, and the humors evaporate. In youth and midlife this dehydration causes all of our vessels to increase in width, and thus all the parts become strong and attain their maximal power. However, as time progresses and the organs become even drier, we experience a gradual loss of function and vitality. This drying also causes us to become thinner and more wrinkled and our limbs to become weak and unsteady in their movements. This condition of old age is the innate destiny of every mortal creature. When at last the dryness is complete and the humors evaporate, the body's vital heat is extinguished.

Christians, Jews, and Islamic Arabs adopted the philosophical basis of Galen's theory. His grand synthesis, representing the culmination of nearly all previous ideas on aging, and his whole medical system, including his approach to aging, were the authoritative influence on medical thought and practice for more than nineteen centuries.

MEDIEVAL EUROPE

The Middle Ages (A.D. 500–1500) were characterized by a strong emphasis on tradition and dogma, with the care and maintenance of the soul considered paramount to the treatment of bodily ailments. As Islam spread through Arabia, the Near East, Africa, and Spain in the seventh century, classical Greek teachings were assimilated into Islamic culture, and medical thought shared Greek, Islamic, Jewish, and Christian influences. Galen's authority remained unchallenged, and indeed, this view was strengthened by the growth of the Christian church and its stifling influence on intellectual thought and original research. During this period the Christian view espoused the belief that disease was punishment for sins, demonic possession, or the result of witchcraft. As a result, the approved therapeutic methods were prayer, penitence, and the assistance of saints. Since medical cure was considered secondary to care of the soul, the Council of Clermont (1130) forbade monks to practice medicine.

At the same time there was naturally a great deal of interest in how to maintain health in old age. The basic medieval view was that phlegm and melancholy were in excess with aging, so lethargy and depression were common geriatric complaints. The contemporary treatments for this humoric imbalance were talking therapy (especially flattery), wearing bright colors, playing games, and listening to music. Maimonides

(1135–1204), a prominent Galenist physician, rabbi, and philosopher, felt that old people should avoid excess, maintain cleanliness, drink wine, and seek medical care at regular intervals. The influential scholar and friar Roger Bacon (ca. 1214–1294) theorized in his *The Cure of Old Age, and Preservation of Youth* that the human life-span is limited because of original sin in the fall of Adam and Eve from the Garden of Eden. He considered aging to be pathological (like a disease) and posited that medicine could delay but never cure it. Bacon's secrets to longevity were controlled diet, proper rest, exercise, moderation, good hygiene, and inhaling the breath of a young virgin.

■ EUROPEAN EARLY RENAISSANCE

In a departure from the scholasticism of the Middle Ages (which placed a strong emphasis on church tradition and dogma), the European Renaissance brought a renewal of humanism, which focuses on human matters rather than the divine. By the early Renaissance universities had begun to grow and medical schools had been established in Paris, Bologna, Oxford, Montpellier, and Padua. Life expectancy gradually lengthened. As old age became less rare, concerns about aging naturally began to increase.

Gabriele Zerbi (1455–1505) was an Italian physician who wrote *Gerontocomia* (1499), the first book exclusively devoted to geriatrics, the care of elderly people. It contains fifty-seven chapters devoted to slowing old age. Zerbi summarized Galen and Islamic contributions and listed three hundred diseases. He felt that only special study of aging could slow its maladies.

Luigi Cornaro (1464–1566) was a Venetian nobleman who at age thirty-five found himself in poor health from excessive drinking and rebellious living. After a near-death experience at age forty he embarked on a calorie-restricted diet consisting of twelve ounces of food and fourteen ounces of fresh wine per day. He wrote his book *The Sure and Certain Methods of Attaining a Long and Healthful Life* when he was eighty-three. Emphasizing moderation, exercise, and dietary restriction, the book became a classic reference and was published in over one hundred editions (probably helped by the author's impressive longevity). Benjamin Franklin wrote several commentaries on this work.

Physician and mystic Paracelsus (1493–1541) advocated a unique philosophy that each body part has a spirit. He believed that life, like a fire, can be extended but to do so would be unchristian. He compared aging to rust on metal (the chemical process of oxidation) and believed that this progression could be slowed by nutrition, geographical location, and ingestion of mystical substances.

THE AGE OF SCIENCE

As the age of science emerged in the sixteenth century, the demand for experimental verification increased. Advances in chemistry, anatomy, physiology, and pathology in the seventeenth and eighteenth centuries enabled scientists to speak with increasing authority on the problems of aging.

Sir John Floyer (1649–1734), a physician from Lichfield, England, who introduced the pulse rate as a vital sign, wrote the first book in English on geriatrics, *Medicina Gerocomica, or, The Galenic Art of Preserving Old Men's Healths*. Floyer advised moderation and hot or cold baths according to the person's temperament. It was probably just a coincidence that his hometown had several famous hot- and cold-water spas. More than a century later the great French physician Jean-Martin Charcot considered Floyer's book to be the first modern text on geriatrics.

The Industrial Revolution brought a new mechanistic paradigm of human physiology and aging. Erasmus Darwin (1731–1802), also from Lichfield and a grandfather of Charles Darwin, proposed a theory of aging as the result of loss of irritability and decreased response to sensation of the tissues. Benjamin Rush (1745–1813), who was a signer of the Declaration of Independence and is considered the father of psychiatry, wrote *Account of the State of the Body and Mind in Old Age; with Observations of Its Diseases and Their Remedies*. Rush believed that diseases, not aging, were responsible for death and held that aging itself is not a disease.

Optimism flourished with Christoph Hufeland's (1762–1836) popular vitalist tract that spawned a German longevity movement. His view was that the life force is capable of continual renewal and that it can be weakened or strengthened through external conditions or exposures. Augmenting the vital force, fortifying organs, slowing consumption, or perfecting regeneration can thus prolong life. This prolongation was not considered indefinite, however, because the theory posited that aging itself dries the body, diminishes and sours the body's humors, narrows the vessels, and causes the body to accumulate "earthy" material.

LATE EIGHTEENTH AND EARLY NINETEENTH CENTURIES

During this period the study of aging profited from rational scientific methods. Burkhard Seiler (1779–1843) published a book in Germany on the anatomy of old age based on postmortem dissections. Carl Canstatt (1807–50) in Germany and René-Clovis Prus (1793–1850) in France simultaneously published systematic descriptions of the diseases in old age. Jean-Martin Charcot (1825–93) worked at the Salpêtrière Hospital, which housed two thousand to three thousand elderly people. Charcot gave specific lectures on old age that were published in 1867. He stressed the distinction between aging and disease, the individuality of aging, and the importance of longitudinal follow-up.

Then in 1859 Charles Darwin published his seminal work on natural selection, *On the Origin of Species*. The ideas in that work and those that followed suggested that aging, rather than being an inescapable process preordained by God, was a side effect of natural selection—one that possibly could be manipulated.

LATE NINETEENTH AND EARLY TWENTIETH CENTURIES

With Darwin's publications on natural selection, people became convinced that aging had a single cause—and thus, tantalizingly, the possibility of a single cure. The search was on. The beauty of modern research was that theories could be tested and confirmed or discarded. Among the proposed "keys to aging" were degeneration of the sexual glands, poisoning by substances produced within the body (autointoxication), hardening of the arteries, and lowered metabolism. Among the pioneers was Charles-Édouard Brown-Séquard, a neuropathologist who worked out much of the physiology of the spinal cord. In his old age he advocated the self-injection of guinea pig and sheep testicular extracts (there were no lasting results). Elie Metchnikoff (1845–1916) introduced the concept of autointoxication from intestinal bacterial flora and together with Paul Ehrlich (1854–1915) received a Nobel Prize in 1908.

Ignatz Nascher (1863–1929) is considered to be the father of geriatric medicine. An American born in Vienna, Nascher became interested in geriatrics as a medical student. He coined the term "geriatrics," from *geras* ("old age") and *iatrikos* ("relating to the physician"), to provide the old age counterpoint to pediatrics in childhood. He created the medical discipline of geriatrics in 1909, founded the Society of Geriatry in New York in 1912, and published his textbook *Geriatrics* in 1914.

CONCLUSIONS

Historical review provides three broad currents of thought. From antiquity to the sixteenth century we have the personal, perceptive observations of Hippocrates, Cicero, Galen, and Cornaro. From the seventeenth to the nineteenth century we have clinical observations on the unique aspects of illness in old age as described by Charcot and many others. Finally, we have the age of modern science in which age is a standard variable.

As I grow to understand life less and less, I learn to love it more and more.
—Jules Renard

You don't stop laughing when you grow old, you grow old when you stop laughing.
—George Bernard Shaw

Chapter 4 **Why We Age**

As we have seen in our exploration of the ancient and not-so-ancient past, people have long sought to determine the cause of aging and to find cures for its associated ailments. Some ancient theories are startlingly prescient; others now seem preposterous to the point of being comical. Before we delve into current thinking on the matter, I must acknowledge that our worldview today cannot be taken as a settled truth so much as our best guess given what we understand about the way the world works. Science is never "finished," so our understanding of aging continues to evolve.

Old age is the last stage of a lifelong process of biological, intellectual, and spiritual change—in many ways, it is the culmination of life. Understanding, to the best of our ability, why we age helps us face our reality and begin the work of strengthening our body, mind, and spirit for the journey ahead.

Over the past century or so, scientists have focused on the molecular, cellular, organic, and social levels of organization in the search for the mechanisms of aging. No single theory has accounted for the observed phenomena, but each holds some tantalizing clues. Two main lines of thought have emerged. The first is that aging results mainly from changes that are programmed or predetermined in our genetic code. The second is that aging essentially results from the act of living—as we go through life, our bodily processes and external environment cause changes in our genes and the functioning of our cells and tissues. The truth is likely a combination of both genetic and non-genetic factors.

GENETIC PROGRAMMING

There is little doubt that genetic mechanisms have an impact on aging. Different species have widely divergent life-spans. Even different breeds within the same species show clear patterns with regard to longevity, implying that relatively few genes may be involved. Using dogs as an example, Norwich terriers live almost twice as long as Scottish deerhounds.

The idea that genes influence aging is also bolstered by the fact that several very rare genetic conditions seem to produce accelerated manifestations of aging. One group is called progeria and progeroid disorders. The words come from Greek roots that mean premature old age. Affected persons appear normal at birth but rapidly lose hair and develop wrinkled skin, heart disease, poor vision, and skeletal fragility. In late adolescence they look like very old people. The cause is a single mutation in a gene called LMNA that ultimately limits cell division by producing an abnormal protein sometimes called progerin. Some senescent cells can activate progerin, leading to speculation that it plays a role in normal aging.

Another genetic condition that seems to produce accelerated aging is Werner syndrome. Affected persons appear to age rapidly in late adolescence, with premature graying of the hair, cataracts, skin atrophy, premature atherosclerosis, and hair loss. Most patients live into their late forties or early fifties and have a mutation of the WRN gene on chromosome 8. The net effect of mutations to this single gene is to reduce the repair of damaged DNA (more on this later).

Broadly speaking, humans are genetically wired to live at the peak of health until we reach sexual maturity. Then, after the reproductive period, health gradually declines until death. But that applies to our entire body. What of our individual cells? Do they also have a life-span? If we are genetically predetermined to age and die, how might this process work at the cellular level?

In the early twentieth century Nobel laureate Alexis Carrel dominated scientific thinking for decades with his forceful personality and claim that cells were immortal. His proof was a culture of embryonic chick heart cells that continued to be viable for more than twenty years, longer than the life-span of a normal chicken. This phenomenon has also been seen numerous times in human cancer cells, which have been known to survive for decades and continue dividing apparently indefinitely.

The claim that all cells are immortal died in 1965 when Leonard Hayflick proved that normal cells have a limited capacity for dividing (about fifty cell divisions). After they reach this point, cells either die or fall into a period of senescence during which they may remain metabolically active but cannot replicate. Cells appear to keep track of the number of cell divisions using repetitive sequences at the ends of their DNA strands called telomeres that resemble the hard ends of a shoelace. Telomeres appear to have no genetic function except to signal the end of the strand. You can picture them as a string of fifty periods at the end of a sentence. Each time the DNA is copied, the two strands making the double helix do not quite line up. A little snip is removed, shortening the telomere. As the telomere diminishes with each successive replication, the DNA strand eventually reaches a point when the cell can no longer divide.

To complicate this natural diminishing of the telomere, there are ways telomeres can be "artificially" lengthened or shortened. Cancer cells, for example, often have a mechanism that keeps the telomeres long, allowing the tumor to grow indefinitely. One such mechanism is telomerase, an enzyme complex that lengthens telomeres and is activated in approximately 90 percent of tumors. Telomeres also can be shortened by oxidative stress from free radicals (more on this later). In fact, damage by free radicals may be a more powerful determinant of telomere length than the number of cell divisions. Stress may also play a role: the telomeres of individuals who feel chronically stressed have been shown to be only half the length of the telomeres of nonstressed individuals. Inflammation and vitamin D deficiency also may shorten telomeres.

Although we now know that telomere length tells cells how many more times they can divide, what is far less certain is the impact of this process on the overall functioning of the human body. Telomere length has been claimed to be associated with arthritis, dementia, osteoporosis, heart disease, and life-span, but the available evidence does not fully support these assertions. Furthermore, there is no evidence of cell failure in two of the most prolific stem cell factories in the body: the cells that line our gut and those in our bone marrow. There is also no correlation in telomere length and age in individuals thirty-eight to one hundred years old for any blood component. In other words, measuring the telomere length does not allow you to determine a person's chronological age. Moreover, most of the systems that are most obviously affected by aging, such as the nervous system, vision, hearing, muscles, bones, and skin, hardly have any cell divisions at all during the course of life.

So the conclusion one might draw from all of this is that there is likely some genetic component to aging and life-span, and we do understand that telomere length influences the life-span of individual cells. But how genetics and telomere length actually affect human aging in practice is not well understood. Based on current knowledge, trying to influence aging by manipulating telomere length is an uncertain use of time and money.

DNA DAMAGE AND REPAIR

It is quite possible that our DNA plays a role in aging somewhat indirectly in that it suffers damage throughout the course of living, and eventually this damage becomes injurious. A number of elements such as ultraviolet light and oxygen free radicals can damage DNA by changing its sequence—altering, moving, or deleting DNA fragments. In addition, the cellular machinery that reproduces our DNA sometimes makes mistakes. With about 70 million cell replications a day in the human body, it is understandable that random errors would occur in DNA replication. If DNA damage is allowed to accumulate, the genetic machinery can break down, leading to abnormal proteins and other cellular components, which in turn cause our tissues and organs to weaken or malfunction. The DNA inside our cells' mitochondria (the cellular "power plants") is more exposed and thus especially likely to become damaged, resulting in reduced energy production and declines in cellular efficiency and performance. Loss of cellular energy may be an underlying feature of aging and several chronic conditions.

Over time we have evolved many defenses to identify and repair DNA damage. Each person's DNA repair rate can vary among cells, and some genes, such as those that regulate cell growth, are repaired more rapidly than others. DNA repair capability appears to be associated with aging. For example, comparative biologists have discovered that DNA repair capability is directly related to species longevity: the more rapid and efficient the DNA repair, the greater the life-span. On the flip side, genetic mutations that compromise DNA repair have been observed in some families with strong histories of cancer.

As discussed earlier, weakened DNA repair is a feature of diseases that are associated with so-called accelerated aging. In a rare disease called Werner syndrome, for example, a single gene defect interferes with DNA replication, causing telomeres to become vastly shorter than normal. Affected individuals show premature graying of the hair and hair loss, skin atrophy, cataracts, atherosclerosis, cancer, diabetes mellitus, and other changes associated with aging. The fact that this one genetic defect results in so many aging-like changes suggests that impaired DNA repair mechanisms may be responsible for some aspects of aging in healthy individuals as well.

The Balancing Act of Gene p53

One DNA repair gene named p53 exemplifies the balancing act seen in many of our body's processes. This is a key gene that regulates the cell cycle and looks for genetic mutations (errors) that might lead to problems. If an error is detected, p53 initiates the DNA repair process, slowing or stopping the cell cycle to allow time for the repairs to occur, or if the damage is too extensive, it initiates the cell death process (apoptosis). In this way p53 keeps cell reproduction under control and prevents abnormal cells from proliferating. Normally p53 is inactive, but it is always "on call" to respond should problems arise. It plays such a crucial role in protecting our DNA that it has earned the nickname "guardian angel of the genome."

Of course, there is always a flip side. An *overactive* p53 gene can cause problems. In such cases, cellular growth and repair are diminished, cellular injury becomes more likely, stem cells are inhibited, and aging is accelerated. As we age, our stem cells become more vulnerable to oxidative stresses, which make p53 even more of a threat to cell growth and repair. In addition, if p53 *itself* is defective, it fails to effectively control cellular replication and can lead to additional genetic errors. Cancer cells, which have escaped the normal controls on the cell cycle, can be the result. Most human cancers have a defective p53 gene. The irony is that cells that achieve youthful immortality by escaping the normal aging process are malignant.

The Role of Sirtuins

Sirtuins are another type of protein that have been shown to influence aging by regulating cell growth, cell death, and cellular resistance to stress. In experiments using yeasts, stimulating the genes that turn on sirtuin production directly slows the aging of the organism and increases the life-span. Sirtuins are found in almost all higher life forms and are responsible for making sure that damaged DNA is not reproduced and that mutations do not accumulate. They do this by slowing down the packing process so that fewer errors are made when DNA is being replicated. Caloric restriction and heat shock proteins appear to activate sirtuin genes, as does the compound resveratrol, found in red wine, muscadine grapes, blueberries, peanuts, and Japanese knotwood.

FREE RADICALS

An old chemistry joke: Two oxygen atoms are walking along the street when one stops and says, "Oh my goodness, I feel more radical. I think I've lost an electron!" "Are you sure?" asks its companion. "Yes," replies the first oxygen atom, "I'm positive."

In our quest to understand the many contributors to human aging, let's now move away from DNA and the genome to consider other influences that accumulate throughout our lives. These factors, which include both natural bodily processes and external exposures in our environment, can affect many aspects of our biological functions, including our genes and how they are expressed. Our first stop is free radicals.

Every cell in our body needs oxygen to survive. At the same time, some forms of oxygen are toxic to our cells and appear to produce a substantial amount of the cellular injury we associate with aging. How our cells handle the oxygen determines whether it functions as life-sustaining energy or life-threatening damage. Much of our interaction with oxygen occurs inside tiny structures within our cells called mitochondria. Mitochondria act as little power plants, burning oxygen and fats or sugars to produce the energy that keeps our cells ticking. At one stage in this process, mitochondria unite oxygen with two hydrogen atoms to form water. While this chemical process is generally well controlled, sometimes things go awry. An unfortunate occasional side effect is the creation of toxic oxygen "pollutants" called free radicals.

A free radical is a molecule that has lost an electron from one or more of its atoms. Electrons are much more stable in pairs, so an oxygen atom with only one electron (a free radical) will shamelessly steal an electron from any nearby source. This creates another unstable molecule (the one victimized by the original free radical) that then joins avidly with other molecules in a chemical chain reaction called oxidation. Under certain circumstances these oxidative reactions are beneficial to our health. For example, our white blood cells release free radicals to kill pathogenic bacteria. However, if not contained and controlled, free radicals can cause widespread damage to proteins, cell membranes, and DNA.

Our mitochondria are the main locus of free radical production and are therefore the primary sites of oxidative damage. As mitochondria become more damaged, they produce less energy and generate more free radicals, creating a vicious circle. Eventually the damage becomes so extensive that our cells begin to malfunction, which could explain many of the changes associated with aging. Denham Harman, a physician who had worked on petroleum-based free radicals as a research chemist for Shell Oil Company, first proposed the oxygen free radical theory of aging in 1956. Free radicals and the damage they produce have been implicated in aging, malignancy, Alzheimer's disease, Parkinson's disease, schizophrenia, certain muscle diseases, cataracts, deafness, and cardiovascular disease. In addition to those naturally produced by our own bodies, we also encounter free radicals in our environment from the sun, manufacturing pollutants, cigarette smoke, and other sources.

Fortunately, an array of antioxidant chemicals can quench free radicals and minimize their damage. These include beta-carotene and vitamins C and E, as well as cellular enzymes such as superoxide dismutase (SOD), catalase, and glutathione peroxidase. The maximum life-span of a variety of mammals has been directly correlated with their relative production of the antioxidant SOD, which basically converts an oxygen free radical into normal oxygen and water. Mice bred to be unable to produce SOD show a reduced life-span and a greater likelihood of developing malignant diseases such as liver cancer and degenerative conditions such as early cataracts and muscle loss. In humans, mutations in the genes that produce SOD can cause amyotrophic lateral sclerosis (also known as Lou Gehrig's disease). In fruit flies, inserting extra copies of the SOD gene can extend the life-span by 30 percent. Naturally high levels of SOD are evident in long-lived nematodes, and scientists have been able to extend the lives of nematodes even further by adding synthetic antioxidants to their growth medium. On the flip side, studies of worms in which the genetics of aging has been well worked out have not shown any life-extending properties of

SOD. No defense is perfect all of the time, and some free radical damage does inevitably occur, eventually leading to cellular aging and cell death. In humans, it remains unclear whether efforts to counter free radicals, such as eating a diet rich in antioxidants or taking antioxidant supplements, can actually reduce disease and extend life.

■ ADVANCED GLYCATION END PRODUCTS

Advanced glycation end products, with the notable abbreviation AGEs, represent another nongenetic factor implicated in aging. AGEs result when glucose and other sugars in the bloodstream directly bind to blood proteins through a chemical process called glycation. Imagine a series of orderly ropes in parallel representing the body's connective tissue. When sugars bind to blood proteins, they act like bands of twine creating knots and wrinkles in the rope netting. Advanced glycation end products are the product of this cross-linking. Over time, AGEs can accumulate and gum things up, causing damage throughout the body. Glycation and oxidation seem to be interrelated, since free radicals and protein cross-links seem to accelerate each other's formation.

AGEs affect nearly every type of cell and molecule in the body and are considered major factors in aging and age-related chronic diseases, such as atherosclerosis, diabetes mellitus, osteoarthritis, coronary artery disease, and peripheral neuropathy. Cross-linked proteins lose their flexibility and become firmer and thicker. This process may explain some of the physical changes that accompany aging. For example, the connective tissue protein collagen becomes stiff and rigid after binding to glucose, contributing to the formation of cataracts and hardening of the arteries. AGEs may also contribute to some forms of dementia, some types of kidney disease, and the vascular and neurological complications of diabetes mellitus. In fact, the AGE-related complications of diabetes are so closely associated with aging that diabetes is sometimes viewed as a model of accelerated aging.

The higher your blood sugar, the greater the number of AGEs your body will naturally produce. AGEs are also used as food additives to improve flavor and appearance and are found in an array of foods, such as grilled meats, doughnuts, soy sauce, cake, and caramel-colored soft drinks. Some white blood cells called macrophages have special receptors to help the body break down AGEs. The degraded AGEs are then released into the bloodstream and excreted into the urine by the kidneys. However, the AGE breakdown products also are biologically active and can cause additional damage, especially to the kidneys. Kidney damage by AGE breakdown products diminishes the subsequent urinary removal of AGEs, forming a vicious circle, creating more kidney damage. As we age, both macrophage function and kidney function decline further and aggravate the process. A number of compounds are being studied to block AGE formation or to increase the breakdown and elimination of AGEs.

■ HEAT SHOCK PROTEINS

In addition to the accumulation of factors that may accelerate aging, we also must consider declines in factors that may slow aging. The natural decline of heat shock proteins (HSPs) is one such example. All living organisms have HSPs that are produced when cells are exposed to various stresses, such as dehydration, starvation, hypoxia, infection, inflammation, toxins, exercise, or psychological stress. The original name was derived from the observation that fruit flies produced HSPs in response to sublethal exposure to heat. The HSPs then allowed the flies to withstand significantly greater heat exposure.

HSPs have several functions, which center on improving the cell's ability to repair itself. For example, they serve as "chaperone" proteins that help newly manufactured proteins to fold and twist into their proper three-dimensional shape and find their place within the cell. HSPs also serve a housekeeping function in disassembling and recycling old or damaged proteins. HSPs are highly expressed in malignant cells and appear to be essential to the survival of cancer cells. In normal cells, the vigor of the HSP response appears to be age related, with more significant declines in HSP production in older cells than in young cells. HSPs also have important roles in muscle contraction, stress hormone regulation, immune response, and the development of malignancy, further bolstering their connection to aging-related changes.

■ HORMONES

Hormones play a crucial role in many of life's stages, but precisely how hormonal factors might regulate human aging is unknown. The term "hormone" comes from the Greek word for "impetus." Hormones are powerful chemical messengers that regulate the function of various tissues and organs and are engaged in reproduction, growth, repair, metabolism, and immune response. Hormones also modulate the body's circadian rhythms and responses to internal and external stimuli.

We are all familiar with the powerful effects hormones have on our minds and bodies. We can see and feel our bodies change as we enter adolescence from childhood and, later, as we approach the latter stages of life (for example, during menopause in women). Several hormones, like growth hormone, estrogen, testosterone, and melatonin, decline as we age, but how these declines relate to aging is less clear.

Hormones also can promote growth and repair. Hormonal growth factors appear to play a role in the longevity of nematodes: in experiments, scientists have extended nematodes' life-spans through mutations in the pathway that produces the hormone known as insulin-like growth factor. But once again, the roles of such hormones in human aging and longevity are not well understood.

What about Hormone Replacement Therapy?

Some hormones naturally decrease with age. Today, despite decades of research on the topic, hormone replacement therapy has remained an uncertain and controversial approach for counteracting aging-related changes.

Men produce lower levels of testosterone as they age, and the notion of hormone replacement seems attractive. Although men with extremely low levels of testosterone may benefit from replacement to restore the levels into the normal range, there is no convincing evidence that raising testosterone levels in normal older men has any beneficial impact, and some studies show that supplementation could be harmful by increasing the risk of heart disease, stroke, and blood clots.

Another area of uncertainty is estrogen replacement therapy for postmenopausal women. The human ovary is genetically programmed to stop producing fertile eggs at approximately age fifty-five, after which estrogen levels fall dramatically. Initial evidence in the 1970s and 1980s suggested that hormone replacement therapy in women could reduce the risks of heart disease, colon cancer, osteoporosis, and other age-related conditions. However, results in 2002 from the first major randomized placebo-controlled clinical trial, the National Institutes of Health's Women's Health Initiative, showed an *increase* in stroke, dementia, heart disease, blood clots, and breast cancer in women taking estrogen and progesterone compared with women taking a placebo. Estrogen replacement did seem to reduce the risk of skeletal fractures, and short-term estrogen replacement during menopause also seemed to reduce hot flashes and fat redistribution.

These results are confusing and controversial in part because there are many different estrogens. The equine estrogens obtained from pregnant mare urine commonly used in the early hormone replacement therapy studies have biological properties different from those of the natural estrogens made in the human ovary. For example, equine estrogens greatly increase the tendency of the blood to clot compared with human estrogens. Moreover, taking the estrogen by mouth, which allows the liver to process it before it gets into the general circulation, increases the risk of serious blood clots by threefold over receiving estrogen through the skin via a patch, which initially bypasses the liver. Based on the accumulated evidence, we simply do not know if the long-term benefits of human estrogen replacement therapy outweigh the risks.

Some hormone replacement therapies are clearly founded more in hype than in reality, so it is wise to be wary. In 1990 endocrinologist Daniel Rudman reported a study in the *New England Journal of Medicine* of twelve men receiving injections of recombinant human growth hormone (rHGH). In contrast to nine men in the control group, the rHGH group had greater bone density, reduced body fat, and increased lean body mass. The media interpreted these findings as antiaging effects, and a multibillion-dollar industry emerged to supply rHGH to weight trainers and as an "antidote" to aging. More recent studies suggest that the main effect of rHGH in older people may be to increase the water content of muscle and not actually increase muscle strength or aerobic capacity. While some athletes have tried to use rHGH as a way to circumvent rules against performance-enhancing drugs, there is no significant evidence that rHGH improves physical performance. In laboratory animals, growth hormone deficiency is related to longevity, whereas excess tends to shorten life—obviously not the longevity hoped for by supplementation enthusiasts. For people who are not deficient in growth hormone, taking rHGH supplements can promote diabetes, peripheral edema, hypertension, heart failure, joint pain, and carpal tunnel syndrome.

THE BIG PICTURE: HOW AGING FITS INTO EVOLUTION

So far this chapter has dealt with the cellular mechanisms of aging—we age because of genetic factors and changes that occur in our DNA, cells, and bodies over time. Examining the "why" of aging from a broader perspective, eventually one arrives at the factor that addresses a great many "why" questions in biology: evolution.

The earliest speculations on the evolutionary role of aging appeared in papers on natural selection by Alfred Russel Wallace and Charles Darwin in the 1860s. They felt that aging was a species characteristic like the stripes on a zebra, with each species having its own age limit. We now know that aging is not programmed into the genes in the same way as other biological processes, but genetic and other evolutionary forces are certainly at work.

Loss of Evolutionary Pressure

In 1952 Sir Peter Medawar published *An Unsolved Problem of Biology*, which addressed the evolution of aging. In it he developed the insight that evolutionary pressures lose their power as animals age. The implication of his ideas is that adaptations that improve the fitness of the young (those who have yet to reproduce) will be favored even if those adaptations result in harmful effects or even death once individuals are past their reproductive prime. Speaking purely in evolutionary terms, the death of an older member of a population often has little downside in terms of species survival. The evolutionary pressure thus favors the development of genes whose negative effects are postponed until after reproduction, and the influence of natural selection diminishes with age.

The power of evolutionary pressure depends on the demands of the ecological niche. For example, animals that face intense survival pressures from predators might favor evolution of the rapid production of large litters, like rabbits or mice. Conversely, circumstances that relieve evolutionary pressures, such as reduced predation because of habitat, size, speed, or the ability to fly, might allow for a lower reproductive volume and an increase in the value that older members bring to the species (such as by nurturing the young).

Disposable Soma

In 1977 English biologist Tom Kirkwood proposed the "disposable soma" (or disposable body) theory. Rather than emphasizing genetically programmed aging or longevity, this theory focuses on the fact that living requires considerable energy and resources. With finite resources, cells and organisms are caught between spending energy on self-maintenance and reproduction. If the adult mortality rate from predators, infection, accident, or starvation is high, then it makes little sense to use precious resources for DNA repair, antioxidant defense, or protein turnover to produce a long-lasting body. As a result, organisms have evolved so that the amount of energy invested in maintaining the body is sufficient to keep the animal alive long enough to reproduce, but less than that which would be required for it to live indefinitely.

With its focus on energy and resources, the disposable soma theory helps to explain the different life-spans among species. A species with a high extrinsic mortality rate (such as from strong predation pressures) should logically invest less energy in cellular maintenance and more energy in rapidly reproducing. By this theory, members of such species will have shorter life-spans if allowed to age, since their energy investment in body maintenance is minimal. Laboratory data and fieldwork from comparative biology support this theory. Animals with adaptations that reduce extrinsic mortality generally have longer life-spans. This difference has even been observed in different populations within the same species. Steven Austad, a cellular biologist, found that Virginia opossums living on an island where extrinsic mortality was low aged at a slower rate than opossums living on the mainland, where there was significant risk of death by predation. There was no evidence that other environmental factors (for example, parasitism, disease, or decreased food availability) contributed to this difference.

The disposable soma theory has been further bolstered by observations that caloric restriction increases longevity in laboratory animals. It makes sense that caloric restriction would shift the energy normally allocated to growth and reproduction toward repair and maintenance. In the wild, starvation is a continual threat that leads to adaptive responses. In times of scarcity, reproduction would be reduced, since the survival of offspring would be threatened. Instead, energy would be invested in maintaining the body to survive until a time when food was more plentiful and reproductive efficiency would be higher.

Population Dynamics

More recently, evolutionary biologist Joshua Mitteldorf has added a demography theory of aging based on population dynamics. He posits that natural selection at the individual level pushes birthrates inexorably higher until the population's growth rate approaches three times the ecosystem's rate of recovery. At that point chaotic population dynamics unavoidably results. Individual selection cannot address this collective problem. The population extinctions that follow will be as frequent as necessary to overpower individual selection and enforce growth restraint, bringing the system back into a more stable state. The emergence of aging as an adaptation fits well within this framework. Aging would become one of the mechanisms by which a species can take control of its death rate, suppressing violent fluctuations that might otherwise lead to extinctions. Aging, together with reproductive and predatory restraint, would help keep population growth at a more stable rate.

It is a shame for a man to grow old without seeing the beauty and strength of which his body is capable.
— Socrates

My grandmother started walking five miles a day when she was sixty. She's ninety-seven now, and we don't know where the heck she is.
— Ellen DeGeneres

Aging Secret 2 Challenge Your Body

Our bodies are the future dwelling places of our own old age. What will this dwelling look like? How well will it function? What will we be able to do? There are no precise answers, but one truth we all must face is that over time we will irreversibly change. Our height, body composition, skin, hair, muscles, and so forth will each undergo gradual shifts as we grow older, though the physical manifestations of aging are highly individual. Within our analogy of the horse, carriage, driver, and master, challenging the body is maintaining the carriage.

For human beings, motion is life. Our bodies are made to move, and without proper stimulation, energy resources are allocated elsewhere, we become frail, we suffer increasing damage from oxygen free radicals, and we become more susceptible to chronic diseases. By exercising modestly on a regular basis, we can change the rate of our aging on a biochemical level. Regular exercise also can improve mood, boost energy levels, and build self-confidence. And by reducing chronic stress and the biochemical responses to stress, our likelihood of experiencing chronic illness is minimized and delayed.

Physical activity is key, because if we do not exercise, we lose function. The issue is not just getting into shape—we must stay in shape. You are never too old to start an exercise program, and significant health benefits have been documented even for octogenarians. Except at the very end of life, significant physical decline is not an inevitable aspect of aging.

Health and vitality in old age are also strongly influenced by what we eat throughout life and as we age. Numerous diets have been associated with longevity, and there is no single answer to the question of what we should eat. Following a few key dietary guidelines, however, can help us avoid the pitfalls of poor nutrition and continue to derive pleasure and satisfaction from food. Combining exercise with a healthful, balanced diet is one of the key ways in which we can take control over our own aging for an enjoyable and active old age.

There is no difference between a young man and an old man as long as they are both sitting.
—Mark Twain

Old Time, that greatest and longest established spinner of all! . . . His factory is a secret place, his work is noiseless, and his hands are mutes.
—Charles Dickens

Chapter 5 How Our Bodies Age

Normal aging in the absence of disease is a remarkably benign process. Physiologically, aging is essentially the gradual but steady erosion of organ system reserves and of the body's built-in capacity to repair itself. In many cases this erosion is evident only during periods of maximal exertion or stress, and many people carry on with their normal daily activities well into old age.

Since none of us can live forever, the overall goal is to keep the body in working order until everything falls apart all at once at the very end of life. Eventually the body reaches a critical point, usually in very advanced age, when minor problems cannot be overcome and result in the person's death in a relatively short time. For example, a urinary tract infection is usually just a nuisance to a college student but may be the harbinger of serious decline in an eighty-five-year-old person. Consequently, a healthy person who is aging normally will often experience serious illness and weakening only in the last period of life. Exceptions to this ideal aging process are typically the result of diseases such as diabetes mellitus, cardiovascular disease, or cancer.

This chapter reviews the main physical changes that you can expect from your aging body. Some of these changes may affect how others perceive you or how you perceive yourself but otherwise have little impact on your quality of life. Some may bring discomfort or inconvenience that is generally manageable if you are prepared and willing to make accommodations. Others can lead to more substantial impacts on your quality of life. Based on this foundation, the next chapters explore how (and why) challenging your body can help you maintain your vitality and independence until the end of life.

■ CHANGES IN HEIGHT

We all lose height as we age, but there is great variability in both the age of onset and the rate of loss. On average, most people lose about two inches by age eighty. Some of this loss happens in the torso due to changes in posture, changes in the growth of vertebrae, a forward bending of the spine, and the compression of the disks between the vertebrae. Changes in the legs and feet also contribute to this loss, including increased curvature of the hips and knees, decreased joint space in the extremities, and flattening of the arches in the feet.

■ CHANGES IN BODY COMPOSITION

Aging causes important changes in body composition and in the structural elements of tissues. The proportion of the body that is made up of fat increases on average from 14 percent to 30 percent between the ages of twenty-five and seventy-five, assuming we are the same weight. If by some chance we have gained weight over this fifty-year span, almost all of the gain is fat. At the same time we experience a decrease in total body water (mainly the water outside our cells, called extracellular water), a substantial loss of lean muscle mass, and a slight decrease in bone and viscera. Specific organs show noticeable losses; the liver and kidneys, for example, lose approximately a third of their weight between ages thirty and ninety. On the other hand, the prostate gland doubles in weight between ages twenty and ninety.

These changes seem to be influenced by hormonal changes. They can have important implications for nutritional planning and the use of medications. For example, a dose of a lipid-soluble drug such as diazepam (Valium) will remain in the body of an older person much longer than it stays in a younger person because proportionally the older person's body contains more fat. Likewise, water-soluble compounds are distributed in a smaller amount of water so the concentration will be increased, sometimes leading to toxicity if the dosage is not reduced.

CHANGES IN SKIN

Skin changes such as wrinkling are one of the physical alterations most readily associated with aging. It may surprise you that the outer layer of the skin, the stratum corneum, changes very little as we age. The main changes occur at a deeper level. Collagen, a basic chemical building block of skin and connective tissue, decreases with age. Its structure also changes. The collagen fibers in younger skin exhibit an orderly arrangement similar to fibers in a rope. These fibers become coarser and more random with aging, eventually resembling a mass of spaghetti. It is this shift that causes a loss of elasticity and produces wrinkles.

In addition, as we age the tissue decreases between the dermis, the inner skin layer, and the epidermis, the layer that covers it. This loss allows increased shearing as the skin (particularly on the arm) moves along a surface. The shearing can rupture small blood vessels, producing a port-wine-colored stain to the skin. There are also reductions in the number of deeper basal cells and pigment-producing cells, the melanocytes, as well as Langerhans cells, which come from the bone marrow and provide assistance to the immune system. The reduction of these cells is striking in skin that has been exposed to sunlight and is thought to contribute to the development of sun-related skin cancers. This process and possibly selenium deficiency can also cause small "aging spots" on the backs of the hands.

CHANGES IN HAIR

Hair changes play a prominent role in how we perceive aging but otherwise have very little impact on one's quality of life. Hair graying results from a progressive loss of pigment cells (melanocytes) from the hair bulbs. Although graying of hair on the head can occur at relatively young ages, the graying of hair in the armpit is thought to be one of the most reliable signs of aging.

There are also age-associated changes in hair growth rate and the amount of hair on various parts of the body. The number of hair follicles on the scalp decreases with age, and the growth rate of scalp, pubic, and armpit hair tends to decline. Elderly men often experience an increased growth of eyebrow, nostril, and ear hair, and elderly women sometimes see an increased growth of facial hair, possibly because of hormonal changes.

■ CHANGES IN MUSCLES AND BONES

Most people lose a substantial amount of muscle as they age. Broadly speaking, muscles decrease in strength, endurance, size, and weight relative to total body weight. However, the late onset of these changes and their unpredictable rate of appearance suggest that they may be due not to aging but, rather, to inactivity, nutritional deficiency, disease, or other long-standing conditions. Curiously, both the diaphragm and the heart, two muscles that work continuously throughout life, appear to be relatively unchanged by aging.

We also experience changes in cartilage, the flexible, cushioning substance that provides the lubricating surface of most joints. Decreased water content and changes in cartilage structure and chemistry may reduce the ability for our cartilage to bounce back during repetitive stress as we grow older.

Bone loss is a universal aspect of aging that occurs at highly individual rates. While bone growth and remodeling occur throughout life, as we age, the growth of bone slows and the bone begins to thin and become more porous. The internal latticework of bones also loses its horizontal supports, which significantly compromises its strength.

The skull, on the other hand, appears to thicken with age. This growth is most apparent deep in the skull and in the frontal sinuses. Bone growth also has been demonstrated well into advanced age in the ribs, the fingers, and the femurs. Changes in the hip may also be important, because growth in the midportion of the bone results in a wider but weaker bone.

Conditioning, nutrition, hormones, and disease have a significant influence on the degeneration of muscles and bones as we age. Conditioning is the most significant because disuse or underuse accelerates declines in bone and muscle structures. Later chapters explore how exercise and nutrition help us maintain strength in the muscles and other bodily systems.

■ CHANGES IN THE NERVOUS SYSTEM

Normal aging is associated with a host of changes in the brain and nervous system, although these changes do not necessarily affect thinking and behavior. From age thirty to seventy the blood flow to the brain decreases by 15 to 20 percent. The brain's weight also decreases with age, but this decline appears to be in a few specific places rather than overall and may be largely due to lower water content. Healthy older people experience a moderate loss of neurons in the gray matter; this loss is much more extensive in people with dementia. Commonly there is also loss of neurons in the cerebellum and the hippocampus, which are involved in some aspects of memory function and spatial navigation. However, there is some indication that hippocampal size and function may be modifiable. A 2000 study of London cab drivers, for example, revealed that drivers had a larger right hippocampus than did the control subjects and that there was a direct correlation between the size of the hippocampus and the length of time on the job. In this case it seems the challenge of routinely memorizing complex routes may have had an actual physical impact on the cabbies' brains.

Less dramatic neuron losses occur in deeper and more primitive brain structures such as the brain stem. For some nerves the density of their interconnections seems to be reduced with aging. However, the dendrites at the ends of nerves (and the connections between them) continue to grow, albeit slowly, even in advanced age, which suggests that some degree of continuous repatterning of the nervous system occurs throughout life.

There are also some age-related changes in certain chemical messengers (neurotransmitters). For example, the enzymes that produce and activate the neurotransmitter acetylcholine decline significantly with age, a decrease that is most prominent in the area of the brain that is involved in learning, memory, language comprehension, and falling in love. Changes in cell membranes can impair cells' ability to send and receive chemical messages. For example, binding sites for serotonin in the frontal cortex and hippocampus are reduced with age, which could affect mood, cognition, learning, sleep, and temperature regulation. There is also a decrease in dopamine-related receptors, which may have effects in motor activity, cognition, memory, motivation, and reward. Similar aging changes have been observed in cortical and pineal beta-adrenergic receptors that may play a role in the sleep-wake cycle.

Although they may sound daunting, these changes are not necessarily detrimental to thinking or behavior. Language skills and sustained attention, for example, are not altered with aging. Some aspects of cognitive ability do seem to change, such as the ability to retain large amounts of information over a long period of time. These changes do not develop uniformly or inevitably, and many older people continue to perform at levels that are comparable to, or even exceed, those of much younger people. Later chapters delve into cognitive changes—and maintenance—in greater detail.

■ CHANGES IN THE SENSES

Vision

We experience a host of changes that affect eye health and vision as we age. The most common aging-associated change in vision is presbyopia, a condition in which it becomes harder to focus on nearby objects. This is mainly due to a reduced elasticity of the lens and weakening of the ciliary muscle, which manipulates the lens shape to control focus. Presbyopia affects men and women equally and often begins in a person's twenties, although it is typically not noticeable until age forty or fifty. Eyeglasses usually correct the problem.

As we age our eyes also adapt more slowly to abrupt changes in light. This correlation is so consistent with age that you can estimate a person's age to within three years based solely on this measure. This change is not trivial: it means that abrupt shifts from darkness to light, such as walking out of a garage onto a sunny driveway, can be temporarily blinding to an older person while the eyes adapt. Aging also reduces the ability to see in dark and semidark situations. After two minutes of reduced illumination, young people's eyes are almost five times as sensitive as older people's eyes; after forty minutes there is a 240-fold difference.

Changes in the eyes also affect our appearance as we age. The tissues around the eyes naturally atrophy and lose fat, often causing the upper lid to droop and the lower lid to turn inward or outward. These changes, combined with a decreased production of tears, increase the risk of eye infection.

As we age we also become more prone to diseases of the eye, including glaucoma, cataracts, and macular degeneration. Glaucoma, an increased pressure in the eye that can progress to blindness, becomes more likely as the iris becomes more rigid, the pupil becomes smaller, and other changes occur in the lens. Cataracts, an extremely common condition caused by a progressive accumulation of various substances in the lens, cause blurred vision and change the way colors are perceived. Because the substances in cataracts are yellow, the lens becomes less transparent to the blue part of the color spectrum, making blue appear greenish blue. Because of this filtering, people dying their hair white or silver often do not notice if their hair takes on a slight blue tint.

It is unclear whether the retina changes as a result of normal aging, although blood vessel disease involving the retina is common. Changes in the blood supply of the retina and possibly in the pigmented layer of the retina can lead to macular degeneration, one of the most common causes of vision loss in older people. Changes in the cornea, the most superficial surface of the eye, also can occur, although they usually are related to disease and not to aging.

Hearing

It is difficult to tease out the hearing changes of normal aging from those that result from excessive noise exposure. Regardless of the distinction, many older people experience significant changes in the shape and structure of the ear and declines in their hearing ability. As we grow older the walls of the ear canal become thinner, the eardrum thickens, the bones and joints in the inner ear often begin to degenerate, and earwax production decreases. In the inner ear there is a loss of hair cells in the organ of Corti, loss of cochlear neurons, a thickening of capillaries, and a degeneration of the spiral ligament. These all contribute to hearing loss.

Hearing loss for pure tones, called presbycusis, becomes more common with age in both men and women, though overall the loss is slightly milder for women. Higher frequencies are more affected than lower frequencies. Aging is also associated with a decreased ability to distinguish between different pitches. Between twenty-five and fifty-five years of age pitch discrimination declines linearly, but after age fifty-five the declines are steeper, especially for very high and low frequencies. This is important because pitch discrimination plays a role in speech perception, even without pure tone hearing loss. Speech intelligibility declines less than 5 percent from age six to sixty but deteriorates rapidly thereafter, dropping more than 25 percent from peak levels after age eighty. This decline is felt even more acutely in situations with ambient noise, such as in a restaurant.

Taste

The evidence regarding taste sensitivity is inconclusive and varies both among individuals and by the substance tested. The tongue atrophies with age, which may result in diminished taste sensation; but the number of taste buds remains unchanged, and the responsiveness of these taste buds appears to be unaltered.

Smell

The sense of smell declines rapidly after age fifty for both men and women, and the parts of the brain involved in smell degenerate significantly. By age eighty smell detection is almost 50 percent poorer than it was at its peak, but complete loss of smell is a sign of illness such as Parkinson's disease and not normal aging. Taste and smell work together to make the discrimination and enjoyment of food possible. Some people find they have trouble recognizing blended foods by taste and smell. Chapter 7 discusses some techniques for overcoming taste and smell limitations.

Touch

Broadly speaking, we become less sensitive to touch as we age, although this occurs at different rates for different types of touch and different parts of the body. In general the response to painful stimuli is diminished with aging. Sensitivity of the cornea of the eye to a light touch declines after the age of fifty, while sensitivity of the nose to touch begins to decline by age fifteen. Pressure touch thresholds on the index finger and on the big toe decline more in men than in women. Touch is a very important aspect of intimacy, and exploring these changes with your partner can be very satisfying and deepening to a relationship. For example, men may require more physical stimulation to maintain an erection but also may be able to sustain intercourse longer for increased pleasure for both partners.

■ CHANGES IN REPRODUCTIVE FUNCTION

While women lose the capacity to reproduce well before they reach the average life-span, men maintain this ability in extreme old age. In women the rapid decline in eggs produced by the ovary is precisely and quantitatively age related. After menopause very few if any eggs can be seen in the ovary, which becomes scarred and withered.

At menopause, the production of ovarian estrogen is markedly reduced. This reduction is responsible for the "hot flashes" felt by some women and for changes in the uterus and vagina. The lining of the uterus (the endometrium) thins, and the connective tissue increases. This thinning of the vaginal lining and reduced secretions can cause pain with sexual intercourse and can contribute to loss of bladder control. Changes in breast tissue are attributed to hormonal factors, and cysts may appear. The stretching of ligaments and loss of muscular tone alter the contour of the breast.

In men, the decline in reproductive function is a gradual process since sperm cells continue to be formed. The prostate tissue is replaced by scar tissue. The gland enlarges, particularly around the urethra. Changes in the concentration of testosterone, particularly its conversion to dihydroxytestosterone, appear to cause the enlargement. Changes in the penis include progressive decline in blood flow and the formation of scar tissue in the inner compartments.

The frequency of sexual activity generally declines with age, but how much this is due to aging and how much to circumstance is not known. The most important factor may be the presence of a willing and able partner. Social and cultural circumstances tend to reinforce the decline in sexual activity, especially for older women.

Biological changes that affect reproductive function, such as reduced responsiveness to erotic stimuli, may also influence sexual activity. It is not possible to predict how menopause will influence a woman's sexuality, although vaginal lubrication diminishes. In men the ability to develop and maintain an erection can be impaired. Older men may experience decreased sensitivity of the penis and thus may require more stimulation.

■ CHANGES IN THE CARDIOVASCULAR SYSTEM

Several aspects of the cardiovascular system change as we age, but in many cases it is unclear whether these changes are the result of normal aging or of disease. Blood pressure, for example, tends to increase with age. It is thought that natural, age-related stiffening of the blood vessels may be the reason. However, an age-associated increase in blood pressure is not found in individuals who live in isolated and less technologically developed societies or in people who grow old in special environments, such as mental institutions, suggesting that there may be environmental or stress-related components as well.

In the heart itself, disease is increasingly common with age. The tissues responsible for producing heartbeats become infiltrated with connective tissue and fat. Similar but less dramatic changes occur in other parts of the heart's electrical conducting system. The elastic properties of the heart muscle are altered with age, and the heart contracts less efficiently, including a prolonged contraction time, decreased response to medications intended to stimulate the heart, and increased resistance to electrical stimulation.

The aging heart also responds less efficiently to stresses. The maximum heart rate decreases in a linear fashion and is typically estimated by subtracting a person's age from 220. The resting heart rate and the amount of blood pumped by the heart (the cardiac output) do not change. When the heart is working hard, cardiac output may increase even though the maximum heart rate decreases, because the amount of blood pumped with each beat, the stroke volume, increases to compensate for the decreased heart rate. After stress it takes longer for an older person's heart rate and blood pressure to return to resting levels.

Changes in the blood vessels also occur with age. Irregularities in size and shape develop in the cells that line blood vessels, and the layers in the blood vessel walls become thickened with connective tissue. The large arteries increase in size and thickness. Blood flow to various organs is decreased, dropping by 50 percent in the kidney and by 15 to 20 percent in the brain.

■ CHANGES IN THE RESPIRATORY SYSTEM

Natural changes in the respiratory system decrease lung function and increase the risk of pulmonary disease over time. However, some of these changes can be mitigated by regular exercise.

The trachea, large airways, and small end units of the airway expand as we age. Counterintuitively, this decreases the vital surface area of the lung while increasing the lung volume of dead space. These changes are exacerbated by reduced lung elasticity and the collapse of small airways. The general effect of all this is that we take in more air but also exhale less fully. The amount of residual air left in the lungs after each breath increases from about 20 percent of the total lung capacity at age twenty to 35 percent at age sixty. In addition, after age eighty the ends of the ribs calcify to the sternum, making the chest wall more rigid and increasing the workload of the respiratory muscles.

Importantly, the lungs also become less efficient at transferring oxygen to the bloodstream. This decrease in oxygenation is largely due to a mismatch between the parts of the lung receiving air and the parts receiving blood flow. The parts of the lung with the greatest blood flow (in the bases of the lungs) are also the parts that tend to collapse with age, causing the mismatch. Carbon monoxide diffusion capacity, a measure of gas exchange capability, also decreases with age. Maximum oxygen consumption, a measure of overall cardiopulmonary function, tends to decline with age but also is influenced substantially by exercise. Endurance training can increase lung capacity and functioning even of previously sedentary older people.

CHANGES IN THE GASTROINTESTINAL SYSTEM

Overall, the gastrointestinal tract (essentially a continuous tube from the mouth to the anus) shows fewer age-associated changes than other body systems. In particular, the lining of the gut, whose total surface is the size of two tennis courts, maintains an extraordinary capacity for regeneration throughout the course of life.

Mouth and Teeth

Natural, age-related changes do not generally lead to the loss of teeth; poor dental hygiene is a much more important factor. Cavities and periodontal (gum) disease are the typical causes of tooth loss, and both can be mitigated by good dental care. There are age-related patterns in the location of cavities as we age, with an increased frequency of root cavities and cavities around sites of previous dental work.

Older people who have lost teeth often experience dietary changes that can increase the likelihood of malnutrition. False teeth reduce taste sensation and do not completely restore normal chewing ability. Older people without teeth also tend to show alterations in swallowing. Even with a full set of teeth, older people do not chew as efficiently as younger people and tend to swallow larger pieces of food. Swallowing can take an older person 50 to 100 percent longer than a younger person, probably because of subtle changes in the swallowing mechanism.

Esophagus and Stomach

Older people experience higher rates of problems with esophageal motility (the movement of food down the esophagus), but these problems appear to stem from diseases such as diabetes mellitus, central nervous system disorders, or neuropathies, rather than aging. In the stomach, aging is associated with a thinning of the stomach lining and smooth muscle and increased white blood cells and aggregations of lymphoid tissue in the gastric wall, but these changes do not appear to affect the movement of food through the stomach. While the secretion of stomach acid decreases with age, a complete loss of stomach acid signifies disease rather than normal aging.

Intestines

Although changes occur with aging in both the small and large intestine, changes in the large intestine have the greatest impact on quality of life.

The lining of the small intestine atrophies slightly with age. When eating, older people show reduced intestinal muscle contractions, although there seems to be no difference in the speed with which substances are transported through the small intestine when a person is not actively eating. The intestines' ability to absorb foods and drugs generally does not change significantly. Older people tend to absorb highly fat-soluble compounds such as vitamin A faster and may absorb and metabolize some sugars, calcium, and iron differently. The activity of some enzymes such as lactase, which helps us digest some sugars (particularly those found in dairy products), appears to decline with age, but the levels of other enzymes remain normal. The absorption of fat may change, but this may relate more to changes in the pancreas than to changes in the intestine.

Changes in the large intestine have more impact. Here the lining atrophies, blood vessel abnormalities become more common, and we experience changes in the muscle layer. These factors contribute to an increased likelihood of diverticula, small outpouchings in the lining of the large intestine. Approximately 30 percent of people over age sixty have diverticula. The condition results from increased pressure inside the intestine caused by a disorder of intestinal muscle function. Weakness in the bowel wall near blood vessels is another contributing factor.

Constipation is a common ailment of old age because food transport in the large intestine slows down and subtle changes occur in the coordination of large intestinal muscle contractions. Mild dehydration compounds the problem. The number of certain narcotic (opiate) receptors increases as we age, and this increase may lead to significant constipation when an older person takes narcotic medications.

The 100 trillion bacteria living in the gut, called the microbiome, are increasingly being studied for their importance in maintaining health and protecting against or producing illnesses such as cancer, inflammatory bowel disease, obesity, and mental health concerns.

The microbiome interacts powerfully with the body's immune system. Recent studies have noted shifts in the microbiome over a person's life that may be detrimental: beneficial organisms seem to decline while pathological species increase.

LIVER AND PANCREAS

The liver and pancreas have a variety of functions, including detoxification, hormone production, and digestion. Broadly speaking, these organs maintain adequate function throughout life. Total failure is due to disease rather than aging.

The liver plays an important role in metabolizing drugs and other compounds, and the efficiency of this process declines with age. The liver also decreases in size with age, and its shape adjusts to the contours of adjacent organs. Aged liver cells contain increased lipofuscin pigment produced by the oxidation of fatty acids, which may be an indicator of cell membrane damage. Liver cells also increase in volume and show reductions in several important cellular functions, such as chemical processing and energy production. Overall, older livers show a reduced ability for regeneration and repair.

In the pancreas, secretion of the digestive enzyme trypsin moderately decreases with age, but other processes appear unchanged. The most common structural change in the pancreas is atrophy of the acinar cells that produce digestive juices. Some reports suggest that older people have more scar tissue in the lobes of the pancreas, but the impact of this is not known.

KIDNEY FUNCTION

The kidneys play a critical role in filtering the blood and removing waste. Their mass decreases by about 25 to 30 percent with age, resulting in reduced filtering surface. Studies have shown that kidney function tends to decline steadily with age, at about 1 percent per year from ages forty to ninety. Some studies suggest a steeper decline at very advanced ages. Reduced filtration leads to reduced clearance of some drugs and reduced urinary acidification. The kidney's abilities to maximally dilute and to maximally concentrate urine are reduced to a greater extent than its ability to filter the blood, called the glomerular filtration rate. In addition, the kidney's hormonal system that regulates salt, water, and blood pressure can be more easily disrupted by dehydration in older people.

Although these changes are typical, they are not inevitable and do not necessarily have a major impact on quality of life. Studies tracking people over more than two decades have found about a third of older people exhibit no decline in kidney function and a few even exhibit functional increases.

BLOOD

Generally, blood volume is maintained throughout life, and the tissues that produce blood retain a remarkable capacity for regeneration. The normal values for red blood cell numbers, size, and hemoglobin concentration are essentially unchanged as we age. The average life-span of red blood cells remains constant, although red cells in older people may be more fragile. The amount of active bone marrow diminishes with age, and marrow fat increases. Older people generally have a reduced capacity to accelerate the production of red blood cells, but the response to major blood loss, although impaired, usually remains adequate.

Anemia, although common, is not a normal physiological consequence of aging. It always has a cause other than age, most commonly malnutrition, blood loss, or the presence of a malignancy. White cell and platelet numbers are unchanged with age, though some of the function of blood cells that protect the body against infections, malignancy, and toxic substances may be affected by aging.

DIFFERENCES BETWEEN MEN AND WOMEN

In most countries and communities in the world today, women tend to live significantly longer than men. When this topic came up at a medical conference on aging, an elderly man came over to me after a presentation and said, "It is perfectly clear why women outlive men: their wives freeze them to death!" In fact, there are differences in mortality between males and females as early as the moment of conception, and different factors influence these patterns throughout the life-span. For example, sperm bearing a Y chromosome are more likely to fertilize an egg than X-bearing sperm, leading to roughly 170 male zygotes for every 100 female zygotes. But embryos of different genders have different rates of spontaneous miscarriage, so by the time of birth there are only slightly more males than females (about 105 males per 100 females). By the beginning of reproductive age, there are generally equal numbers of males and females, and from that point on females outnumber males.

Beyond middle age, men have about 75 to 80 percent of the longevity remaining for comparably aged women, although there is considerable societal diversity. For example, the gender differential in life expectancy from birth is about six and a half years greater for women in the United States, five and a third years in the United Kingdom, twelve years in Russia, and about half a year in India. This diversity implies that social factors have an influence on male and female longevity. While the evidence seems to suggest that women have a biological advantage, living conditions and social customs in some cultures have tended to negate this benefit. For example, social differences in how men and women are treated, their eating and work habits, or how often they are subjected to violence can have a significant impact on health and longevity. In addition, challenges related to motherhood can further compromise women's biological advantage.

The biological basis for female longevity is clear: the female of almost every species outlives the male, with very few exceptions. Having two X chromosomes provides women a backup when a genetic mutation occurs on one of the genes, while men have only a single X chromosome to express all these genes, whether damaged or not. Perhaps this genetic reserve allows a greater repertoire of effective neural, endocrine, and immune responses that gives women an edge in coping with potentially deleterious environmental demands.

Female hormones, particularly estrogen, and the resiliency of the female body to accommodate pregnancy and breast-feeding are also thought to promote longevity. Estrogens have beneficial effects on lipids in the blood and seem to protect women from premature heart disease.

There are also significant differences in the brains of men and women. For example, ultrasound images of a developing fetus at around twenty-six weeks suggest that the corpus callosum—a critical point of communication between the brain's right and left hemispheres—is larger in girls than in boys. In adults, female brains show language activity on both sides of the brain, while male brains tend to use mainly the left side. Learning disabilities, dyslexia, and stuttering are all more common in boys than in girls. Some evidence suggests that the male brain may be favored in the areas of geometry and mathematics. The portions of the brain devoted to controlling impulses of aggression and anger tend to be larger in women.

Men and women also show different patterns of behavior that may influence longevity. Boys and men tend to take more risks than girls and women, and men tend to be more often exposed to hazards in the workplace. Men also tend to drive more aggressively, experience more motor vehicle accidents, and have higher rates of alcoholism and smoking. In addition to their obvious immediate mortality risks, these behaviors can increase the likelihood of heart disease and malignancy. Women, on the other hand, tend to be more health conscious, do not expose themselves to as much risk, and attend to their bodies, seeking preventive health care and practicing healthier lifestyles compared with men.

Another way to approach the longevity differential between women and men is to look at the causes of death across the life-span. Graphs of mortality ratios by gender show excess male mortality by violence that peaks at four to one around age thirty. Gender-specific mortality rates for the top ten causes of death show an excess male-to-female ratio for all conditions except diabetes mellitus (where the risk is identical). Whether this gender gap relates to biological differences or lifestyle choices (such as cigarette smoking) is a matter of debate.

■ WHAT DOES ALL THIS MEAN FOR YOU?

This chapter presents an overview of the normal changes that you are likely to experience as you grow older, as well as some of the increased health risks you may face. What are the general implications of these changes in terms of your own aging and vitality?

One lesson that I've drawn from my decades as a geriatrician is that aging is far from homogeneous. In fact, as we age we become increasingly differentiated and biologically unique. There is much more biological variability among octogenarians than among neonates. Because of this increasing differentiation over time, algorithmic approaches, clinical pathways, rigid guidelines, and other one-size-fits-all strategies of diagnostic investigation, treatments, and resource allocation are likely to be less than optimal if they are based solely on age. Health providers, clinical investigators, and health policy makers must begin to recognize this and take it into account. As a patient, you should work to build relationships with your health care providers and ensure they are considering your whole health picture rather than only your age.

A second lesson is that biological systems that are minimally affected by age are often profoundly influenced by lifestyle factors such as smoking, physical activity, nutrition, and economic advantage. Although the precise mechanisms by which these factors induce physiological changes are unknown, chronic stress is a likely contributor, and it is often worth trying, where possible, to reduce those factors that seem to accelerate aging.

A third lesson is that we must—as individuals and as a society—recognize the inherent challenges of living with progressively diminishing resources while our environmental demands become increasingly complicated. Age-related functional declines are often compounded by losses of social status, income, self-esteem, and family support (such as through the death of a spouse). Disease processes, increasingly common with age, may further reduce physical or mental capabilities. These changes in capacity may appear magnified or have greater impacts as a result of societal changes. For example, computer literacy is becoming an increasingly important social skill but can be challenging for some older people due to such barriers as vision problems or financial constraints. The complexity of changing social expectations may be especially problematic for those who have developed a self-reliant lifestyle and self-image. In addition, some older people are victims of changes in the physical environment, such as the deterioration of a once-fashionable neighborhood and resulting increases in crime.

Aging is not the accumulation of disease, although aging and disease are related in subtle and complex ways. The fundamental principle to keep in mind is that biological and chronological age are not the same. Each of us ages at a different rate, and within each person aging affects different systems in different ways, primarily as a result of environmental factors such as lifestyle. Because aging is so variable and individual, we must each develop and implement an individualized personal aging plan. A one-size-fits-all strategy simply will not work.

Lack of activity destroys the good condition of every human being, while movement and methodical physical exercise save it and preserve it.
—Plato

It is exercise alone that supports the spirits, and keeps the mind in vigor.
—Cicero

Chapter 6 **Why Bother Exercising?**

Chapters 4 and 5 offer a taste of the science behind aging and introduce the major physical changes we can expect from our aging bodies. Although there are patterns and trends in human aging, I hope that I have effectively conveyed the overarching point that how we age—and specifically the degree to which we maintain our function and vitality—is extremely variable from person to person and largely within our control. One of the primary ways we can influence our aging is through exercise.

Illustration 5 shows what we accomplish with exercise. The upper line represents the maximal potential performance throughout life for a given system, such as the musculoskeletal system or the cardiovascular system. In a healthy person who maintains fitness, this curve is almost horizontal, with minimal decrements over time. The position and slope of this curve are affected by various environmental factors and possibly genetics. For example, cigarette smoking in youth may irreversibly reduce your respiratory potential in later years. The lower line represents the rate of atrophy if the system stays primarily in a resting state and is never stressed. The system always functions at some point between the two curves.

The divergence of these lines over time leads to three important inferences. First, the natural declines that occur with age are generally of a lesser magnitude than declines associated with physical conditioning and environmental factors. Second, the possibility of significant decline increases as we age, so self-maintenance becomes more

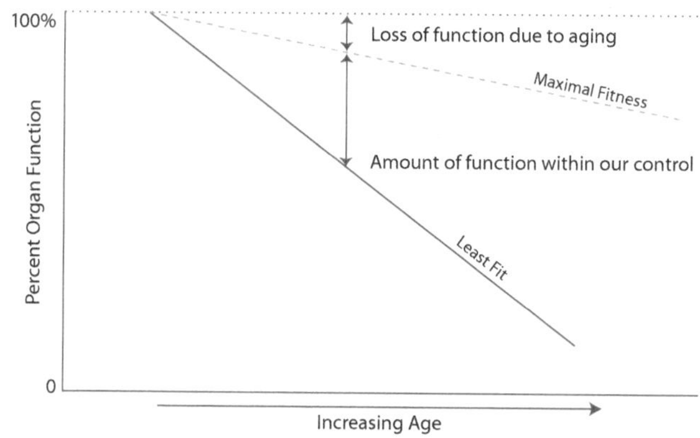

Illustration 5. The effects of age on organ function. The upper line shows the theoretical maximal possible function throughout life, and the lower line shows the rate of atrophy when the system is never stressed. The fact that these two lines diverge with time leads to important inferences. (From M. E. Williams, "Clinical Implications of Aging Physiology," *American Journal of Medicine* 76, no. 6 [1984]: 1049–54)

important. Finally, unless you are already in near-optimal condition, you have a greater opportunity for improvement as you grow older. For example, consider a very deconditioned person functioning near the lower line. With exercise and improved physical conditioning, the person could move up the functioning curve closer to the top line and function at a much higher level, perhaps even higher than sedentary younger people.

In addition to its effects on system functioning and quality of life, exercise is also one way to reduce the risk for debilitating diseases and premature death. For example, investigators in the Netherlands calculated that moderate exercise at age fifty increases life-span by one and a half years, and high levels of exercise doubles that to more than three additional years. Moreover, exercise can reduce the likelihood of dependency. The average sixty-five-year-old can expect to live about thirteen more years without disability. Highly active sixty-five-year-olds, however, remain disability-free on average for at least another eighteen years.

■ WHY EXERCISE WORKS

Exercise has potent effects on the body's biochemical mechanisms of growth and repair, which are constantly counterpoised against the biological processes that cause decline and decay. Our biological systems are not static but are in a continual state of renewal.

When we are young the default biochemical systems seem to be genetically programmed for growth and repair. As we age, decline and decay become the predominant biological effects. Without regular physical activity, our muscles atrophy and we begin to walk with a slow and shuffling gait. We become short of breath with minimal exertion and feel less steady on our feet. Fortunately, this cascade can be minimized. In other words, the frailty we sometimes associate with old age is to a large extent preventable and, in the early stages, even reversible. The key is to challenge the body through regular exercise. What we do and how long we do it makes a considerable difference.

Let's delve a little deeper into the biochemistry of exercise to see how we can promote growth and repair and overcome the tendency for decline and decay. Inflammation is the body's chemical response to insults and normally is a natural protective mechanism for healing. It can be a double-edged sword, however, and an overzealous inflammatory response is implicated in numerous common ailments. Inflammation stimulates chemical signals to initiate growth and repair to begin healing. At the same time, an associated biochemical cascade produces redness, swelling, heat, pain, and tissue destruction.

Exercise can harness the benefits of the inflammatory response. With each body movement our muscles send chemical messengers to communicate with the rest of the body. One of the most important chemical signals related to muscle and inflammation is interleukin-6 (IL-6). During an inflammatory response, other chemical messengers such as IL-1 and tumor necrosis factor (TNF)-alpha trigger the release of IL-6. During exercise, IL-6 (and not these other chemicals) is released into the bloodstream with every muscle contraction. IL-6 appears to be *anti*-inflammatory when released from skeletal muscle in high concentrations without TNF-alpha and IL-1 stimulation. Muscle contraction activates the genes controlling IL-6 production in a manner directly proportional to the amount of muscle being contracted: the more muscle is exercised, the more IL-6 is produced. In addition, the amount of IL-6 released increases as the muscle energy stores are depleted. Taken together, continuous muscle contractions and depletion of muscle energy during exercise can induce an increase of plasma IL-6 that is twenty to one hundred times greater than at inactive levels.

Now here comes the important part. After about thirty minutes of continuous exercise, these high levels of IL-6 appear to flip a metabolic switch telling the body to burn fat, control energy regulation, and stimulate the growth and repair cycle through the release mediators such as IL-10. The good news is that the switch stays flipped for about twenty-four hours. As a result, the low background noise of decline and decay is reversed by the release of IL-10. This is part of the biochemical basis for the beneficial effects of exercise on reduced inflammation, improvement of glucose tolerance, and the repair of body tissues. This mechanism also explains why one thirty-minute walk is better than three fifteen-minute walks because the shorter walks never flip the metabolic switch. By exercising daily for at least thirty continuous minutes, we can shift the body's underlying chemistry from decline and decay to growth and repair.

■ FIGHTING FREE RADICALS

As we saw in Chapter 4, oxygen free radicals appear to be one of the primary causes of age-related declines. Because free radicals are an important biochemical basis of aging, it naturally follows that activities that reduce free radicals may moderate the effects of aging.

The degradation caused by oxidation is visibly evident in the rust on a steel pipe or the brown discoloration on a slice of apple or avocado left in the air. Most of the oxygen free radicals found in our bodies originate in the mitochondria, the tiny "power plant" found in each of our cells. Mitochondria sometimes create free radicals as a side effect of the energy production process. Free radical production increases dramatically with environmental factors such as excess sunlight exposure and probably during times of emotional stress. These additional free radicals can damage the mitochondria (leading to even more free radical production), as well as other cellular components, such as cell membranes and DNA.

Because dealing with oxygen is such a hazardous undertaking, our bodies have evolved sophisticated chemical processes to quench free radicals. Exercise and good nutrition are the two most important tools we have in preventing the free radical damage associated with aging. As we age, some of the body's natural antioxidant mechanisms weaken. Exercise can actually reverse some of these losses by boosting the body's antioxidant defense system. In this way exercise increases the efficiency of oxygen utilization while reducing the production of oxygen free radicals. In addition, some foods such as fruits, vegetables, green tea, and dark chocolate contain high levels of antioxidants to help with the process.

Not all exercise is created equal, however. Strenuous exercise actually increases the production of free radicals, but regular physical exercise protects against free radical damage by boosting the defenses to a greater extent. The important point to draw from this is that occasional, intense exercise by a usually sedentary "weekend warrior" can overwhelm the antioxidant defenses. This circumstance results in increased free radical damage and may do more harm than good. The key is to build an exercise program systematically, and it is even more important to exercise every day to maintain the beneficial effects. The net result can be a reduction of free radical damage combined with enhanced growth and repair mechanisms.

■ USING EVOLUTION TO YOUR ADVANTAGE

Roughly 2.5 million years ago our ancestors faced the daunting task of finding enough food to support life and family on a daily basis. The main daily activities were gathering, hunting, and walking long distances to find new food locations. Hunting involved sprinting at top speed for forty to one hundred yards to catch and kill prey, perhaps by throwing a rock or a sharpened stick. The animal would then have to be carried back to the camp. These two types of physical activity—short, intense bursts and longer endurance activities—place very different demands on the body. As a result, humans evolved to burn energy in different ways depending on the situation.

The important lesson for us is that different types of exercise stimulate different chemical processes within the body that might slow down the aging process. When we perform activities akin to gathering food or walking long distances, the body uses fat for fuel. Sprinting and rapid-response activities, however, use glucose. Skeletal muscle usually likes to burn fat because fat is denser energy and is more efficient to metabolize, but due to physical constraints there is a limit to the rate at which we can burn fat. As we all know, fat is stored not in muscle but in adipose cells located primarily in the waist, buttocks, and thighs. Under periods of low metabolic demand fat must be transported to muscle through the circulation using big transporter molecules called triglycerides. Structurally these compounds resemble a kite with three long fatty acid tails, and they serve the purpose of making fats soluble in the blood. Like massive eighteen-wheelers on a tight mountain road, only a few triglycerides at a time can snake through the muscle capillaries to deliver the fuel. New capillaries can be added with regular exercise over time, but there is still a limit to the amount of fat metabolism that can occur.

If the metabolic demands are greater than can be supplied by fat (such as when a person is chasing down a buffalo or exercising at high intensity), the mitochondria begin to utilize glucose as well as fat. Our bodies prepare for this quick energy response by storing glucose in the muscle cells in the form of glycogen; during intense activity muscle cells break down their stores of glycogen to produce lactic acid. The net effect is to allow our aging muscles and bones to maintain their biological vigor despite the losses that occur with aging.

Another capacity that evolved early in human evolution was the ability to remove body heat and waste products through sweating. Without this capability, protracted exertion is not possible. This capacity gave our early human ancestors a crucial evolutionary edge by allowing them to pursue game for long intervals. Sweating decreases as we age, and regular exercise may slow down the rate of this loss. In other words, with regular exercise we can exercise for longer periods if we wish or if circumstances demand it. One of my patients complained that when going to Europe on an annual cruise she "gave out" before other members of her slightly younger party and found herself staying on the ship rather than going on excursions. We discussed her wishes, and she committed to a regular daily exercise program. When I saw her in clinic after her last Mediterranean tour she beamed that she could keep up with all of her friends climbing stairs and walking down long cobblestone streets and noted in passing that she sweated more than she remembered on earlier trips.

Our food should be our medicine and our medicine should be our food.
— Hippocrates

To eat is a necessity, but to eat intelligently is an art.
— La Rochefoucauld

Chapter 7 What Should We Eat?

Nutrition has an undeniable role in health and illness. Food is also a lifelong pleasure and has psychological as well as physiological impacts. Happily, there is generally no reason to change the way we eat as we grow older. Studies indicate that, barring certain illnesses, older people need exactly the same foods as everyone else, although perhaps in slightly smaller quantities. As is true throughout the lifespan, oversimplified advice for or against various foods and nutrients will not work for everyone, and as discussed in Chapter 1, dieting can actually be hazardous to your health. Moreover, one person's success with one diet does not mean that other diets are inferior. There simply is no single "correct" diet for health and longevity.

Graham Lusk, one of the founders of the science of nutrition, said in 1927, "I can summarize everything that the science of nutrition can tell you in one sentence. Tell your patients to eat plenty of food, varied food, well prepared, attractively served and in good company." Nearly ninety years later this advice is still modern. The admonition to consume varied foods is especially useful to safeguard against nutrient deficiencies known and unknown. It is good advice at any age but may be particularly so for older people.

Although our diet as a whole can likely stay the same as we grow older, there are some age-related changes to be aware of. For example, as we age we tend to burn fewer calories and therefore need to eat a little less. Also, because the risk of certain chronic diseases increases as we age, the quality of our dietary choices becomes more important than ever.

■ TAKE NUTRITIONAL ADVICE WITH A GRAIN OF SALT

A remarkable mythology has evolved around the subject of food. This folklore is not too surprising, given the potent influences food has on our lives and experiences. In all honesty we know relatively little about the complex relationships among food, genetics, gut flora, specific illnesses, and overall health. Limitations of knowledge, however, have not restrained the enthusiasm of countless writers over the centuries, both professional and layman, from espousing the latest miracle diet as a panacea for most human ills. Let's take a brief sojourn through a few nutritional theories of the past to put modern nutritional thinking in some context.

In 1829 the Reverend Sylvester Graham, a Presbyterian minister inspired by the temperance movement of the mid-nineteenth century, invented a form of bread made of finely ground white flour and coarsely ground wheat bran and germ. His intent was to produce a food that helped to curb the carnal urges of alcoholism and sexual lust, which he felt were related to improper diet. His discovery was termed Graham crackers, and he rests securely in eponymous immortality. Around the turn of the twentieth century cod-liver oil, which was known to treat rickets (vitamin D deficiency in childhood), became the standard remedy for any child who was feeling puny. Blackstrap molasses was another cure-all popularized in the early twentieth century by good health movements.

A revolutionary discovery in medical history made in the early nineteenth century was that minute amounts of vitamins, named from the contraction of "vital minerals," were essential for health. Interestingly, people have been utilizing vitamin-based therapies for millennia, although they likely didn't understand why these therapies worked. The ancient Egyptians, for example, recommended eating liver, which is rich in vitamin A, for treating night blindness, a condition we now know is produced by vitamin A deficiency. In 1753 Scottish surgeon James Lind published a treatise showing that citrus fruits prevented scurvy, a condition causing bleeding, poor wound healing, and death, although he didn't know that vitamin C was at the root of the cause and cure for the condition. Studies in the late eighteenth and early nineteenth centuries led to the identification of the vitamin deficiencies producing beriberi (thiamine or vitamin B1), pellagra (niacin or vitamin B3), and rickets (vitamin D).

Human nature being what it is, it did not take long once vitamins were discovered for the public to be bombarded with nutritional advertisements and propaganda from diet faddists, drug companies, and charlatans promoting vitamins to provide improved health, increased energy, resistance to infection, enhanced virility, and even improved body odor. We now know that large amounts of some vitamins like A and D can be toxic and can cause significant illness or even death.

Modern science supports taking a single multivitamin because large longitudinal studies convincingly show that as we age we are more likely to develop subtle nutrient deficiencies. However, the billions of dollars spent annually for vitamin supplements are largely wasted. As one of my mentors, Dr. Mack Lipkin Sr., used to say, "The people who take them [extra vitamins] become the middlemen between pill bottle and toilet."

One of the more recent nutritional passions is for organically grown foods, with supporters espousing the benefits of chemical-free fruits and vegetables in particular. Although there is evidence that toxic pesticides and bacterial pathogens can be detrimental to our health, it has been more challenging to find any evidence that foods sold as organic have any special nutritional virtue over conventionally grown foods.

A SENSIBLE APPROACH TO A BALANCED DIET

Careful studies show that a number of diets are compatible with longevity and good health. Communities eating mainly fish tend to have longevity, as do those that eat mostly vegetables and fruits. Groups that live primarily on grains also seem to do well. There are even a few communities, such as the Masai in Africa, that maintained health with relatively little atherosclerosis despite consuming large amounts of meat and a high-saturated-fat, high-cholesterol diet. As their diet "Westernized" in the very recent past, they may have lost their previous advantage.

Just as there appears to be no single diet that promotes longevity, there does not appear to be an ideal meal structure, either. Some people thrive on one meal per day; others eat as many as six. Some groups hardly ever have a full meal and survive on light and frequent nibbling. They also seem to age well.

Although there is no single "ideal" diet at the population level, some individuals benefit from particular dietary restrictions or approaches based on their genetic predispositions. For example, people with a family history of heart attack or stroke at a young age are sometimes not able to handle fats well, and for them a diet low in cholesterol and saturated fat combined with lipid-lowering medication may be beneficial and life extending. Another example is people with celiac disease, who benefit from excluding glutens from their diet to avoid triggering an immune reaction that damages the small intestine.

The fact that there is no single answer to the question of diet does not mean that we should all just eat whatever we want. There are certainly dietary choices that directly promote ill health, disease, and even premature death. What we eat can have a significant impact on the rate and severity of aging-related declines. The nutritional advice presented here summarizes what current research tells us about the broad dietary approaches that can best help us avoid debilitating disease and live a full, long life.

Follow MyPlate

MyPlate, developed by the Center for Policy and Nutrition of the U.S. Department of Agriculture, offers a quick summary of basic nutritional principles. Following MyPlate essentially boils down to making sure that most of your diet is nutritious, with limited amounts of saturated fats and processed sugar and flour. This guidance suggests filling half of your plate with fruits and vegetables. Although this can include any kind of vegetable or fruit, be careful about juices because many popular choices contain very little actual fruit juice (look for those that are 100 percent juice). Generally men and women over age fifty need roughly one and a half to two cups of fruit, two to two and a half cups of vegetables, three ounces of grains, five to five and a half ounces of protein, and three servings of dairy products daily. The ChooseMyPlate.gov website provides additional information, as well as the definitions of serving sizes. Beans and peas (except for string beans, lima beans, and green peas, which are considered vegetables) are excellent sources of plant proteins and are considered in the protein category rather than the vegetable group. Grains are divided into whole grains (which contain all of the grain) and refined grains (which are milled and have lost the germ and the bran from the grain). Make sure at least half of your three-ounce daily portion of grains is whole grains. Pasta is considered a grain. Dietary proteins include meat, seafood, eggs, poultry, nuts, seeds, beans, and peas. The dairy group includes milk or foods made from milk such as butter, cheese, yogurt, puddings, and ice cream. Soymilk is also considered a dairy product.

Know What You Are Eating

Many of the best foods, like fresh fruits and vegetables, don't come with a nutrition label. That's generally fine, since they are naturally quite nutritious. On most packaged foods, however, you will find a little Nutrition Facts label listing nutritional information and the product's ingredients. If you know how to read this label, you will find it is actually quite handy for helping you make healthy choices about what products to buy. Understanding food labels becomes especially important as you grow older and need to choose the best nutritional value for your health and budget. This information is often in microscopic print and is sometimes printed in a noncontrasting color, like red print on a dark orange background. Consider taking a magnifying glass with you when you go shopping.

The first thing to notice is the serving size, because all of the other numbers are based on it. The next items to check are the number of calories per serving and the number of calories from fat. A useful rule of thumb is to minimize foods with more than 30 percent of their calories from fat. The percentage daily value (%DV) gives you an idea of the percentage of specific nutrients based on a 2,000-calorie daily diet. If the %DV is more than 20 percent, then the food is considered a reasonable source for that nutrient. On the other hand, if the %DV is less than 5 percent, then the food is not a reliable source for that nutrient.

The ingredients are listed in order, by weight, from the most to the least. Try not to be misled by different names given to sugars and fats. For example, words that end with "-ose" mean a type of sugar, such as sucrose, dextrose, or fructose. In addition, sugars can be called by their origin, such as corn syrup, evaporated cane juice, molasses, or honey. Synonyms for fat include lard, butter, margarine, hydrogenated vegetable shortening, and "oil," such as coconut oil, palm oil, and safflower oil.

Find Your Fiber

There is an old saying that you are what you eat. To me this saying is only half true—you are not what you ingest but what you digest. Fiber, also known as roughage, is the part of plant-based foods that your body does not digest. Despite passing through your gastrointestinal tract essentially intact, fiber has plenty of important roles in maintaining health, some of which become more important as we grow older. For example, fiber helps to alleviate constipation, promotes bowel regularity, helps to reduce variations in blood sugar after eating, reduces appetite, and may lower the risk of heart disease and colon cancer.

The U.S. Institute of Medicine recommends twenty to thirty-five grams of dietary fiber daily. Most of us fall well short of this goal, with the average person consuming only twelve to eighteen grams. An easy way to get lots of natural fiber is with Power Pudding, a recipe I learned from an astute geriatric nurse practitioner: mix together one cup prune juice, one cup bran flakes, and one cup applesauce and put the mixture in the refrigerator. Start with a "dose" of two tablespoons each morning. Some of my patients eat it straight out of the container, some smear it on a piece of whole wheat bread, and some dollop it on their cereal. The dose can be increased every three to four days until you are achieving the desired results.

Put Color on Your Plate

As we discussed earlier, half of your plate should be loaded with fruits and vegetables, which along with whole grains provide fiber as well as complex carbohydrates and micronutrients. An easy way to make sure you have a good variety of fruits and vegetables is to think color. Naturally brightly colorful fruits and vegetables are full of powerful antioxidants and disease fighters such as zinc, vitamins C and E, and the phytochemicals lutein, zeaxanthin, and beta-carotene. For berries a good rule of thumb is the darker the berry, the greater the antioxidant effect. Your daily goal is at least four or five different colors (try to get at least three different colors per meal). It's okay to count different shades of red, orange, and green as separate colors.

Power Up with Protein

Protein is needed to sustain and rebuild muscles, as well as to maintain the immune system. Our body's need for protein does not appear to change much as we age, although research has yielded some mixed results on this topic. It can be challenging to balance protein needs and restrictions, particularly during travel and eating out. Good sources of low-fat high-quality protein are poultry, fish, eggs, soybeans, nuts, and dairy products. Just two ounces of fish per day can reduce the risk of heart disease in people at high risk. The omega-3 fatty acids in fish also may offer benefits for people with diabetes mellitus, hypertension, and arthritis. Chronic infections or diseases can affect the amount of protein needed. For example, excess protein can stress the kidneys, so people with chronic kidney disease often have to restrict protein intake.

Go Nuts for Nuts, Beans, and Legumes

Nuts are an integral part of a healthy diet and are rich in unsaturated fats, magnesium, and copper. The challenge is that they tend to be high in calories and are hard to eat in small quantities. The target serving size is a quarter cup, which is four level tablespoons. There is no difference in calories or nutritional value whether the nuts are raw, dry roasted, or roasted with or without oil. Salted nuts can be loaded with sodium, so check the nutrition label to make sure your daily sodium intake stays in the appropriate range.

Beans and legumes are another healthful source of protein, as well as many other nutrients. Adding a variety of beans, lentils, and peas to your diet is a great way to put texture on your plate and help you feel full after meals.

Use Care with Carbohydrates

Carbohydrates—particularly in the form of whole grains—have an important role in a balanced diet. Carbohydrates in overly refined, processed forms, on the other hand, can promote overeating and lead to ill health. In recent years carbohydrates have gotten a huge amount of attention from science, the media, and peddlers of fad diets. Although some of the claims are quite overblown, a quick look at the physiology of eating and some historical context reveals why some starchy foods are more healthful than others.

The types of foods we eat produce chemical signals that strongly influence how our body handles nutrition. The diet of our ancestors had constant ratios of carbohydrate to protein and fat regardless of whether the primary nutritional source was plant or animal. When we ingest sufficient quantities of protein and fat, the body sends chemical messages that signal us to stop eating. Carbohydrates, on the other hand, do not send this "full" signal. This is because carbohydrates in nature are found in foods like whole grains, beans, and fruits that have few calories per pound. As long as the carbohydrates are unprocessed, we get a pleasant sense of satiety from the sheer volume of the carbohydrates we eat, so a chemical signal is not needed.

Another evolutionary legacy is that our bodies use a rise in blood sugar after we eat as an important and sensitive marker of the number of calories we have ingested. The body uses this chemical signal to determine how much work the digestive system needs to do. When eating low-density, unprocessed carbohydrates, a small rise in blood sugar signals that a large meal has just been ingested and tells the body to prepare to digest the food and absorb the nutrients. At the same time, the stomach and upper intestine signal the pancreas to produce insulin, which helps to control the rise in blood sugar.

Approximately ten thousand years ago agriculture had advanced to the point where cultivated crops were high in carbohydrates, like rice, wheat, and potatoes. As far as the evolution of our body chemistry is concerned, ten thousand years is not long enough for any meaningful adaptation to changes in diet. High-starch foods tend to be white in color from refinement and are essentially very dense sugars. In fact, ingesting some starches causes a rise in blood sugar that is more rapid than eating refined table sugar.

The amount of easily digested sugar in food is rated by the glycemic index, which reflects the rise in blood sugar after ingestion. Foods with a low glycemic index produce a low rise in blood sugar, and those with a high glycemic index generate a significant increase in blood sugar. Starches with a low glycemic index are whole grains, beans, lentils, and high-fiber cereals. Baked goods, processed cereals, and anything made with refined flour are likely to have a high glycemic index. As a general rule foods with a glycemic index over fifty-five are considered not as healthy as foods with lower indices. Epidemiologic studies suggest that people who consume lower glycemic index diets tend to have lower rates of major age-related disabilities, such as diabetes mellitus, heart disease, and macular degeneration. Recent studies in mice show that high glycemic diets are associated with a threefold increase of advanced glycation end products (remember the AGEs from Chapter 4?) in the lens, retina, liver, and brain.

Get the Skinny on Fat

There are two basic types of fat. Unsaturated fat is the essential active fat that our bodies use on a daily basis to restore cell membranes, maintain neurological tissues, produce hormonal messengers, and provide energy. The fats are called "unsaturated" because they have some double bonds in their chemical structure, which basically means

Illustration 6. Glycemic index and portion size for select foods.

Food	*Portion Size*	*Glycemic Index*
Broccoli	Half cup	10
Peanuts	Three tablespoons	14
Lentils	Half cup	29
Spaghetti	One cup	41
Banana	One large	53
White bread	Two slices	70
Corn flakes	One cup	84
Baked potato	One cup	85
Instant rice	Two-thirds cup	91

Sources: K. Foster-Powell, S. H. Holt, and J. C. Brand-Miller, "International Table of Glycemic Index and Glycemic Load Values," *American Journal of Clinical Nutrition* 76 (2002): 5–56; F. S. Atkinson, K. Foster-Powell, and J. C. Brand-Miller, "International Table of Glycemic Index and Glycemic Load Values," *Diabetes Care* 31 (2008): 2281–83; http://www.lowgihealth.com.au/glycemic-index-list-of-foods/.
Note: Various sources give slightly different values.

that they are not fully saturated with hydrogen. Unsaturated fats are liquid at room temperature because the double bond causes the structure to bend, and as a result, the fats cannot stack neatly. Foods high in unsaturated fats are fatty fish like salmon and sardines, nuts, avocados, and olive oil, among many others.

The other type of fat is saturated fat, which is the fat the body stores for future energy needs. Saturated with hydrogen, these fats are straight and can stack tightly, which leads to their tendency to be solid at room temperature. They also do not spoil as quickly as unsaturated fats. This property gives food products made with saturated fats a longer shelf life and facilitates the transportation of large quantities of merchandise made with it. Foods high in saturated fats are red meat, dairy products, pies, cookies, crackers, doughnuts, and almost all fried foods.

While unsaturated fats provide valuable energy and other benefits for the body, the major problem with saturated fats is that they promote inflammation, which underlies the development of heart disease, stroke, malignancy, arthritis, and perhaps some forms of dementia. In addition, the presence of excess saturated fats leads the body to substitute saturated fats for unsaturated fats for the purpose of repairing cell membranes. This chemical process of trying to force a straight structure into a curved space not only is ineffective but also sets the stage for local inflammation wherever the saturated fats are deposited, which is often in the walls of blood vessels.

Hydrate, Hydrate, Hydrate

We may not consider water a nutrient, but in many ways it is the most important one. Adequate water intake becomes increasingly essential as kidney function declines with age. Even mild dehydration can predispose you to constipation, and adequate fluid intake can help relieve this tendency. Do not wait until you are thirsty to drink. The thirst mechanism declines with age, so you face a greater risk of dehydration as you grow older if you do not put conscious effort into drinking enough water.

Aim for about two liters (roughly a half gallon) of fluid per day. One patient of mine keeps a two-liter container in her refrigerator. She fills it with fresh water every evening and makes sure that she finishes all of it by the end of the next day.

Get Creative

Declines in taste and smell may make nutritious food seem less appetizing as we grow older. One way to compensate for these changes is to eat a variety of foods of differing textures and flavors. Avoid overcooking vegetables, which can produce a bland mush. Experiment with seasonings like curry, dill, or other herbs and spices to brighten flavors, and find cooking techniques that can make food more appealing.

Watch Out for Malnutrition

In contemporary America obesity is becoming a greater public health concern than malnutrition, and obesity can exacerbate many aging-related physical changes. On the flip side, malnutrition can become an important concern among elderly people, especially because many older people are living on a small, fixed income, and some experience decreased taste and appetite or illnesses that interfere with eating. The loss of teeth can also lead to malnutrition because food choices become more constricted. People who are malnourished have reduced reserves for fighting an illness or injury and generally take longer to fully recover. Poor nutrition also can lead to additional complications, such as pressure ulcers, infections, muscle weakness, unsteady gait, or falls.

If you have trouble keeping your weight up, it is critical that you discuss your situation with your doctor. Be sure to eat three meals a day and consider adding three snacks. Do not skip a meal. During meals eat the highest-calorie foods first and consider liquid supplements. If you have a blender, try mixing an instant breakfast product with whole milk and adding a banana and other fresh fruit for a nutritious snack. Commercial supplements also can be helpful.

THE DELICATE DANCE OF DIET AND EXERCISE

Chapter 6 explored the physiological basis for exercise as it relates to healthy aging. This chapter focuses on the impact of the foods we eat. But diet and exercise are not wholly separate things. In fact, there is considerable interplay between what we eat and how we move, and the combination of these factors has a strong influence on health and vitality as we age.

Over millennia our ancestors evolved under conditions in which every meal was special and each calorie was valuable. As a result, our bodies are not used to food excess. Given the unpredictable nature of finding food and the seasonal variations in food supply, our ancient ancestors adapted to periods of impending famine by storing nutrition as fat and by significantly reducing energy expenditure through inactivity. What this means for us modern humans is that our prehistoric body interprets inactivity as a signal of famine, triggering it to fervently store fat to weather the (perceived) impending period of starvation.

This fat storage process, signaled by a sedentary lifestyle, occurs irrespective of the amount of food we eat. In fact, eating large amounts of food triggers another biochemical process that only exacerbates unhealthy eating. Consuming a typical 1,000-calorie fast-food entrée of a giant cheeseburger, soda, and fries, for example, causes your blood sugar to rise so rapidly that your body behaves as if you have just eaten a huge "natural" feast of 8,000 to 10,000 calories. To address this largesse the digestive system goes into overdrive, pouring gastric juices into the gastrointestinal tract and insulin into the bloodstream. Because our body is not set up for excess, it absorbs every calorie and stores the overage as fat, figuring that another feast this large is unlikely to occur anytime soon. But instead of feeling sated for a good long time, the rapid surge in blood sugar is followed by a sudden drop in blood sugar not long afterward, as the excess insulin kicks in, making us feel hungry again and prompting another meal. In this way our body ricochets between perceived feast (signaled by caloric excess) to perceived famine (signaled by inactivity and plummeting blood sugar). Over years this pattern can lead to obesity, heart disease, diabetes mellitus, and other chronic diseases that lower quality of life and shorten the life-span.

The simple way to reverse this basic biology is to exercise regularly. Exercise tells the body that starvation is not imminent and therefore energy does not need to be stored as fat. Despite the focus on calorie burning in the popular media, the real benefit of exercise is not so much in the calories burned as in conveying to the body that it is safe to grow and maintain itself instead of storing fat to survive impending famine. We can help overcome the clashes between our modern lifestyles and the evolutionary legacies of our prehistoric ancestors by exercising, avoiding overly processed foods, reducing the amount of starch and saturated fat in the diet, and eating foods with a low glycemic index.

I am pushing sixty. That is enough exercise for me.
— Mark Twain

All truly great thoughts are conceived while walking.
— Friedrich Nietzsche

Chapter 8 Specific Ways to Challenge Your Body

As in the analogy of the horse, carriage, driver, and master, nobody is going to step in and maintain your carriage for you. It takes conscious action and dedication on your part. It also takes hard work, especially if you are not naturally inclined toward physical activity. But the rewards for your body and brain are well worth the effort.

Before you begin an exercise regimen, see your doctor to be sure it is safe for you. Some people have hidden heart disease, and if you are at risk, your physician might recommend cardiac stress testing before you begin a strenuous exercise program. In addition, if you do not already exercise regularly, you may be deconditioned, especially if you have been sedentary for a long time. Start out slowly and work yourself up gradually to your exercise targets. Warm up and cool down before and after each workout to reduce the likelihood of injury.

■ GINNING UP MOTIVATION

In the interest of full disclosure, I must confess that I am not a naturally motivated exerciser. I can intellectually appreciate the benefits and understand the biochemistry of how regular exercise is essential to my health and my well-being. But it is still an uphill struggle. I simply do not find motion for the sake of motion that appealing, and I admire "gym rats" who seem to crave and thrive on regular physical activity. For many of us, the main challenge with exercise is getting started and then sticking with it.

If you find it hard to get motivated to exercise, I can tell you from experience that exercise woven into other integrated activities can be satisfying and fun. Several years ago my family and I spent quite a long time achieving our black belts in the martial art Tae Kwon Do. Each session left us dripping with sweat and feeling tired and satisfied. For me, the endeavor of learning a useful skill, building self-discipline, and participating with my family workout partners provided the necessary motivation to stick with the program and finally reach the goal.

Getting started on an exercise program is often half the battle. In some ways it simply boils down to "Just do it!" The rest of this chapter offers a number of specific exercise options, but the reality is that getting regular exercise matters more than the details of your workout. You must create an exercise habit. Fortunately, our brains are hardwired to develop habits through the action of the chemical dopamine. Dopamine is stimulated by learning and basically helps to tell your brain what you desire and how to get that desire fulfilled. You can use this biochemistry to your advantage by giving yourself some minor reward each time you exercise. This will stimulate dopamine and help you transform exercise from a goal-directed to a habit-directed activity.

These goals or rewards you associate with exercise can be tangible or psychological, anything that motivates you to get started. For example, you might appreciate exercise more if you think of it as a time to be by yourself, meditate, or relieve stress. You might remind yourself how good it feels to finish or motivate yourself by setting specific strength achievements or weight loss goals. Or you might promise yourself a more immediate reward such as a new smartphone app, favorite television show, or nutritious snack. Regular exercise reduces your risk of a premature death, and perhaps for some people that is motivation enough.

HOW MUCH EXERCISE IS ENOUGH?

For more than thirty years I have tried to ask each of my very elderly patients to share their personal secrets to longevity. Several years ago I was seeing an elderly farmer from a remote rural community. His sixty-five-year-old daughter felt that her ninety-year-old father needed a checkup since he had not seen a physician in more than forty years (possibly his real secret). The older man was generally in good shape, and I asked him for his secret to good health and longevity. He thought for a moment and then said, "I really do not have a secret to getting into old age, but I will tell you one fact. I worked up a good sweat every day." I think it is hard to distill the answer to the question of how much exercise is enough any better than that.

A study of 17,000 Harvard alumni basically concluded that any exercise was better than none. Those who burned more than 700 calories a week through exercise lived longer than those who did not. Moderately paced walking for thirty minutes burns about 150 calories, so a daily half-hour walk will surpass that 700 calorie threshold. The study also showed that the more intense the activity, the greater the benefit, up to about 2,000 calories burned weekly. These findings are supported by other studies, as well.

I should note that the people included in exercise studies are often relatively affluent and well educated. Despite its substantial impact on health, exercise cannot necessarily overcome all of the other environmental factors we encounter that also influence our health, often in detrimental ways. For example, I have provided medical care for many migrant workers who got plenty of vigorous exercise daily for years and who still experienced premature disability and death. I would not posit that more exercise would have improved the outlook for these individuals. But this fact does not diminish the benefits of exercise for most people, especially those of us who tend toward a more sedentary lifestyle.

■ CREATING YOUR ROUTINE

Your ideal exercise routine depends on your personal preferences, physical capabilities, and scheduling constraints. No two people are alike in this regard. Illustration 7 offers general guidance about the recommended types and amounts of exercise that have been found to be beneficial for most people. But more important than following this guide exactly is creating an exercise routine that you find motivating and sustainable. Some people thrive on routine, while others crave variation. For some people it's best to set specific times and places to do particular exercises, while others get more enjoyment and motivation by mixing it up. You'll need to find your own ways to enjoy exercise. It also may help to listen to podcasts, audio books, or music while you exercise. You will feel like you have accomplished twice as much, which you have, and the time will pass quickly.

Illustration 7. Types and benefits of exercise.

Exercise Type	*Key Benefits*	*Target Amount*
Warm up	Reduces risk of injury; improves performance	5–10 minutes per workout
Aerobic exercise	Supports heart, lungs, and vascular system	30–45 minutes daily (3 times per week minimum)
Resistance exercise	Strengthens muscles; reduces frailty	30–45 minutes (2–3 times per week)
Flexibility exercise	Reduces risk of injury; promotes relaxation	15 minutes daily
Balance exercise	Reduces risk of falling	10 minutes daily
Cool down	Reduces fatigue and soreness	5–10 minutes per workout

Sources: https://go4life.nia.nih.gov/4-types-exercise; http://www.nytimes.com/health/guides/specialtopic/physical-activity/print.html

The Warm-Up

Warming up is literally the process of increasing your body temperature by one or two degrees Celsius (about one and a half to three degrees Fahrenheit) to prepare for exercise. Warming up relaxes taut muscles, prepares the heart and lungs for increased activity, and can improve your physical performance and reduce your risk of injury. Always warm up as the first step of your workout.

Begin with basic joint-lubricating movements, going from your hands and arms and working down to your toes. Use slow, simple rotations clockwise and counterclockwise until the joint feels relaxed and the movement is smooth. Take your time.

Once your joints feel lubricated and relaxed, perform three to five minutes of light aerobic exercise such as jumping jacks, push-ups, or jogging in place. The goal is to get your circulation moving toward your muscles and to increase body temperature. Remember that this is the warm-up and not the vigorous portion of your exercise routine.

Finally, perform some warm-up stretching. Wait until your muscles are warmed up and more elastic before you stretch, to reduce the likelihood of injury. Remember that stretching is the final phase of the warm-up and is not the entire warm-up. In other words, do not begin your workout with stretching. Stretch your back, sides, neck, chest, thighs, and calves. Be sure to stretch those muscles that you intend to exercise. Let your muscles stretch naturally by keeping movements slow and relaxed—never bounce or jerk a stretch. A mild pulling sensation during the stretch is normal, but stretching should never cause pain—stop immediately if you notice pain. When you have finished stretching you are ready to begin your main workout.

Aerobic Exercise

Aerobic exercise is essentially any activity that increases your heart rate and causes you to breathe more deeply. Common examples are running, swimming, cycling, and vigorous dancing. Aerobic exercises help the heart, lungs, and vascular system and, after walking thirty minutes a day, should form the core of your exercise regimen.

The main way to gauge the intensity of an aerobic workout is based on a calculation of maximum heart rate, or the number of times your heart beats per minute when you are at peak exertion. The basic formula for maximum heart rate is 220 minus your age, so if you are sixty, your maximum heart rate is 160, although this formula may be slightly different for men and women. Until you are in peak condition, do not attempt to reach your maximum heart rate because you could seriously injure yourself.

Most aerobic workouts have you reach 60 to 80 percent of your maximum (96 to 128 beats per minute for a sixty-year-old) and hold it in that range for at least thirty minutes. As noted in Chapter 6, it takes at least thirty minutes of exercise to get your IL-6 levels up the point at which your basic biochemistry will switch from decline and decay to growth and repair. At around 60 percent of your maximum heart rate, you are primarily burning fat. A person in good shape is able to handle this pace for a couple of hours. At around 80 percent of your maximum heart rate you are burning oxygen (hence the term aerobic). Once you are in good shape you will be able to keep this pace for an hour. At this level you are pushing your mitochondria to multiply and to increase your defenses against oxygen free radicals.

It bears emphasis that the most important way to begin your workout is to warm up. Do not be impatient and jump vigorously on your exercise equipment or race down the block. All major athletes have a warm-up program, and so should you. The main reason is to reduce the likelihood of exercise-induced injury.

One important detail when beginning an aerobic exercise program is to invest in a heart rate monitor—it is impossible to determine your own heart rate during exercise without one. The monitor can tell you when you have reached your limit by showing an *abrupt* jump in your pulse of 10 to 20 beats per minute. For example, your heart rate is steady at 98 beats per minute and suddenly pops up to 115—that is the signal to stop and cool down for the day. Your heart is telling you that you have done enough even if it was only ten minutes. Do not try to push it through that point.

Resistance Exercise

Resistance exercise is essentially lifting weights to increase the strength of your muscles. It can be done with resistance machines, free weights, resistance bands, or other similar equipment. Doing thirty to forty-five minutes of resistance exercises two to three times a week can significantly enhance your core aerobic workout.

The earliest notation of progressive resistance training is Milo of Croton, the sixth-century-B.C. Greek athletic champion and friend of Pythagoras. He reportedly carried a four-year-old bull on his shoulders for miles. He was able to accomplish the feat by carrying a newborn ox on his shoulders daily until it grew into adulthood.

Although you probably don't need to be able to carry a full-grown bull on your shoulders, it may surprise you to hear that the older you are, the greater the benefits of resistance exercise. One study of ninety-year-olds in a nursing home showed remarkable increases in strength, balance, flexibility, and aerobic capacity from regular resistance exercise. Muscle size and strength nearly tripled, and the rate of falling dropped significantly. Part of the definition of frailty is a loss of muscle mass, so it is not surprising that strengthening the muscles reduces frailty.

Resistance exercise may also have benefits for your mental health. There is evidence that resistance training causes the skeletal muscles to release glutamate, which is the most potent excitatory chemical messenger in the brain and is involved in learning and memory. Interestingly, one study showed that nursing home patients with Alzheimer's disease who participated in an exercise program had slower declines in mental and physical function than did those who did not exercise, although there is no proof that glutamate was involved in this change.

It is prudent to work with an experienced trainer before beginning resistance training, to reduce the risk of injury. Once you have the feel of the program you can continue on your own. Exercise physiologists suggest that we get the most benefit from resistance exercise when our muscles work at 80 percent of their single maximum effort. For example, if you can perform one biceps curl with fifty pounds, then your ideal lifting regimen would be forty pounds with six to ten repetitions. When you are able to perform ten repetitions, you then increase the amount of weight and drop back to six repetitions. Speed is not the point and can cause injuries, so do your repetitions slowly.

Flexibility Exercise

Flexibility exercises are gentle stretching exercises that reduce your risk of joint injury and aid in relaxation and stress reduction. Examples of flexibility exercises are Tai Chi, Qigong, and yoga. Work up to fifteen continuous minutes of flexibility exercises per day. Certified instructors can help with proper technique.

How does flexibility exercise work? As your muscles are stretched, each muscle fiber is extended to its maximal length, and the connective tissue (tendons and ligaments) takes up the remaining slack. This process straightens any disordered or damaged fibers by realigning them toward the tension. This realignment is a key to improving joint and muscle health. Generally the stretch is held for about twenty seconds, released for fifteen to thirty seconds, and then repeated for a total of three to five stretches. Try to relax and exhale during each stretch. A regular program of flexibility exercise will show results in upper body flexibility in four to six weeks. It may take two to three months to improve lower body flexibility.

Balance Exercise

Balance becomes increasingly important as we age. Balance exercises are designed to improve your ability to stay steady and reduce the risk of falling.

The simplest balance exercise is to stand on one leg. Try to hold steady on each leg for at least one minute, three or four times per leg. If necessary, rest one hand lightly on a chair to keep yourself from falling while you build up your balance. Once you feel comfortable standing on one leg, try doing this with your arms crossed across your chest. If that becomes too easy, try it with your eyes closed. Finally, for maximal difficulty try standing on a pillow or other soft surface. The goal is to find a challenging level but not one that is too difficult or dangerous for you. Once you feel fairly stable, integrate this exercise into your daily routine by standing on one leg while you brush your teeth in the morning.

Another good balance exercise is called tandem walking: walking heel to toe in a straight line as if you were walking on a tightrope. It is what the police sometimes ask suspected intoxicated drivers to do to test sobriety. The slower you go, the more difficult the task becomes, like the difficulty in trying to ride a bicycle very slowly. You can increase the difficulty by crossing your arms across your chest.

If these exercises are difficult for you, you can improve your balance by working on your thighs and calves. Stand erect with your hands on the back of a chair. Lift your right leg backward while keeping it straight and do not bend your knee or lean forward. This will stretch your hip extensors, which are a key to good balance. Repeat ten to twelve times with each leg. Then slowly lift your right leg to the side while keeping your knee straight until it is six to eight inches above the ground. Hold it there for fifteen seconds, and then lower it. Repeat ten to twelve times on each side. To make these exercises more difficult, touch the chair with only one finger for support, or try them without using any chair support. Now raise your leg straight up as if you are marching and hold it in place while keeping your thigh parallel to the ground, to exercise the hip flexors. Finally, rise slowly up on your tiptoes and hold there for fifteen seconds. Repeat this ten to twelve times.

The Cool-Down

Once your workout is finished, perform a five-minute cool-down to reduce muscle fatigue, cramping, tightening, and soreness caused by the production of lactic acid from your maximal or near-maximal muscle exertion. This cooling down is a mirror image of your warm-up. Perform some light stretches until your heart rate slows down to its normal rate.

■ THINKING CREATIVELY ABOUT EXERCISE

If all this sounds like a lot to keep track of, do not be dismayed. There are numerous ways to integrate aerobic, resistance, flexibility, and balance exercises into your daily routine. Experiment and take the time to find a combination of activities that you enjoy and that fit your schedule. Some people enjoy exercising in groups for social reasons or to help motivate each other. Others prefer to use exercise as a time for solitude or relaxation. Keep experimenting until you find what works for you.

There are also many overlaps among the different types of exercise. For example, Tai Chi and Qigong support both balance and flexibility. Yoga, Pilates, and various martial arts can often fulfill these roles, as well as aerobic or resistance exercise. If you are finding it hard to work an adequate amount of each exercise into your schedule, try to find combination exercises that will allow you to do multiple types of training at once. Or think creatively about how to combine exercise with other activities. For example, you and a friend could replace a weekly coffee date with a walk instead.

The most important part of exercise is simply to do it. The twelfth-century poet Saadi said in his *Rose Garden*, "He who studies wisdom and does not practice is like a man who ploughs a field but does not sow it." Pick something you like to do and establish a daily routine. No excuses—just get started.

God gave us memory so that we might have roses
in December.
— J. M. Barrie

Reading furnishes the mind only with materials of knowledge;
it is thinking that makes what we read ours.
— John Locke

Aging Secret 3 Stimulate Your Intellect

Michelangelo Buonarroti, the extraordinary genius of the Italian Renaissance, had an artistic career that spanned seventy years. The last thirty years of his life was a period of prolific creativity that continued until the day of his death at the age of eighty-nine on February 18, 1564. He attributed his skill to his brain and not his hands. In 1508 Michelangelo was commissioned by Pope Julius II to paint the magnificent frescoes of the Sistine Chapel. One of the most famous is the *Creation of Adam*.

In this familiar fresco we see Adam and God reaching toward each other as though Adam is to receive something from God. But what is the gift? He is already fully developed, alive with open eyes. For nearly five centuries scholars overlooked a special message hidden by Michelangelo that explains the mystery. In the late 1970s, Indiana surgeon Frank Lynn Meshberger realized that the image showed God arising from the right side of a human brain. The image has the approximate shape and anatomical features, including the frontal lobe, pons, optic chiasm, pituitary gland, cerebellum, and basilar artery. In Michelangelo's symbolism, God's gift to Adam and all mankind is the gift of intellect.

Changes in mental function are perhaps the most feared aspect of aging. Significant mental dysfunction threatens our lives and our independence because we use our brains to perceive and act on risks in the environment. In most people this fear of becoming mentally incompetent is groundless. Much harm results from the assumption that all mental functions decline with age. Every little slip is given the worst interpretation, and people begin to believe the stereotype, which encourages social isolation and loss of self-esteem.

By stimulating our intellect as we grow older, we can in fact expand our creativity, deepen our wisdom and sensibility, and become *more*, not less. As we explore how the brain changes with age, we will see that mental function does not have to decline and that learning capacity can continue throughout life. The intellectual contributions of a host of old people—Michelangelo, Monet, Renoir, Benjamin Franklin, Walt Whitman, and so many others—reinforce a view of aging as a potent time of variety, creativity, and fulfillment.

The way we use our mental abilities may change as we age. Some kinds of memory change very little if at all, while others change more substantially. Research indicates there is a tendency for our reasoning to become less abstract and more concrete and complex. On the other hand, old people tend to perform less well when stressed or put under time pressure.

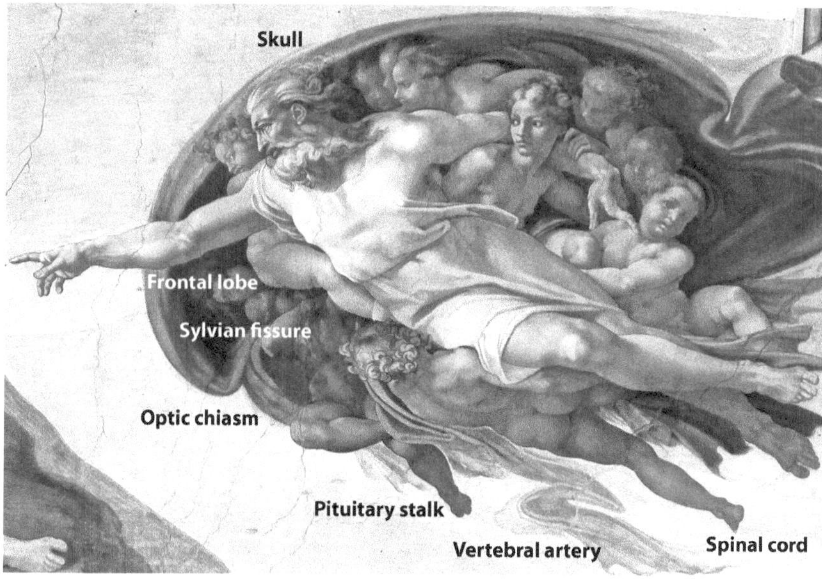

Illustration 8. The parts of the right side of the brain superimposed on Michelangelo's fresco on the ceiling of the Sistine Chapel. (After Frank Meshberger, "An Interpretation of Michelangelo's Creation of Adam Based on Neuroanatomy," *Journal of the American Medical Association* 264 [1990]: 1837–41. Image from https://en.wikipedia.org/wiki/File:Creaci%C3%B3n_de_Ad%C3%A1n_%28Miguel_%C3%81ngel%29.jpg, with modifications by the author.)

You may need to change your coping strategies toward more thoughtful and deliberate action and greater mastery over emotional responses. With years of rich experience and reflection, some achieve transcendence of their own circumstances, which we call wisdom, the ability to appreciate the truth in the light of the moment, the reality behind the appearance.

The timeless in you is aware of life's timelessness. And knows that yesterday is but today's memory and tomorrow is today's dream.
—Kahlil Gibran

Why is it that our memory is good enough to retain the least triviality that happens to us, and yet not good enough to recollect how often we have told it to the same person?
—La Rochefoucauld

Chapter 9 Aging and Memory

On March 27, 1827, one day after the death of Ludwig van Beethoven, an autopsy was performed. It showed, among other things, that his brain had remarkably larger and significantly denser folds than did normal human brains. Were these exaggerated findings in Beethoven's brain merely an interesting coincidence, or did they reflect decades of nearly continuous high-level cognitive activity?

The human capacity for learning and memory is truly remarkable. These abilities continue throughout life, and the brain never stops building new neural connections. Our brains are not, however, unchanged by aging, and older people often experience subtle shifts in processing speed, short-term memory, and retention and recall of some types of long-term memories. We also face an increased risk of dementing diseases such as Alzheimer's disease as we age, but these conditions do not by any means affect every person. Although learning can take more time and require more effort when we are old than when we were younger, the joy of learning new things—and the joy of remembering the past—can significantly enhance our quality of life.

The strength of a person's memory is strongly influenced by overall health, interest, motivation, and activity. Let's take a look at how memories are formed, the changes we might expect to experience with aging, and what conclusions we might draw about the value and importance of memory.

HOW THE BRAIN WORKS

As a useful oversimplification, think of your brain as being divided into two halves called hemispheres, with each performing different tasks. As Aretaeus of Cappadocia noted in the first century A.D., the left hemisphere controls the right side of the body, while the right hemisphere controls the left side of the body. In addition, the left hemisphere is sequential and analytical, and often judgmental, while the right hemisphere is more holistic, intuitive, and contextual and integrates information simultaneously. The left brain works with symbols and words, while the right brain deals in images.

At the basic level our brains are a collection of interconnected nerve cells, or neurons. The brain as a whole shrinks as we age, but this appears to be primarily due to a loss of water within the neurons. While some neurons are lost in late life, more are lost in early childhood. Brain atrophy and severe loss of neurons, previously thought to be due to old age, are now believed to be due to diseases, such as Alzheimer's disease. The rate of loss of neurons varies for different parts of the brain. The hippocampus, for example, which plays a role in memory, tends to lose neurons more rapidly than areas like the brain stem, which governs basic processes like breathing.

We appear to have many more nerve cells than we actually use. For example, normal intelligence has been documented in people with remarkably little gray matter. And many functions, such as regulating body water or fine muscle movements, are not impaired until 80 to 90 percent of the neurons are lost. It may be that the type and number of interconnections among nerves matter more than simply the sheer number of nerve cells.

Neurons communicate through complex interconnections called synapses. The very ends of the cells, called dendrites (from the Greek word for "treelike"), branch out like trees in a forest to touch the ends of other neurons. It appears that these connections continue to propagate throughout life. When a tree falls in the forest, the trees surrounding the newly vacated hole tend to sprout new branches to fill in the canopy. In the same way, it seems our brain cells continue to grow and repattern themselves to account for changing circumstances. The powerful implication of this is that our brain is not static and slowly decaying as we age but, rather, has the potential to become *more* complex through new and diverse interconnections. Could this continual repatterning form the underlying neural architecture of wisdom?

Illustration 9. Types of memory based on aspects of brain function.

Memory Type			**Brain Center**		
	Instinctive center	*Moving center*	*Physical center*	*Emotional center*	*Intellectual center*
Instinctive memory	Cellular function	Sensation	Basic awareness	Basic emotions	Intuitions
Physical memory	Reflexes	Imitations	Coordination	Adaptation	Learning new movements
Emotional memory	Mechanical expression	Likes and dislikes	Usual awareness	Conscience	Artistic creation
Intellectual memory	Phrase repetition	Appreciating novelty	Appreciating danger	Desire to know	Creative construction

Sources: M. Nicoll, *Psychological Commenteries on the Teachings of Gurdjieff and Ouspensky*, 5 vols. (London: Robinson & Watkins, 1952–56); adapted from K. R. Speeth, *The Gurdjieff Work* (Berkeley, Calif.: And/Or Press, 1976), 37.

To what degrees do biological changes in the brain influence thinking and behavior, and what changes in mental function can we realistically expect? As with the physical changes that occur with aging, there is considerable variety and variability in the mental changes each of us experiences. There is also clear interplay between physical and cognitive aging. Some people, facing increasing physical constraints, tend to dwell increasingly in the inner world of the mind, reflecting on the accumulation of life experiences and awareness of a finite life-span. We can also use the mind to help counteract or compensate for physical vulnerabilities, or use physical activity and maintenance activities like sleep to stimulate and cultivate the mind.

As the command center for the body, the brain operates simultaneously at many levels, which reflect our organizing analogy of the horse, carriage, driver, and master. Illustration 9 shows examples of some of the relationships of the brain's functions and their types of memories. Notice that these memories become more complex as we move from the instinctive and physical realms at the upper left into the emotional and intellectual levels at the lower right. The goal in stimulating our intellect is to nurture and rebalance the processes that maintain the instinctive, physical, emotional, and intellectual abilities. The key point

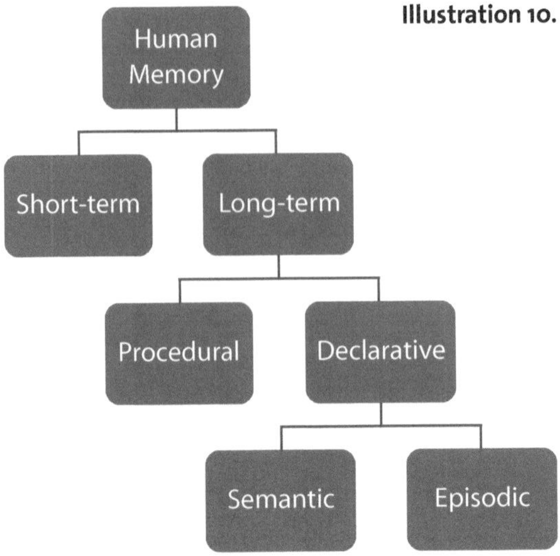

Illustration 10. Flowchart of human memory.

of the table is that many types of memory relate to various aspects of physical, emotional, and mental function. For example, the type of memory used to learn how to ride a bicycle (the intersection of physical memory and the intellectual center) is different from the memory of sensations.

HOW MEMORY WORKS

Memory is essentially the storing and retrieving of information. Functionally, it is based in the brain's neural connections. There are several different types of memory that together help us accomplish our daily tasks and learn new things.

Short-term memory, sometimes called working memory, is the term for memories that last about a minute, such as remembering a telephone number before dialing. Short-term memory declines with age, so it becomes increasingly difficult to remember the details of recent events, such as where you parked your car in the grocery store lot.

Long-term memory, on the other hand, handles memories we hold for a longer period of time, from days to decades. One type is known as instinctive or *procedural memory*. Procedural memory is what allows us to operate without conscious action, such as riding a bicycle, driving a car, playing a musical instrument, or typing a letter. This type of memory helps us perform various skills, tasks, or procedures and often stays intact even when other types of memory are declining. For example, an elderly patient of mine with severe dementia could not recognize or name a potato peeler, but if you gave her a potato she could skillfully peel it. Despite significant memory impairments, her procedural memory was intact.

The other type of long-term memory is known as conscious or *declarative memory*. Declarative memory involves recall, the search and retrieval of factual information that requires our awareness and thought. One type of declarative memory, called *semantic memory*, draws upon our general fund of knowledge to remember facts, such as that London is the capital of England, zebras have stripes, and most birds can fly. The facts are not necessarily linked to how or when we learned them. We use this semantic memory to match stored information with information in the environment. This capability does not decline significantly with age.

Another type of declarative memory is *episodic memory*, which draws upon specific episodes or events from life experience, such as what happened on your sixteenth birthday. Episodic memory seems to be located in the hippocampus and may decline with aging. Generally, the most powerful episodic memories are those in which we were jolted out of our usual egocentric waking state, often by a strong emotion, resulting in a new way of seeing the world. By capturing these experiences of heightened awareness, episodic memories in a way serve as a record of our personal conscious evolution.

The basic mechanisms for memory on a genetic and biochemical level have been largely conserved from the common ancestors we share with mollusks and snails. Eric Kandel, along with Arvid Carlsson and Paul Greengard, won a Nobel Prize in 2000 for his pioneering work on the physiology and biochemistry of memory. His work linked short-term memory with functional changes in existing synapses and long-term memory with the number of synaptic interconnections.

Our brains appear to have several gigabits of storage capacity, but there is clearly a limit. Like a computer, we can load new information (such as facts or experiences), as well as new programs (or ways to process and use stored information). We do not gain more memory capacity, but we can reprogram our brains to store and use information in new ways.

The Spacing Effect

There are some distinct patterns in how we form and retain memories. One is called the spacing effect: for events that occur repeatedly, we are best able to remember the events that have a longer time interval between them. Why is this? Perhaps from an evolutionary perspective this strategy allows very frequent, repetitive events (such as collecting water from a stream) to be lost rather than stored, saving brain power and energy for more important and less frequent events (such as remembering what happened during your last buffalo hunt).

The spacing effect was discovered by German psychologist Hermann Ebbinghaus and published in 1885. His exhaustive methodology for investigating memory included creating 2,700 nonsense syllables, like BOK or YAT, and then attempting to memorize random combinations of them. The process was incredibly tedious: he memorized and then recited two and a half nonsense syllables per second using a metronome for scientific rigor. One study alone required 15,000 recitations. He conducted these experiments daily for a year and then three years later repeated them all again!

In addition to revealing the spacing effect, his experiments led to the learning and forgetting curves, which describe how memory drops off over time. He found that retention declined the most after twenty minutes, then declined again after an hour, and so on. After a day the memory curve begins to level off. He also investigated how the position of an item within a list affects the likelihood of recalling the item. For example, we are often best able to remember the most recent information (the "recency" effect) or the first items in a list (the "primacy" effect). Modern researchers agree on the general points of Ebbinghaus's research, although there is some controversy regarding the precise shape of the remembering and forgetting curves. For example, an intense emotional memory such as September 11, 2001, may change the shape of the curves.

Retrievability and Stability

Two other important memory concepts are retrievability and stability. At the cellular level, retrievability describes how efficiently neurons respond to stimuli. It is the biochemical basis for recall, the ability to search and retrieve information from memory storage. Stability reflects the durability of memories, or how long they stick around. As stability decreases, the rate of retrievability declines as well. Different items have differing retrievability and stability characteristics for different individuals. For example, a show-off might be more apt to favor the retention of trivia in order to better maintain attention in social settings.

If you never recall an item, retrievability declines to zero and you forget it. However, if you restore the association before retrievability hits zero, its stability increases substantially. This means the repetition interval is now longer before forgetting takes place. When retrievability is already high, additional repetitions do not increase the durability of memory because of the spacing effect. Longer time intervals between repetitions produce more durable memories.

The Value of Forgetting

Memory requires forgetfulness, because physically we do not have enough room to store the totality of experience. We can't deal with storing all incoming sensory and imaginary information, so we filter the input and forget what we do not think we need. But is there any order or pattern to our forgetting? We probably forget in terms of relevance since successive stimulation confers increasing relevance. However, since evolution proceeds in the absence of the volitional aspects of human behavior—we evolved not by choice but by forces of nature—we do not have the capacity to forget at will. For example, you cannot decide to free memory space by forgetting an elderly neighbor because you heard that he died or the number 173 because you hardly ever use it.

■ HOW MEMORY CHANGES WITH AGE

Broadly speaking, aging affects the speed of information processing in the brain and body. Most of this change occurs in the central nervous system, where sensory input is translated into responses. In addition, the conduction velocity of sensory and motor nerves located throughout the body slows with age. The result is that older people tend to be slower than younger people in processing sensory information and reacting to stimuli. Older people are particularly slow to respond when an event comes as a surprise. Practice can help, but older people will generally not be able to match the processing speed of young people, so it is helpful to compensate by slowing down, making lists, avoiding challenging circumstances, rehearsing key elements, and trying other memory aids. On the other hand, older people seem to place a greater value on accuracy, so as we age our responses are slower but often more accurate.

Aging affects different aspects of memory in different ways. Recall that searching for and retrieving factual information from storage worsens over time. But recognition, the matching of stored information with information in the environment, changes very little. Encoding, the process of preparing information for memory, takes more time and effort as we grow older, in part because of the slowing of sensory processing.

What to Watch For

At any age, we have all had the experience of forgetting things, such as someone's name at a social event, where you put your car keys, or what you were supposed to get from the refrigerator. These episodes of forgetfulness are completely normal and are not the early signs of dementia.

We often confuse the normal aging process with diseases that affect the brain. Much harm results from the erroneous assumption that all mental function declines with age. In contemporary society old people cannot make a mistake without the specter of decline hanging over them. If your hand shakes a little after drinking an afternoon coffee, you might worry about developing Parkinson's disease. Those around you might interpret normal forgetfulness as a sign of early Alzheimer's disease. My advice to young people is this: if you have a secret fantasy, indulge it now. For example, if you have always wanted to gamble in a casino but wait until you are age seventy-five to visit Las Vegas, your family will begin to wonder about your cognition and mental status. Many examples of older people "losing their grip" are simply normal, rational decisions that are perceived through a lens that assumes the older person is mentally declining.

The tragedy of these damaging stereotypes is that if you come to believe you are mentally declining even when you are not, you may unnecessarily withdraw from social interaction, become more isolated, and lose self-esteem, resulting in significant declines in quality of life. You may become convinced that the problem is within you rather than in the society around you. In a way, aging is a myth: we start to look old in other people's eyes, and slowly they convince us of that fact.

That said, people do develop diseases that lead to abnormal cognition or memory loss, and the risk of these diseases increases with age. When, then, should you seek professional evaluation? If a person is unaware of memory loss or is having difficulty with the names of close friends or family members, then a potential problem exists. Difficulty with familiar daily activities such as using a telephone or making a meal also is of concern, as is getting lost in a familiar setting. Abrupt changes in mood, personality, or language or increasing frustration and anger are additional signs of illness and are not part of normal aging. Putting objects in odd places, such as car keys or a cereal box in the refrigerator, signify a possible disease process and the need for comprehensive evaluation. These symptoms are typically most obvious to people around you. In my clinical practice, I find that patients who come to my office alone and complain of memory loss often turn out to be relatively normal. But if spouses or family members accompany patients to the clinic and relate memory concerns regarding their relative, a dementing illness is more likely.

What to Aim For

Does memory have to decline with aging? Absolutely not! Like anything else, the more you neglect memory, the worse it gets. Usually when people leave educational settings they do not use their memories as actively. Information in real life is seldom packaged as neatly or organized as efficiently as it is in academia, and many jobs depend on compliance, loyalty, predictability, and reliability far more than learning, creativity, or imagination. Memory may get worse with aging, but primarily because we allow it to deteriorate by our ingrained habits.

There are certainly activities we can do to actively strengthen our memories or accommodate minor losses. Chapter 12 discusses specific examples. In general, these techniques work because they help us become more mindful and counteract the seductive power of habit. Lifelong learning is absolutely attainable for most older adults.

The Duplicitous Nature of Habit

Habits are the accustomed attitudes, familiar behaviors, and conditioned reflexes that keep us comfortable in everyday life. We acquire them from late childhood and through our schooling and cultural conditioning. We imitate those behaviors that we admire in others, and we develop additional comforting, cushioning habits of thought, word, and deed. Habits are remarkably robust over time and have both positive and negative impacts on memory and mental health as we age. Our mental, physical, and emotional repertoire consists almost completely of habits, and we cannot fully know ourselves until we have studied all our habits. As such, taking a critical look at our own habits is an important step in the aging journey.

Habits are what help us establish routines. Routines use the template of yesterday and reproduce it over and over. They provide mental economy since pondering unimportant matters is a waste of time and effort. In addition, there is safety in certain habitual actions, such as looking both ways before crossing the street. For people whose mental capabilities are diminishing, habit becomes even more important because its predictable structure helps to relieve mental shortcomings. Sometimes people with advanced dementia can interact with others without revealing the severity of the impairment because their generic social habits and routines are so polished. For young people the rules of life are indistinct, and there is plenty of room for risk taking, spontaneity, and improvisation. For some older people it is more comfortable to rely on tried formulas and familiar methods. Habits provide comfort, security, and reduced anxiety. They allow each action to be a safe and expected repetition.

But habit also inhibits, and relying entirely on habit to maintain functioning works only when circumstances are stable and predictable. Habit comfortably takes the place of creativity and shields you from a deeper knowledge of yourself. The desire to maintain a comfortable and stable life cushions you from unpleasantness and uncertainty. It is like you are wearing earphones continually playing your favorite music while masking the soft inner voice of your spirit telling you to wake up and get on with your destiny. In the analogy of the horse, carriage, driver, and master, habit is what keeps the driver stuck in the pub.

To get out of the pub, you must observe and study your habits. This is especially difficult because they are so familiar and so engrained. It is like being a fish and trying to appreciate the nature of water. Find a way to create a space where you can observe the nature of your habits and the profound impact they have on you and on your behavior. Initially this will be a nonjudgmental recording of your reactions to various circumstances. It may be useful as well as surprisingly accurate to assume that all your actions are habitual and watch the nature, type, and extent of your prepatterned reactions and conditioned responses.

It is very difficult to function without habits, and that is not necessarily the goal. But becoming aware of our habits can be a powerful step toward reducing their cushioning influence. Our inner life cannot grow and mature without surprises, shocks, and jolts to our awareness and changes in our daily routines. The mystic poet Rumi said, "If you are irritated by every rub, how will your mirror be polished?" We do not whet a knife with a warm stick of butter or strike a flint with a feather to produce a spark. Only unsettling inner events can help to awaken us and sharpen our memory and thinking.

THINKING REALISTICALLY ABOUT MEMORY

In thinking about memory many people assume the ideal is to be able to remember everything from your entire life in perfect detail. But apart from being unattainable, this ideal misses the point. It is helpful to take a step back and think about the limitations of memory and what it is exactly that memory has to offer our present and future selves.

Memories that may seem rich still have an essential poverty about them. Our memories are not a library of digital images that we can comfortably replay to rediscover their secrets. In reality they are suspended in time and space and do not re-create the real world, just as seeing butterflies pinned in a museum collection does not inform us how butterflies perform when they flit in the meadow. We seem to combine bits and pieces of memories to weave one large memory like a patchwork quilt. The patches are stereotypic views that persist despite a changing world. They are almost like dreams and almost certainly could not have been photographed as we remember them. Suppose we were asked to remember a famous place we had visited, like the U.S. Capitol. Can we tell from our recollection how many steps there are from the street to the entrance? Our memories do not contain that level of detail. When asked a comparable question later in life, we might assume that we have forgotten the number of steps when the information was never there in the first place. We simply do not observe the world with that level of awareness.

Shared memories often reveal our limitations. Have you ever discussed a shared experience with someone else and been surprised by how much you have forgotten? Different people retain different memories of the same event, so others can remind us of events and circumstances that we would never have remembered on our own. How could we have forgotten so much that seemed so important at the time? When a close friend or relative dies, part of ourselves is lost forever because these dear people held the keys to memories we have forgotten.

Time can also embellish memories. Age changes our relationship with time: our future shortens and our past grows heavier. As *Peanuts* cartoonist Charles M. Schulz remarked, "Once you're over the hill, you begin to pick up speed." The past was experienced at a time when anything was possible, and now when looking back memories are frozen in time. There is a kind of magic in remembering an event from when we were younger because today we can combine the sense of who we were at the time with the broader context we did not have when we were having the actual experience. In Charlottesville, Virginia, the taxis have witty slogans on their trunks like "Faulty boomerangs are nonreturnable" or "Corduroy pillows are making headlines." One of my favorites is "The older I get, the better I was." Mark Twain wrote in his expansive autobiography, "When I was younger, I could remember anything, whether it had happened or not; but my faculties are decaying now and soon I shall be so I cannot remember any but the things that never happened."

The past defines the present, which is the outlet to the future. As we age our future changes from being indefinite and infinite to definitive and finite. To advance we must acknowledge the evolution that inevitably has taken place in us over time—we are not the same person we were before. Some, failing to admit this development, set up a fixed and unchanging personality that continues to diverge from reality. But if we can revive the state of mind first experienced in childhood in which we can live in the moment and see the world as it is, we can escape from the power of age, for that mind-set is the fountain of youth. Pablo Picasso once said, "It took me four years to paint like Raphael, but a lifetime to paint like a child." For Christians this sentiment is spread throughout the New Testament. For example, "Verily I say unto you, Whosoever shall not receive the kingdom of God as a little child, he shall not enter therein" (Mark 10:15).

With age we can become trapped by our memories and in our own uniqueness as individuals. We cannot escape from the people we have been. A long life can hold us captive if we cling to the unchanging past and experience life mainly through the rearview mirror. Sometimes dwelling in memory is necessary and pleasurable, but it does not in general lead us forward. The cement is setting, but what is its shape? What is left for us to do with a limited future and an almost solidified past? Should we use our remaining time to improve our memory or look ahead and pursue our dreams? Perhaps we can do both.

You can tell whether a man is clever by his answers. You can tell whether a man is wise by his questions.
— Naguib Mahfouz

Learning acquired in youth arrests the evil of old age; and if you understand that old age has wisdom for its food, you will so conduct yourself in youth that your old age will not lack for nourishment.
— Leonardo da Vinci

Chapter 10 Intelligence and Creativity

According to anthropologists, millennia ago *Homo sapiens* made an evolutionary leap in brain capacity, from which emerged three crucial capacities. One of these is consciousness—our awareness of the self and our ability not just to know but to know that we know.

In modern times the sculptor Auguste Rodin powerfully celebrated this consciousness in his statue *The Thinker*. In the arts and philosophy, human consciousness has often been applied to appreciating the sheer wonder of the world, the power of sexuality, and the mystery of death. Man is perhaps the only animal that knows his ultimate fate: he is going to die.

The second capacity is language, the ability to symbolize the world and arrange word symbols into a discourse. Playing with those mental symbols, we create first stories and then abstractions—in short, we create our worlds. Language has an enormous influence over what we think of as reality, as evidenced by the vastly different worldviews of different peoples and cultures. It is with word-based pictures of our physical, emotional, and social worlds that the consciousness of the young can be molded. The third crucial capacity of humans is the creation of culture, which derives from self-awareness and language capacities.

What these capacities mean for us is that our minds—the ability to think, remember, and create—are at the essence of who we are. The nuances in our intellects and creativity change in old age just as they do in every stage of life. But by and large, old age for most people brings not a diminishing of thought and consciousness but a deepening.

DOES INTELLIGENCE DECLINE WITH AGE?

This question has been hotly debated. When testing groups, researchers have found that older people seem to do less well than younger people on standard intelligence tests. But when individuals are followed over time, very little decline is seen. Tests of verbal skill such as information retention, vocabulary, and comprehension appear to remain steady. On the other hand, tests of performance such as the speed of copying a complex diagram seem to decline over time.

It may be that traditional intelligence tests are not appropriate to measure intellectual functioning as we age. First, the fact that the speed of the response is given significant weight in these tests puts older people at a disadvantage. As discussed in Chapter 9, processing speed naturally diminishes with time, though that does not necessarily mean that an older person would fail to arrive at the correct answer. Moreover, as we age we tend to be more cautious and less willing than younger people to make a mistake in judgment. In real-life situations such caution has important survival value, but in an experimental setting it may bias psychological test results in favor of younger people.

Some have posited that intellectual achievements seem to occur on a curve that rises swiftly during the early twenties, peaks in the mid-forties, and gradually declines thereafter. There is a widespread perception in disciplines like physics and mathematics that people tend to do their best work earlier in life. Recent research, however, has to a large extent debunked those claims. An analysis of Nobel Prizes awarded in physics, chemistry, and physiology or medicine between 1900 and 2008, for example, found a clear upward trend in the age at which researchers produce their best work. There are many ways to measure intellectual contributions, and these vary greatly from field to field and with different career structures. Some have suggested that younger people may do well with theoretical work while older people are better equipped for experimental work, particularly in fields requiring the accumulation of a great deal of knowledge. One recent book, *Outliers: The Story of Success*, by Malcolm Gladwell, suggests that mastery of an area where one wants to succeed requires about 10,000 hours of practice—a claim that would suggest old age and intellectual achievement are indeed compatible.

WHAT ABOUT CREATIVITY?

There is no reason to expect creative intellectual accomplishment to decline in old age. To the contrary, it is remarkably easy to find monumental achievements inspired by very old minds. Sophocles was eighty-nine when his oldest son brought suit against him in an Athenian court. The son claimed that Sophocles had grown senile and was unable to manage his estate. In defense, Sophocles read aloud to the court a draft of a play he was working on. It was *Oedipus at Colonus,* which is, with Shakespeare's *King Lear*, one of the two great plays about old age. The case was instantly dismissed.

Galileo did his best writing, *Dialogues Concerning Two New Sciences*, at seventy-two; Benjamin Franklin invented bifocals and studied lead poisoning at seventy-nine. Bach, Beethoven, Monteverdi, Verdi, and Stravinsky produced some of their greatest works in old age. The Solomon R. Guggenheim museum in New York City was the last commission of Frank Lloyd Wright, which occupied him until his death at the age of ninety-two. Georgia O'Keeffe continued to paint despite failing eyesight into her late nineties.

In creativity, deepening wisdom, and sensibility we can actually become more, not less. German scholars use the word *Altersstil* to describe the development of a distinctive style in old age. It is characterized by a reduction to essential forms and a quality of transcendence. The late works of Donatello, Michelangelo, Rembrandt, and Goya provide outstanding examples of this old age sensibility. They reveal the essence of human experience and give expression to the ultimate spiritual reality.

Consider the classical forms and sensuous beauty of the *Pietà* in St. Peter's Basilica in Rome, sculpted by Michelangelo in 1499, when he was twenty-four. Note the delicacy of Mary's grief, with her bowed head and extended left arm. She seems younger than Jesus, and he appears almost asleep. Compare this work with the *Deposition*, also called the *Florentine Pietà*, with its incredibly moving and profound expression. Michelangelo completed the *Deposition* when he was over eighty. The large supporting figure with the hood is thought to be a self-portrait. There is a simplicity and power in this *Pietà* that communicates deep emotion and pathos that we can feel. Note the lack of symmetry and the serpentine quality of the composition. This is *Altersstil*.

Illustrations 11 and 12. Michelangelo's *Pietà* (left), completed when the artist was twenty-four, and *Deposition*, or *Florentine Pietà* (right), completed when the artist was in his eighties. Notice the profound differences in style and creative expression of Michelangelo's artistic genius. (https://commons.wikimedia.org/wiki/File:Michelangelo%27s_Pieta_5450.jpg; Stanislav Traykov / Creative Commons Attribution 2.5 Generic [ill. 11], and https://en.wikipedia.org/wiki/File:Pieta_Bandini_Opera_Duomo_Florence_n01.jpg; © Marie-Lan Nguyen / Wikimedia Commons / CC-BY 2.5 [ill. 12])

Profound creative accomplishments can occur in old age, and if extrinsic factors interfere with creativity, they often can be mitigated. Goya was deaf, wore two pairs of eyeglasses, and used a magnifying glass to paint his *Milkmaid of Bordeaux*.

Although we obviously are not all great artists, these examples are relevant to how we think about and plan for old age. There is no reason for old age to block our creative energies in their journey to expression. The process of self-actualization that drives creativity depends upon overcoming barriers by accepting certain limitations. No system of artistic thought includes a boundless life.

ACTIVELY MAINTAINING MENTAL PRODUCTIVITY

Continual evolution of the intellect and consciousness is not guaranteed. It does not occur mechanically the way genes regulate our physical development. There are stages of our conscious development. As a child we are dependent on others, and we learn discipline and obedience. With maturity we transcend this so that as adults we live with self-responsible authority. As we age further we may need to yield some of the possessions and independence we have accumulated. We quit thinking primarily about ourselves and our self-preservation, and we sacrifice the desires and fears of the body to that which spiritually supports the body. For some, this contributes to an awakening of the heart that leads to a shift from self-interest to a concern for humanity. With years of rich experience and reflection, some of us can transcend our own circumstances and become wise.

Maintaining intellectual productivity, nurturing creativity, and cultivating wisdom come down to knowing how to operate optimally within our limitations. They stem from our ability to appreciate the truth in the light of the moment, the reality behind the appearance. So as we age and grow we must make a choice: are we going to identify with our physical bodies and our memories that will ultimately decline and fade, or do we identify with consciousness that is carried within the body? To paraphrase the American mythologist and author Joseph Campbell, "Am I the bulb that carries the light or am I the light of which the bulb is only the vehicle?"

Each night, when I go to sleep, I die. And the next morning, when I wake up, I am reborn.
— Mahatma Gandhi

You know you're in love when you can't fall asleep because reality is finally better than your dreams.
— Dr. Seuss

Chapter 11 The Value of Sleep

Getting enough restful sleep is not a personal luxury but a biological necessity. Sleep is far more than giving the body some rest. It is the time when your brain forms new neural connections. This means that sleep is crucial for learning and maintaining memory. Getting—or not getting—adequate sleep also has a substantial impact on our physical fitness and emotional state. As such, it is an integral part of our physical, intellectual, and emotional maintenance throughout life and as we age.

■ HOW SLEEP WORKS

Although it feels like a very inert or dormant state, sleep is actually a time of great activity in the brain. It is through sleep that the brain incorporates and stores new information (learning) by revising or updating the neural network. During sleep some of the synaptic connections between nerve cells seem to weaken, while others strengthen. We sometimes use the phrase "let me sleep on it" while pondering a decision. This actually has a biological basis because the opportunity for the brain to incorporate new knowledge and reorganize existing memories may well help us make more informed decisions the next day!

As a result of this physiology, sleep has a strong influence on the quantity and quality of the learning we can achieve when we are awake. The relationship goes the other way as well. The more we stimulate our intellect while we are awake, the better we sleep. And the better we sleep, the more we remember and learn. Sleep deprivation not only compromises performance but also increases the likelihood of errors and forgetfulness.

The typical sleep cycle starts with ten to twenty minutes of drowsiness and very light sleep. This is followed by an hour or so of very deep sleep, followed by a rapid eye movement (REM) period when dreaming occurs. As the cycle repeats throughout the night, the length of deep sleep decreases and REM periods increase.

Two basic factors govern the nature of sleepiness and the quality of sleep: our body's circadian rhythm and the amount of time we have been awake. The interaction of these two factors determines the best time for us to sleep. The body's internal clocks were dubbed the circadian ("about a day") rhythm in 1959 by Franz Halberg, a pioneering scientist who founded the science of chronobiology. Circadian rhythms exert powerful influences on the regulation of sleep and drive our daily patterns of sleepiness and alertness. One of the physical manifestations of the circadian rhythm is body temperature, which tends to fall when we need to sleep and rise during waking periods. Other factors such as the amount of time we have been awake, exercise, caffeine, light, and stress also affect sleepiness. Greater cognitive stimulation during waking hours also seems to enhance sleep. Manipulating these factors can allow us to stay awake when we need to or effectively prepare ourselves for bed.

Experiments show that the natural human circadian rhythm runs on a twenty-five-hour cycle. You can flow with the normal cycle, which can become challenging from a social perspective, or try to reset your rhythm into a twenty-four-hour cycle using techniques like bright morning light and exercise. If you try to sleep too early within your natural cycle, you will experience insomnia. The solution is to wait until you feel sleepy. This means that Benjamin Franklin's aphorism "early to bed, early to rise, makes a man healthy, wealthy, and wise" is not true for everyone. The maxim that "sleep is more valuable before midnight" is also a myth. You need to sleep when your natural rhythms tell you to. The trick is to fit your natural sleepiness within the demands of modern life.

Sleep problems abound in modern society. Stress about sleeping compounds the sleeping difficulty by revving up the stress hormones that keep you aroused. Sleeping pills really do not solve the problem in the long term and usually increase the risk of confusion, memory loss, and falls. They are best used for very specific short-term circumstances, like a brief hospitalization.

SLEEP AND AGING

Our sleep patterns naturally change as we age. The most important changes include a decreased continuity of sleep (an increase in the number of arousals during sleep), a tendency for the largest period of sleep (and the most REM sleep) to occur earlier in the night, a decrease or loss of the deepest parts of non-REM sleep, increased napping, and a tendency to spend more time in bed. This type of sleeping pattern with a single, early period of deep sleep followed by more frequent arousals may have been important for our ancestors because lighter sleepers would have been more sensitive to nocturnal environmental threats such as predatory animals.

Some people find it harder to get to sleep and stay asleep as they grow older. In part this may be due to decreased cognitive stimulation during waking hours. Spending more time in bed, particularly during the day, also seems to reduce sleep quality. Studies of sleep in healthy elderly people also suggest some gender differences: elderly men show poorer sleep maintenance than do elderly women. But older women are more likely than men to complain of sleep problems and to take sleeping pills, possibly because they are more likely to share their concerns, or perhaps they are more sensitive to sleep quality and sleep loss than are older men.

Diseases such as depression, dementia, and sleep-disordered breathing (sometimes called sleep apnea) produce characteristic changes in the way we sleep. Depressed people show a shortened time between the onset of sleep and REM sleep, various changes in brainwave patterns, and early morning awakening. Patients with Alzheimer's disease can have a disrupted sleep-wake cycle that worsens as the disease progresses. They can exhibit longer napping, decreased eye movements in the REM period, and increased breathing problems during sleep.

Sleep apnea is a common problem among older people. While it has several causes, the major effect is relaxation of the throat muscles and tongue during sleep that closes off airflow through the nose and throat. People with sleep apnea typically snore loudly, and their breathing periodically stops during sleep. They may be completely unaware of the problem, although if they have a bed partner the partner is certainly aware. It is an important condition that usually responds to medical therapy but untreated can increase the risk of hypertension, heart attack, and stroke.

■ PRACTICAL WAYS TO IMPROVE YOUR SLEEP

Given the important relationships between sleep, memory, physical health, and emotional stability, how can you influence your sleep for better health? Essentially, it comes down to working with your natural circadian rhythm to take advantage of your natural periods of sleepiness. When you need to sleep, it is best to avoid those factors that will keep you awake, such as light or caffeine, and to take steps to reduce stress and make your environment conducive to sleep.

Regular exercise can have a significant impact on sleep, helping you to get to sleep more quickly and sleep more restfully. However, the timing of exercise is important and should not occur within three hours of sleep. This is because exercise increases your body temperature, awareness, and alertness. Exercise also helps to modify the sleep cycle. For example, early morning exercise in sunlight will help you to sleep better in the evening.

Alcohol and caffeine can both interfere with sleep. Limit alcohol at least three hours before bedtime. Alcohol reduces the amount of deep sleep and REM sleep, increases the number of awakenings, and further fragments sleep. In addition, alcohol can exacerbate sleep apnea. Avoid caffeinated beverages and foods except right after you awaken.

Sex at bedtime with your loving partner is a pleasurable aid to restful sleep, though obviously it can be disruptive to sleep in some passionate circumstances. If you go to bed but after thirty minutes find yourself tossing and turning and unable to get to sleep, get up and do some nonstimulating activity. Wait until you feel sleepy, to get back in synch with your circadian rhythms, and then go back to bed.

A normal feature of the circadian sleep cycle is to feel slightly sleepy right after lunchtime. A high-carbohydrate meal or a weak alcoholic beverage exacerbates this tendency. Not everyone feels this temporary fading in alertness, especially if overcaffeinated or working in a stressful setting. If you find yourself wanting to sleep after lunch, a short "siesta" of twenty to thirty minutes can be refreshing without disrupting your nighttime sleep cycle. A longer nap or napping later in the afternoon, however, may fragment the sleep-wake cycle, worsen insomnia, and produce a sense of fuzziness and disorientation on arising.

I see and I forget, I hear and I remember, I do and I understand.
— Chinese Proverb

The true art of memory is the art of attention.
— Samuel Johnson

Chapter 12 Specific Ways to Stimulate Your Intellect

There are myriad ways to stimulate your mind, foster your creativity, and improve your memory at any stage of life. Before deciding what specific techniques you might use to advance these goals as you age, it is important to first clarify your intentions. What is the reason to improve your memory? Do you want to minimize forgetfulness, maintain your independence, or preserve your identity? For some, cultivating memory holds value in helping maintain identity as life circumstances change. Stimulating thinking and creativity can also greatly expand your worldview and enjoyment of life. Is there something you have always wanted to learn about but never had the time? In facing increasing physical limitations, maintaining an active mental life can become especially beneficial.

The number of interconnections within our brains is mind-boggling. A typical three-pound human brain has about 100 billion nerve cells, each with interconnections up to 10,000 other neurons! As individual nerves die, new connections sprout, increasing the complexity of the neural network. Our brains literally grow with experience, and certain things that we do can stimulate and energize our brains significantly.

Broadly speaking, the quality of the intellect and memory depends to a large extent on overall health, clarity of intention, and the level of attention given to cultivating the mind. Attention is how well you can maintain your mental focus, while intention is the conscious will to participate in what you focus on. In 1937 international grand master George Koltanowski played chess blindfolded against thirty-four players simultaneously. He won twenty-four games and had ten draws while never seeing the chessboard, setting a world record for blindfolded chess that stood for seventy-four years. According to his obituary in the *New York Times,* his wife, Leah, said that his memory was so poor that he could not remember to bring a loaf of bread home from the market! Clearly the man had great capacity for attention when the intention was there, but like the rest of us, his focus in the absence of intention was not very impressive.

While each of us has differing mental capabilities, everyone's mental productivity and achievement can be improved with motivation and training. In general it is submitting to habit, laziness, inaction, or environmental distractions that keeps us from reaching our full potential. In terms of the brain's anatomy, there is no correlation between the size of brain areas and intellectual ability, and as we have seen in Chapters 9 and 10, there is no reason to believe that you will necessarily face insurmountable mental declines as you grow older.

In fact, your brain is well equipped to respond eagerly to new challenges, especially when you believe in yourself. It is possible to improve your memory and train your brain to work more efficiently. A recent study by the Mayo Clinic found that after eight weeks of practicing daily memory exercises, a group of healthy adults sixty-five years and older improved the speed of their overall brain processing substantially. While the study focused on the brain's auditory processing (memorizing sounds of different pitches), participants also showed general improvements in speed and accuracy for attention and memory. The important take-home message from this study is that improving your cognitive skills through practice can lead to generalized gains in problem solving and accomplishing daily activities. Again, the key is motivation, training, and believing that change is possible.

Alvan Feinstein, an internationally acclaimed epidemiologist and clinical research mentor, once told me that medical research was 90 percent drudgery (literature reviews, data collection, note taking, etc.), 9 percent good fun, and 1 percent sheer ecstasy when the results are finally apparent. His point is that you must choose an area of focus that will motivate you to continue through the inevitable drudgery to reach your goal. As Thomas Edison summed it up: "Genius is 1 percent inspiration and 99 percent perspiration."

PRACTICAL WAYS TO IMPROVE YOUR MEMORY

The more you use your memory, the better it gets. As we saw in Chapter 9, if a memory is never recalled, its stability declines to zero and it disappears. Keep your brain active, and reinforce existing neural connections by challenging your memory on a regular basis.

Practice Memorizing Things

Practice memorizing a short poem and repeating it every day for two weeks. Then memorize another poem. There are endless possibilities and vast archives of beautiful work to draw from. If poetry doesn't strike your fancy, try sports statistics, world leaders, or any other subject that interests you.

Another good memory booster is to work crossword puzzles every day. Odd words get recycled regularly, and with practice they are easily remembered. Puzzles in the newspapers are easiest on Monday and get more difficult as the week progresses. You can often find inexpensive puzzle books on the magazine shelves at grocery stores. Other word puzzles and Sudoku are also useful mental exercises.

A more social approach is to join a local acting group or take an acting class. In addition to forcing you to memorize lines, this has the added bonus of giving you a chance to make new friends, get out of your comfort zone, and be part of an interesting mix of people.

The important point in finding ways to challenge your memory is to pick something that is doable yet challenging without being overly frustrating or trivial. Your memory exercises should occasionally shock your system like a brief cool shower invigorates tired muscles. And, most important, they should be fun and stimulating. Eleanor Roosevelt is said to have offered this advice: "Do one thing every day that scares you."

How to Remember Names

Forgetting names is probably one of the most common and embarrassing memory complaints. Remembering has two opposing criteria: how much detail we wish to retrieve later (maximum retention) and how much effort we wish to exert in repetitions (minimum learning time). If you really want to remember someone's name you first must *intend* to remember the name. Then you must pay attention to the person's name and be sure you heard it correctly. To me this is where most of us drop the cognitive ball because at the moment of truth, when the person is telling us his or her name, our brain is not really in gear because we are distracted by beautiful eyes, an interesting outfit, or our own social anxiety.

Suppose someone held a loaded gun to your head and said, "In thirty minutes I am going to ask you this person's name, and if you cannot recall it, I am pulling the trigger." With that level of motivation, virtually all of us would be likely to remember a person's name. But we seldom are that vigilant, and we fool ourselves into thinking we really intend to remember the name. Approach an introduction with mindful intention to hear, process, and remember the person's name. Another basic strategy is to repeat the person's name right after you hear it, use the person's name at least twice during the conversation, and then use it again as you are parting.

ENRICHING YOUR MENTAL LIFE

Stimulating your intellect must become a daily practice if you wish to take maximum advantage of opportunities to learn, create, and remember. Often one of the best ways to stay mentally active is to enrich your brain with new knowledge, experiences, and skills.

Create New Experiences

Our brains are stimulated by new experiences, which is why it is beneficial to be aware of the muffling effects of our habits. Habits allow us to slip into a familiar context and spare ourselves the necessity of adaptation or dealing with uncertainty. Being cognizant of your habits, and occasionally actively breaking them, can help you stimulate brain growth and create new neural connections.

You may have noticed that when you travel time seems to slow down. If you keep a journal on a trip, which I highly recommend, you can review it when you return home and marvel at all the things you experienced and accomplished. Travel is an excellent way to stimulate brain activity because it forces you out of your habits and puts you in situations where you have to take note of the minor things you might ordinarily ignore.

Creating new experiences stimulates the brain and increases the release of a substance called brain-derived neurotrophic factor (BDNF). This substance is vital to memory and, like fertilizer, helps nerve cells grow and connect. BDNF levels are low in mentally impaired patients with Alzheimer's disease and Huntington's disease. Stimulating BDNF is one part of the biochemical underpinning of memory maintenance and improvement strategies. But you don't necessarily have to venture abroad to tap into the power of BDNF. Simply altering your daily routines can stimulate its release, as can exercise and eating curcumin, contained in the Indian spice turmeric that is used in curry.

A useful first step is to make occasional small random changes in your routine or your environment. For example, drive or walk to work using a different route, sit in a different seat at your dining table, or find a different location to watch television. Interpersonal communication and interaction also help to create new experiences and build new neural connections. New social activities create a number of novel and interesting experiences. For example, you might join an interest group such as an investment club, book club, or Bible study group. Or simply take advantage of opportunities to interact with others: pick up the telephone rather than send an email, or interact with the teller inside the bank rather than using the ATM.

Teaching is another powerful way to stimulate your intellect. Teaching forces you organize information and communicate with others. Perhaps you can share a hobby or skill, volunteer to coach an athletic team, or serve as a mentor through a local or national organization in your field. Teach literacy. Even reading books to children in school or in a public library can stimulate your brain.

Learn Something New

One challenging and satisfying way to stimulate your intellect is to learn a new skill or body of knowledge. Try learning a foreign language or playing a musical instrument. Take up painting or poetry. Learn how to dance. Or you might develop a hobby, such as model railroading, scrapbooking, genealogy, magic, or collecting. One of my older patients enjoys painting watercolor flowers. She could not continue with large commissioned projects and now creates personal greeting and gift cards. She told me designing the cards is fun but what she most enjoys is the reaction she sees when someone opens a card in her presence and realizes that it is a lovely handmade gift.

There are also many ways to gain knowledge about a topic that interests you. For example, you can take an online class, watch educational videos, or take in lectures either online or at free local events.

Expand on Something You Already Know

If you already enjoy a hobby or activity, try broadening your knowledge and repertoire. One of my nonagenarian patients was an accomplished concert pianist. When she became bored practicing her classical favorites, she made a switch to improvisational jazz. A change of pace like this can be challenging and fun.

■ USING YOUR BODY TO SHARPEN YOUR MIND

The mind, of course, does not exist in a vacuum. It supports and is supported by the body. Getting enough sleep, exercising regularly, and eating a well-balanced diet all help to keep your brain healthy. In addition, you can use the mind-body linkages to challenge your brain in ways that bolster and expand the neural network.

Deprive a Sense

When one or more of your senses is not functioning up to par, your brain creates new neural networks. Historical examples show how great artists and mathematicians overcame the loss of a sense and produced some of their most compelling work. Ludwig van Beethoven began to lose his hearing in his twenties and continued performing and composing his music despite an increasing disability. He was completely deaf when he composed and then conducted the premier of his Ninth Symphony in Vienna in 1824. The fourth movement of the work contains the famous "Ode to Joy." At the end of the performance he is said to have wept because he could not hear the applause. The audience threw handkerchiefs in the air for him to see their reaction and gave the performance five standing ovations.

Leonhard Euler, one of the greatest mathematicians of all time, experienced blindness in his right eye when he was twenty-eight. A cataract on his left eye left him totally blind at the age of fifty-nine. Nonetheless, his mathematical productivity increased to nearly fifty original papers a year, and it takes a book just to catalog his eight hundred prodigious contributions. He could recite all twelve books of Virgil's *Aeneid* from memory, and once he reportedly calculated the first six powers of the first hundred integers in his head as a remedy for insomnia. A few days later he repeated the entire table from memory for his assistants to write down.

To use a sensory deprivation strategy to stimulate your intellect, try spending some time with cotton stuffed into your ears when you are not engaged in driving or other potentially hazardous activities. Watch television with the sound muted and see if you can follow an athletic event or a political talk show by using your eyes and watching actions and people's facial expressions and gestures. Try tasting various foods and drinks while blindfolded or holding your nose. Pay particular attention to changes in texture and other ways to differentiate various flavors.

Use Your Nondominant Hand

One simple and safe way to stimulate your brain is to perform certain routine tasks with your nondominant hand. If you are right-handed, try eating with your left hand twice a week in the privacy of your home. Brushing your teeth is another good exercise for your nondominant hand. Try a more difficult activity like writing a letter or opening your mail while using your nondominant hand. Keep your dominant hand behind your back or in your lap.

Laugh and Play

We cannot age successfully unless we can laugh and play and have fun. The philosopher Alan W. Watts observed, "This is the real secret of life—to be completely engaged with what you are doing in the here and now. And instead of calling it work, realize it is play." Think about childhood. During that stage of life, learning and having fun often were part of the same activity. Plato once remarked, "The most effective kind of education is that a child should play amongst lovely things." It is no different in old age. Our conscious development depends on having a sense of humor and being willing to laugh and see the other side of things, and a person with no sense of humor is stuck. Satchel Paige, the great pitcher and oldest man to debut in Major League Baseball, at age forty-one, reportedly said, "We don't stop playing because we turn old, we turn old because we stop playing."

For example, try playing a computer game. Every conceivable format of gaming is available, from interactive board games to realistic fantasy and role-playing games. Some games use special sensors to allow you to participate physically in an activity, such as simulated bowling, tennis, or golf. In 2014 the Entertainment Software Association compiled some interesting statistics: 65 percent of households play computer games; 29 percent of gamers are over fifty; nearly half are women; and 59 percent play interactive games with other gamers. There are even games designed specifically to enhance cognitive skills for older people.

If computer games do not appeal to you, consider finding a brain-training app, solving jigsaw puzzles, playing chess, or pursuing other brain-stimulating recreational activities. Jigsaw puzzles are especially good for improving visual-spatial skills. You can make the task more difficult by studying the image on the box for a few minutes and then attempting to work the puzzle without referring to the image. The goal is to have fun and sharpen your perceptions and skills at the same time.

Practicing Laughter Yoga is another enjoyable and offbeat activity that may help to improve memory. Laughter Yoga clubs are spreading around the world, with laughing and having fun as the primary goal. The movement originated in India in 1995, led by Indian physician Madan Kataria, who reasoned that laughter was essential to wellness. The clubs are nonprofit and exist purely to allow people to laugh together. Many large communities have a laughter club, and the movement has continued to grow. The purpose is not just to have fun but to reach your goals of broadening and increasing your intellect, cultivating creativity, and improving your life and the lives of others.

As for old age, embrace and love it. It abounds with pleasure if you know how to use it. The gradually declining years are among the sweetest in a man's life, and I maintain that, even when they have reached the extreme limit, they have their pleasure still.
— Seneca the Younger (4 B.C.–A.D. 65)

The best and most beautiful things in the world cannot be seen or even touched. They must be felt with the heart.
— Helen Keller

Aging Secret 4 Manage Your Emotions

There is an excellent chance that you will live into old age. How will you confront being old? What will old age mean to you? How will you deal with losses? Who do you want to become, and who are you becoming?

Earlier chapters explored the influence of aging on biological and mental processes. These changes do not occur in a vacuum: they all take place in a rich cultural context that defines roles and expectations for us as we age. The transition to old age can have enormous emotional significance. How we handle it is central to determining whether we will age with grace and contentment, or with misery and despair.

From ancient times people have had a complex emotional relationship with aging. The roles and expectations of older people have fluctuated widely over the centuries, and they have been alternately treated with ridicule or adulation, often depending on economic forces, religious views, and class differences. Self-portraits of aged painters allow us to appreciate how they express their relationship with their aging selves and the world. Numerous famous thinkers have dealt with old age, and not surprisingly, they have had very different points of view. Aristotle, for example, found little use for older people in society and advocated withdrawal or disengagement in old age. Cicero and Montaigne proposed maintaining the pursuits of middle age as long as possible. Plato suggested a middle course in which the older persons are valued for their unique wisdom and continue to contribute to society but do not hold the same expectations for activity and engagement as in middle age. Today as in ancient times, we must choose our own path in aging within the context of the subtle (and not so subtle) messages we get from our culture and society.

Meaningful work and a sense of purpose strongly influence your emotional state as you age. What does work mean to you? Is traditional retirement the appropriate course for you and for society? What pursuits will bring your life meaning after retirement? Satisfactions from work are central to self-definition, self-esteem, and social status. People who accept the view that they no longer matter deny *themselves* a meaningful future. Our views of work and contribution to society must be enlarged to encompass a wide variety of occupations, personal projects, volunteer activities, and community involvement.

Combined with work or personal purpose, our complex web of interpersonal relationships—family and friendships—is largely what shapes and gives meaning to our lives. The relationships between generations can be a particularly powerful influence; with aging many of us must navigate what it means to become the oldest generation in the family. In the ideal relationship older people receive support, care, respect, status, and a sense of purpose. In return they provide cultural meaning, stability, and continuity with the past. What roles do old people play in family life? How have these roles differed across cultures? How can we manage our own shifting roles in a positive way?

Some of the most common emotional challenges among older people are stress, anger, worry, anxiety, depression, grief, and loneliness. Pride and vanity can also cause stress and exacerbate emotional challenges. Men and women often differ in how they respond to their changing bodies and circumstances. How can we manage our emotions when confronted with a constant barrage of negative social stereotypes about aging?

Our hearts are made to give away love and compassion. They are not designed to store anger and hostility. Keeping negative emotions locked inside can be an aging accelerator. It is like driving down the highway with one foot slammed down on the gas pedal and the other foot riding the brakes. You may travel at the speed limit, but the journey will be short and stressful and the vehicle will wear out prematurely. It is crucial to address and manage negative emotions to help find harmony and balance in your life. In doing so you will also save yourself a tremendous amount of wasted energy. In the allegorical framework of the horse, carriage, driver, and master, managing your emotions is training and maintaining the horse so that you may have the vitality, energy, and passion to welcome the master and move forward with your journey.

What's past is prologue.
—William Shakespeare

One ought to hold on to one's heart; for if one lets it go, one soon loses control of the head too.
—Friedrich Nietzsche

Chapter 13 Recognizing the Emotional Baggage of Aging

Throughout our lives we tend to view old age through the lens of our younger selves and all of the expectations and prejudices that our society embeds in us. The first step in managing our emotions is to recognize the faulty assumptions and ageism we are up against. This requires a critical perspective on how our families, cultures, and social systems view aging and the value of older people.

From ancient history through modern times, people have had a complicated emotional relationship with aging. Older people are variously viewed as worthless and feeble or wise and honorable. Recognize this history and the emotional baggage of aging, and you will be one step closer to shedding unnecessarily negative views and freeing yourself to enjoy a productive and fulfilling old age.

The poet and philosopher George Santayana said, "Those who cannot remember the past are condemned to repeat it." Chapter 3 reflected on how people have explained and understood aging throughout history and across cultures. Here we consider how past attitudes toward aging and older people contribute to the emotional baggage of aging today.

WHAT HISTORY CAN TEACH US

Old age has meant vastly different things in different historical periods, cultures, and social classes. Searching for clues about how aging was perceived and experienced in the past is challenging because the sources are distorted: only the upper class has tended to publish enduring work on this topic, and until the nineteenth century the record largely reflects aristocratic situations. Winston Churchill said, "History will be kind to me for I intend to write it." In addition, I must acknowledge that the scholarship presented here primarily focuses on Western and mainly European history and leans heavily on the work of Simone de Beauvoir. However, even these limited windows reveal valuable insights about our perceptions of and relationship with aging.

Often, even privileged old people have been an idle minority whose fate depends on the will and power of the active majority. When politically convenient, elders (almost always men) have been made intermediaries, judges, or advisers. But this honor can be fleeting, and younger adversaries also have removed older people from their posts. As a general rule, old people have been most disenfranchised in times of upheaval, expansion, or revolution.

All civilizations have exploited others, particularly vulnerable groups like the very young and the very old. Through the ages old people were a minority, as life expectancy was far shorter than it is now. For much of human history the treatment and care of older people have largely depended on the family. Naturally this resulted in tremendous variability in the treatment of older people, with some well cared for, others given sporadic care, others left to die in isolation, and some intentionally killed. Poor old people faced the worst prospects and often were seen as useless and burdensome. On the other hand, older people with wealth or high status in the community were afforded more respect. In some societies and classes old age itself has been perceived as a virtue, representing the culmination of life. In societies that institutionalize property and other rights in laws, old people gain power because laws are indifferent to physical prowess. Looking back at the evolution of views on aging over time, we can take a new, critical perspective on our current assumptions, ideologies, and social structures.

ANCIENT GREECE AND ROME

Some of the earliest accounts of attitudes toward aging appear in the mythology, art, philosophy, and political records of ancient

Greece and Rome. The themes in these accounts are often strongly negative toward aging, focusing on conflicts between young and old, disdain for the declines of aging, and the desire for continued youth. But political records and the writings of philosophers also reflect an association of age with wisdom, honor, and at times, political power. Both societies appear to have had a continuous tug-of-war on this issue, with older people simultaneously exalted as wise and ridiculed as weak.

Greece

In Greek mythology, immortality is highly desirable but means nothing without eternal youth. One example is the love affair of Eos, the goddess of dawn (an immortal), and Tithonus (a mortal). As Tithonus grows older, the pair realize what will happen to him, and Eos asks Zeus, the king of the gods, to grant Tithonus immortality. Zeus grants this wish but does not grant him eternal youth. When Tithonus becomes very old, debilitated, and demented, Eos turns him into a grasshopper, a life form the Greeks considered to be immortal and a form Eos presumably thought preferable to extreme old age in a human body.

Greek plays reflect similar ambivalence with aging: as the body fails, misfortunes sometimes offset even superhuman greatness. In Aristophanes's comedies, old age is used as a comic resource. The first use of the theme of the old man being beaten and mocked was in his play *The Clouds*. Interestingly, that work came in last place in a literary competition when it was first produced. The popular playwright Menander, known for perceptive observations of everyday life, also promulgated negative views of aging, stating that "people should die before they get too old" and "it is sad that old men should consider a sexual life." But even as Menander treated the characteristics of old age as ludicrous and unbearable, he also considered aging to be accompanied by wisdom and kindness.

Disparagement of aging is also found in Greek art and sculpture. Visit the Louvre in Paris today, for example, and you can see Greek vases depicting Hercules fighting Geras—old age represented by a wrinkled, bald figure of a man begging for mercy.

Attitudes toward aging were more diverse in the realm of philosophy. Of particular note is the divergence of views between two of the greats—Plato and his student Aristotle. In *The Republic* and *Laws* Plato posits that happiness is a virtue based on the knowledge of truth, which takes education and time—in other words, age. In his view physical decline does not limit and in fact enhances spiritual growth: "The spiritual eyesight improves as the physical eyesight declines." In his view, truth lives in the soul, the body is an illusion, and physical decay brings the soul greater freedom. Plato believed that, because of the experience and superior knowledge of older people, the elder should command and the young obey: "A man learns by being in the company of the old." Historians estimate that Plato lived to around age eighty.

Aristotle, on the other hand, had a strong preference for youth. He posited that humans exist by union of the soul and the body and thus that a person can be happy only as long as the body remains fit. In his *Rhetoric*, youth is glowing while old age is cold and ill-natured. Experience is not progress but degradation. He asserts that youth is better because fewer mistakes have been made. In *Politics* he expresses a wish to remove elderly people from power and suggests old men should be priests rather than politicians so that their roles will be limited to giving wise advice. Aristotle died at age sixty-two.

The tensions between disdain and praise for elderly people are also reflected in Greek politics. The Greek words *gera* and *geron* (the roots of our modern-day "geriatrics" and "gerontology") mean great age. In the seventh century B.C Greek city-states were ruled by councils of elders called *gerusia*, some of which had a minimum age requirement of sixty years. However, these councils may have had more honor than real power, and the rights and power of older people in ancient Greece oscillated over time. In Athens, for example, the laws of Solon gave significant power to older citizens, but that power was lost about a century later when Cleisthenes established democracy in 508 B.C.

Rome

Ancient Rome, which was a strong and stable society for many centuries, on the whole placed high value on elders, yet in its arts and culture there is evidence of much of the same ambivalence toward aging as was found in Greece. In Roman politics and matters of property, older people typically held considerable power. Among the wealthy were many old men who held the prestige and dominance of wealth. Until the second century B.C Rome was powerful, and much of the power rested in the hands of high offices that could be attained only at an advanced age. Political structures were carefully arranged so there were no shortcuts or "fast tracks." Old men's roles conferred more weight than young men's votes, so legal majority was not the same as a numerical majority. The Roman patriarch had privileged status in the family; he could kill, mutilate, or sell. To marry, a man needed his father's and grandfather's permission.

However, there is evidence that custom and public opinion limited this otherwise absolute authority of older men. Older people were regularly mocked in plays, especially those by Plautus, one of the most popular of the Roman playwrights. In portraying father-son relationships, Plautus's basic formula was that the father's miserliness hinders the son and the old and young compete as rivals. The father uses his wealth and position and employs dirty tricks, but his plots always fail. Age itself is respectable, but a man proves unworthy if he uses his power to satisfy his vices. One can also find negative views of the aging process itself sprinkled throughout Roman literature. The Roman poets Horace and Ovid wrote that everything that gives pleasure disappears in old age; the satirist Juvenal offered a vicious description of old age: "Growing old means seeing the death of those we love."

Toward the end of the empire, Roman conquests brought about social and political changes that diminished the power of elders. The esteemed Senate lost power to young soldiers, the magistrates. Under Gallienus's rule around 260–268 A.D., the Senate lost financial privileges. In hindsight, these developments near the empire's dissolution make especially poignant the statement of the Roman philosopher Cicero from several centuries earlier: "States have always been ruined by young men and saved by the old."

The political systems of ancient Greece and Rome did have one notable effect on older people that has largely endured over the centuries. It is these societies that developed the concept that property ownership is based in law and institutions rather than on personal strength. When the physical characteristics of the owner become irrelevant, rights matter more than individual abilities. Since wealth usually increases with age, this legal development has provided a mechanism in many societies for older people (men, in particular) to secure and maintain a high social status despite physical declines.

■ THE MIDDLE AGES

The Middle Ages were not a particularly nice time to be old. Attitudes toward aging were quite pessimistic, as reflected in art and ideology, and older people were essentially excluded from society while the young ruled the world. Very few people even survived until old age; for most peasants in this period age thirty was near the upper limit of the expected life-span.

Early Middle Ages

During the early Middle Ages in particular, governance derived more from the fortunes of battle than from stable institutions. This left little room for the richly experienced elder, with only two exceptions: Khindaswintz, who was chosen king of the seventh-century Visigoths at age seventy-nine, and Charlemagne, who ruled various parts of western Europe in the eighth and ninth centuries until his death at age seventy-two. Even popes were young. Gregory I, one of the most important early pontiffs, was fifty when elected in 590 and died at age sixty-four.

Various Germanic and Scandinavian tribes determined an individual's value by age with a scale of blood money to be paid if a free person was killed. For sixth-century Visigoths, for example, the rate was 60 gold coins for a child, 150 for a boy aged fifteen to twenty, 300 for a man aged twenty to fifty, 200 for a man aged fifty to sixty-five, 100 for a man over sixty-five, 250 for a woman aged fifteen to forty, and 200 for a woman forty to sixty. Burgundian law was simpler: 300 gold coins for those between twenty and fifty, 200 for those fifty to sixty-five, and 150 for people over sixty-five.

Middle Middle Ages

Feudal society became more organized around 1000, and people were mostly divided into three major orders: those who fought, those who worked, and those who prayed. The sword (not traditionally the realm of older individuals) was rated above work and prayer, and the roles of elderly people were trivial. The typically elderly chief magistrate, or doge, of Venice represented a unique exception. Epic poems from this era such as chansons de geste put young men in the role of heroes, and though they are often long-lived, these characters often have a timeless, comic strip quality.

In this period a man generally worked his land as long as he was able and then passed it to his oldest son. The older couple would then retire to a designated room in the home; in Ireland, this space was traditionally located in the western chamber. Elderly people without families sometimes received help from the lord or the monastery, and from the fourth century the church built asylums and hospitals, which probably benefited elderly people. Many, however, were reduced to paupers. The legend of King Lear told of a king of the Britons who had no male heir and three daughters who treated him badly in his old age. The tale was very popular, since it addressed everyday circumstances and complex, dysfunctional family relationships.

The medieval world cherished the dream of victory over old age through rejuvenation. Often in legends this takes the form of a rejuvenating talisman such as a magical fruit, an elixir, or entrance to the Isle of Avalon, the island of life where no one ever dies or grows old. In Scandinavian mythology battles between generations are common, and the young consistently win. Interestingly, the gods in Norse myths are not immortal and must eat youth-restoring apples for rejuvenation. Several myths deal with the apples being stolen or unavailable and the quest to get them back.

The concepts of the superiority of youth and the transfer of power from father to son influenced Christianity, especially from the eleventh century. In the period's stained glass windows and illustrated Bibles, Christ rather than God the Father is the central figure, and each stage of life is equidistant from the center. This pattern gives rise to an interesting comparison between Eastern and Western religions. Buddha, for example, is said to have passed through all stages of life and reached his highest point of perfection in dying at age eighty. Jesus, on the other hand, performed his tasks at a relatively young age before dying at age thirty-three.

Iconography in the Middle Ages was important, since it spoke clearly to illiterate people. In this art we find strains of the same ambivalence toward aging that was evidenced in ancient Greece and Rome. Elders are sometimes shown as wise counselors, prophets, or saints. Other times they are depicted as thin, bearded hermits. Father Time, for example, is sometimes shown as winged and thin, carrying a scythe. In the eleventh and twelfth centuries Death holds the scythe and Time, the enemy of life, is allied with Death.

Astrologers thought Saturn, the slowest and most remote planet, was cold and dry and associated the planet with poverty, senility, and death. In art Saturn is usually represented as a gloomy old man holding a scythe, pick, and shovel and leaning on a crutch. He sometimes has a wooden leg, is castrated, or is represented as decrepit Time with wings and an hourglass. In one image Saturn rides across the heavens while eating his son!

In general the portrayal of aging in medieval literature is rather grim. Philippe de Novare in 1265 wrote of four stages of life, commenting that "the life of the old is but pain and labor." A thirteenth-century poem says, "In October he is sixty and no more. Then he becomes old and hoary and so he must remember that time leads him towards his death." Some writers reflect a general sense of the world growing old and decaying. German bishop Otho of Freising wrote in his *Chronicle or History of Two Cities*, "We see the world failing, and as it were, breathing out its last sign of extreme old age." Focusing on the original sin of Adam and Eve, many believed that mankind was doomed to unhappiness. Decisions were often made day by day, with no long-term view; everyone was equally close to death. Hopes were outside time; man had to free himself from earthly life and look to his salvation.

Late Middle Ages

Even in the late Middle Ages longevity was still highly unusual. Charles V of France was considered to be a wise old man when he died in 1380 at forty-two. But gradually social and cultural factors began to shift, leading to subtle improvements in the status and experience of older people. The church legitimized the quest for profit, and commerce began to thrive. Contracts, rather than physical strength, began to play a larger role in property ownership, allowing people to accumulate possessions and money and to enjoy more financial stability. In the upper classes this changed things significantly for old people since they could increase their power by gathering wealth.

The treatment of old age in thought and literature grew somewhat gentler. In his *Convivio* Dante compares life to a curve rising from the earth to a culminating point in the sky and then coming down again. The zenith is at age thirty-five, with forty-five to seventy as the time of old age. In another analogy, aging is depicted by a mariner who, upon seeing land, lowers his sail and drifts into the harbor. From 1400 on there was a deluge of *ars moriendi*, illustrated books on how to prepare for death. They presented old age as a time to ensure your salvation and advised reading devotional books and making a will (leaving some to the church, of course).

There remained, however, a strong thread of negativity toward aging in the popular literature. Two writers of the time, Boccaccio (Italian) and Chaucer (English), made fun of old people and in particular present the sexuality of old men as disgusting. In Boccaccio's work, for example, the old man is impotent, while in Chaucer's he has a revolting mock virility. Society ridiculed old women as well. The south tower of

Bayeux Cathedral in Normandy contains a contemporary inscription in graffiti concerning Isabelle de Douvres, the mother of a bishop, that reads, "Why couldn't one hundred old women be buried here instead of only one?" Stories of this period also exploited the link between old age and blindness, a link with roots in reality, since cataracts blinded many old people. In literature this blindness often symbolized exile and loneliness while conferring spiritual insight.

In fifteenth-century France, there seemed to be a preoccupation with death, evidenced by numerous macabre illustrations representing "dances of death" or "triumphs of death." Death and Time are often represented as skeletons with scythes and hourglasses; man is merely a living corpse.

THE RENAISSANCE

One of the distinguishing features of the Renaissance was a rediscovery of the ancient world in which thinkers and artists melded classical values with the gospels and integrated a love of life and beauty with Christianity. As the arts flourished, however, old age continued to be presented in stereotypes, most of which were negative. Gray hair signaled ice, the winter of life compared to the green blossoming of youth. Old age was not generally considered desirable and was often viewed as a foil or boundary on the periphery of the human state.

Similar to the preceding centuries, the Renaissance praised physical beauty and detested the changes associated with aging. The misogyny of the Middle Ages was carried forward, and the influence of the ancients was significant. Fernando de Rojas's 1492 play *Celestina* is the first time an old woman appears as the main heroine. The author heaps on her all of the vices (and some of the assets) attributed to old women: she is wise, hedonistic, miserly, and sexually manipulative.

Comic theater in this period continued to ridicule old men. The most vitriolic attacks were often directed at the nouveau riche, merchants who became rich in their last years. To the penniless middle-aged man this seemed like an injustice, a scandal that became particularly unbearable if elder merchants bought young wives and frustrated the desires of young men.

Some writers treated aging more kindly. The popular scholar Erasmus devoted a dialogue in his *Colloquies* to aged people in which he described the consummate old man at sixty with white hair, good eyesight, a ruddy complexion, and no wrinkles. Luigi Cornaro, called the Apostle of Aging, wrote *A Treatise of Health and Long Life, with the Sure Means of Attaining It* in 1547 when he was eighty-three. His book emphasized moderation, exercise, and dietary restriction and had over one hundred editions. Cornaro, who reportedly lived to 102, said that "a wise life leads to a fine old age."

The poet Agrippa d'Aubigné (1552–1630) led a full and adventurous life and ultimately wrote many poems extolling the virtues of old age. He lost his first wife early and was part of the Huguenot conspiracy to kidnap the young French king François II. When Marie de Médicis assumed the crown, d'Aubigné was a target for revenge and retired to Chateau Crest in Geneva with his new, much younger wife. Living the life of a country gentleman, he wrote of age as a winter of calm leisure or a peaceful harbor, rather than a period of frigid sterility. In his masterpiece, *Les Tragiques*, he states that an autumn rose is lovelier than any other.

Another writer and philosopher, Michel de Montaigne, provided a fresh look at the reality most people wanted to disguise: "Kings and philosophers defecate, and so do ladies." Although he did not think aging enriched him, his essays became deeper and more intimate, original, and philosophical as he aged. It was when he felt his powers were waning that he was at his peak.

In Renaissance iconography, aging is often represented in terms of the seasons. November, for example, is drawn as a sick, old man who then neared death in December.

Another artistic theme of the Renaissance was the Fountain of Youth. In a depiction by Cranach the Elder, elderly women play in the fountain and emerge young on the other side. When Cranach was asked why women were the major focus, he reportedly replied that if women felt young then men would automatically be young. The myth of the Fountain of Youth became so popular that Ponce de León searched for it in 1512 and ended up discovering Florida; contemporary Florida's influx of elderly people is perhaps more fitting than many realize.

The seventeenth century brought about some new cultural developments that were in some ways detrimental to the status of old people. With the exceptions of Louis XIV and the series of popes elected after the Council of Trent (1545–63), who were mostly in their sixties and seventies, young warriors held the power, and life was hard on old people. The average life-span was around twenty-five. Half the children died in infancy, and most adults died around thirty-five. People often endured brutal treatment in childhood and a life of exhausting labor,

Illustration 13. *The Fountain of Youth* by Lucas Cranach the Elder in 1546. Notice the aging figures entering the pool on the left and being transformed into young people as they bathe and leave the water on the right. (https://en.wikipedia.org/wiki/Fountain_of_Youth#/media/File:Lucas_Cranach_%28I%29_-_Jungbrunnen_-_Gem%C3%A4ldegalerie_Berlin.jpg)

malnutrition, and poor hygiene. By age thirty the typical peasant was bent and wrinkled. Those who made it to old age were usually confined to their homes; men of the upper classes often either retired to their estates or took holy orders.

In England in 1603 Queen Elizabeth instituted the Poor Law to combat devastating poverty and harsh living conditions by establishing charitable institutions such as almshouses and hospitals. Prior to the Poor Law, parishes had helped only their own paupers, and crippled and old people were placed in terrible asylums. The Poor Law built upon the religious view that the rich should give generously to charity. This was a time of significant social upheaval, and several decades later the Puritans, merchants strangled by crown-granted monopolies, revolted. With no integrated middle class, rebellion broke out and the British Crown was defeated during the English Civil War.

The rise of Puritan values markedly affected old people and those in poverty. Puritanism adapted Christianity to the spirit of industrial competition and considered idleness a sin: "He who doesn't work doesn't eat." At the same time, aged middle-class Puritans were better off as a result of the culture's idealized family structure and respect for the grandfather in particular. The philosophy of Jean Bodin influenced the Anglican convention of 1606 in which life and death rights of children were given to the father. Many Puritan sermons had the theme of "government of the household," in which authority should belong to elderly people. Old people were thought to be set free from lusty passions and therefore able to practice the key virtue of asceticism. Since success meant divine blessing, old age was a clear sign of virtue.

The English Restoration, beginning in 1660, was a violent reaction against the Puritans. King Charles II opened theaters that challenged Puritan values by presenting plays concerning generational conflict and disparagement of old age (for example, William Congreve's *Love for Love*). Literature of the period treats elderly people as a laughingstock, mocking old women and directing the sharp edge of sarcasm at old men. There are instances in which the treatment of old men becomes more nuanced: in some works, the older man remains a man and no human feelings are forbidden to him. The French dramatist Pierre Corneille in his play *Le Cid*, for example, espoused a more positive sentiment that aged man should have a place and has the right to be loved. The play contains many remarkable statements about love and age.

For his part, Shakespeare displayed a significant negativity toward aging. Applying all the classic aging clichés such as winter and twilight, his sonnets show an acute bitterness against age. The soliloquy of Jaques with the seven ages of man in *As You Like It*, act 2, scene 7, is particularly pessimistic:

All the world's a stage,
And all the men and women merely players:
They have their exits and their entrances;
And one man in his time plays many parts,
His acts being seven ages. At first the infant,
Mewling and puking in the nurse's arms.
And then the whining school-boy, with his satchel
And shining morning face, creeping like snail
Unwillingly to school. And then the lover,

Sighing like furnace, with a woeful ballad
Made to his mistress' eyebrow. Then a soldier,
Full of strange oaths and bearded like the bard,
Jealous in honour, sudden and quick in quarrel,
Seeking the bubble reputation
Even in the cannon's mouth. And then the justice,
In fair round belly with good capon lined,
With eyes severe and beard of formal cut,
Full of wise saws and modern instances;
And so he plays his part. The sixth age shifts
Into the lean and slipper'd pantaloon,
With spectacles on nose and pouch on side,
His youthful hose, well saved, a world too wide
For his shrunk shank; and his big manly voice,
Turning again toward childish treble, pipes
And whistles in his sound. Last scene of all,
That ends this strange eventful history,
Is second childishness and mere oblivion,
Sans teeth, sans eyes, sans taste, sans everything.

Shakespeare's *King Lear* is the only great historic work other than Sophocles's *Oedipus at Colonus* in which the hero is an old man. Old age is here presented as the truth of the human state, the basis for understanding man and life. With old age, Shakespeare saw a wandering mind—not wisdom. The old man is banished.

■ THE EIGHTEENTH CENTURY THROUGH MODERN TIMES

Scientific, economic, cultural, and social changes drove substantial improvements in the quality of life for elderly people starting in the eighteenth century, although no doubt many continued to face poverty, hardship, and maltreatment—problems that persist to this day.

Eighteenth Century

Since the 1700s significant improvements in hygiene dramatically lowered the rate of premature death, paving the way for many more people to survive until old age. Also in this period, people have more and more begun to view poverty as a societal problem, not the individual's fault. The English Relief of the Poor Act of 1782, for example, gave parishes the right to form unions to collect and spend for the benefit of poor people. Magistrates of Speenhamland in rural England issued the Relief to the Poor Law in 1795, which stated that if a man cannot earn a living, society must provide, laying the groundwork for basic welfare for elderly people, as well as for widows, orphans, and those who were ill or unemployed.

Eighteenth-century technological progress expanded industry, finance, and trade and created a rich and powerful new merchant class. In the European image of the day, the ideal man was honest, straightforward, and productive. A rich old merchant was now viewed as worthy of respect, displacing the old Chaucerian stereotype that directed envy and revenge against successful businessmen. Becoming old and rich conferred special respect because a man's prosperity was considered to be the result of his wisdom and virtue. Wealthy merchants placed moral value above artistic considerations, and they hated showiness.

For the wealthy, life became increasingly comfortable. Travel became easier, and a successful business or rich social life required intelligence and experience, relying less on strength or physical exertion. For example, Maurice, Count of Saxony (1696–1750), won a decisive victory against the Duke of Cumberland at the Battle of Fontenoy despite a major flare-up of his gout and peripheral edema. The active life-span grew longer, and society was not surprised to see an older man with a younger wife.

Literature reflects a mixture of attitudes toward older people. In eighteenth-century France the literature is full of conflicts in which man is harsh and malicious, for example, in the works of the Marquis de Sade. Others displayed more optimism and humanitarianism; the Genevan writer and philosopher Rousseau, for example, reminded adults that they had been children once. An elderly man symbolized the stability, continuity, and unity of the family. Families became wealthy through inheritance, and respect for the elderly head of the household became a basis for capitalism. One's happiness could be purchased through the practice of philanthropy.

In some ways the eighteenth century can be seen as an age of feeling: truth was sought in the heart, and virtue was praised; vulnerable family members like elderly parents and young children were objects of tender emotion. Happiness was associated with moderation and leisure, making old age seem a happy and exemplary period. Although wealth was increasing, absence of desire was considered more valuable than possessions. The Figaro plays of Pierre Beaumarchais showed various shades of character in elderly people. In *Barber of Seville*, for example, people mostly become good as they grow older, with the exception of those who are dreadfully wicked from birth.

There remained, however, plenty of pessimism toward aging. Jonathan Swift in *Gulliver's Travels* created one of the harshest portraits of old age ever drawn, with its incredibly pessimistic descriptions of decrepit senility. His Struldbrugs are wretched individuals who are immortal and perpetually aging. Old age to Swift meant not only decrepitude but being a solitary outcast, left behind as the world evolves. The notion of being "a foreigner in your own country" was a new concept that he contributed.

Pessimism toward old age is also reflected in the continued search for rejuvenation. As we have seen throughout history, people have never wished to be undying old men and old women; instead, they dreamed of a Fountain of Youth. Goethe's *Faust* echoes this theme. If Mephisto gives Faust back his youth, he will not be so deceived by pleasures that he will want to stop Time. Goethe wanted to be able to change his skin, and the key was the possibility of rejuvenation.

Nineteenth Century

The Industrial Revolution, migration to urban areas, and the rise of a new class—the proletariat of industrial workers—transformed Europe in the nineteenth century. Populations soared: 187 million in 1800 swelled to 266 million in 1850 and 300 million in 1870. Population growth plus increased life-spans meant that there were now too many old people to be ignored. Scientific progress shattered some myths, and medical advances made it possible to provide more substantial care for old people. Nonetheless, it seems older people for the most part did not receive significantly better treatment as a result of these changes.

Between 1840 and 1850 the countryside could no longer feed those who lived on it, and technological progress made it hard for the poor to compete in industrial areas. These changes were catastrophic for most old people. The Industrial Revolution yielded an incredible waste of human life. Workers died at young ages, and those who survived were reduced to poverty when their age kept them from working. England and France saw an enormous increase in aged vagabonds, mendicants, and destitute old people. Old people were at the mercy of their families. Although the law tried to protect old people from exploitation and neglect, these efforts largely backfired, and some old people disappeared under suspicious circumstances, perhaps to parricide.

The Grimms' fairy tales, published in 1812, capture German folklore and offer a remarkably disparaging view of older people. The old men typically are portrayed as pitiful and impoverished; the old women are often wicked and dangerous. One tale, "The Duration of Life," is particularly poignant. In this work all creatures are given a life-span of thirty years. The donkey, dog, and monkey ask God to reduce their life-span by eighteen, twelve, and ten years, respectively, since too long a life is wearisome. Man asks for more life to be added to his thirty years. He gets the first thirty years as his own, then the donkey's eighteen when he carries burdens, the dog's twelve when he growls and crawls around with no teeth, and finally the monkey's ten years in which he has no wits and is laughed at by children.

This disparagement is by no means universal, however. In some stories the image of aging is of transcendence, growth, and wisdom. Younger heroes and heroines need the virtues of patience, courage, self-discipline, and restraint, while older heroes and heroines exhibit awareness, sincerity, curiosity, and broad-mindedness. The adversary of the older protagonist is an inner demon, not an external threat, and the battle is one of personal transformation. The spoils of victory are illumination and transcendence rather than jewels and material treasure. And the result of this struggle is beneficial to all of mankind, not just to the victor. The enemy is often vanity, self-importance, or misunderstanding.

Despite persistent negative stereotypes and the abysmal conditions faced by poor old people, elderly people at the top of the social structure were very well treated. The gap between rich and poor elderly people was striking during the late nineteenth century. Royalists of the French Restoration set up a gerontocracy, with political power based on property. Investment became the primary method for generating profit, replacing rent as the major economic influence. Common interests symbolized by the elderly grandfather bound family members.

By the mid-1800s banks and industries held the political power. Generational conflicts tended to disappear in the upper class and provided solidarity against the threatening lower classes. Often the son gained a higher position than his father, and the father was proud of his son's success. Life was more complex, and in many areas seniority became a prerequisite. In the Victorian era, England held puritanical values: strict morality, profit, and austerity. All of these benefited older men. The contemporary view of aging morphed: with age came increased associations, knowledge, and wisdom.

Artistic representations continue to show the staircase of life, with middle age at the top and increasing age as a decline.

Nineteenth-century literature began to reflect a more genuine view of old age, for the first time dealing in a realistic manner with all classes, especially the exploited classes. A new theme appears: that of the devoted old servant. The aged poor made a timid entry into literature! Early nineteenth-century melodramas adopted stately and touching old men who make mistakes but atone for them by having noble hearts. Charles Dickens opposed the view that old age and childhood were similar processes. Arthur Schopenhauer professed total pessimism but set high value on old age as a consequence of his pessimism. In chapter 6 of *Wisdom of Life* he wrote, "The burden of life is lighter in old age than in youth." Ralph Waldo Emerson praised the value of old age in these terms: "Rejoice in escape from dangers; No strain for achievement; No more doubt or uneasiness; and Acquired experience and knowledge." Victor Hugo also glorified old age. He used the image of a worn-out body and a lofty soul in *Les Misérables* and carefully displayed the affinities between children and old people.

Twentieth Century

The twentieth century brought continued urbanization and incredible diversity of experience. People continued to leave the family farm and small town to seek better prospects in the city, upending traditional family structures. Patriarchy entered a state of decline. Young men advanced violent political movements. More recently, the growth of technology has meant that personal knowledge does not grow with time but becomes obsolete. Age in some ways has become less of an advantage, and youth is prized.

In each era of human history, it seems, everything changes yet everything remains the same. Modern variations of ancient clichés emerge again and are recycled. Though life-spans have increased substantially and living conditions have drastically improved in many parts of the world, there remain persistent emotional, social, and cultural threads that alternately disparage old people as weak or wicked or exalt them as wise and virtuous. The truth is that we are all people—regardless of age—and in order to live to our fullest potential we must confront and shed the negative assumptions that have endured for centuries. With a realistic and respectful perspective on aging, we can control our own destiny.

> **Age only matters when one is aging. Now that I have arrived at a great age, I might as well be twenty.**
> **— Pablo Picasso**

> **How old would you be if you didn't know how old you was?**
> **— Satchel Paige**

Chapter 14 **Self-Image and Shifting Roles**

For young people, the horizons seem boundless. Then the years pass, and suddenly you cross a threshold and realize that your number of remaining years is limited. What does it mean to have most of your life-span gone? Can you ever really change from who you have been? What is left to do with a finite future? How does one adjust to changing roles in work, family, and society? What factors influence the private inner experience of aging?

Negative aging stereotypes can become a self-fulfilling prophecy: if you view aging and elderly people with hostility, then you have sealed your own fate. As we age we seem to become more like ourselves: our underlying chief personality characteristics become more and more apparent. Older people with a suspicious streak may suspect that those near them will hasten their decline rather than help to reduce it. Fears of illness, infirmity, and economic instability can become all-consuming, poisoning one's relationships with others and enjoyment of life. Or a more generous spirit can blossom in old age as one takes the time to appreciate the small things and live with gratitude in the heart. Those who are comfortable in their own skin and optimistic about the future can derive ever greater joy from their inner experiences, work, and family. Awakening yourself to your own self-image and confronting the influences of society free you to cultivate a rich and healthy emotional life.

THE VIEW FROM WITHIN

Our bodies undergo continual physical changes throughout life, though these are often especially apparent in the very young and the very old. When we look in the mirror we cannot see ourselves in the objective way a stranger would view us. As a result, old age often takes us by surprise, and the realization that one is now old can be traumatic.

But it does not have to be. American writer Max De Pree said, "We cannot become what we need to be by remaining what we are." For the most self-assured among us, age can remain theoretical; as Mark Twain wrote, "There is no difference between a young man and an old man as long as they are both sitting." If you look at yourself with contentment and appreciation and are comfortable with the aging process, age is only of small account.

Self-portraits of aged painters reveal some of the diverse ways different people perceive their own aging. For example, Anna Mary Robertson Moses (Grandma Moses) at around ninety has a bright, sensitive expression. Leonardo da Vinci at age sixty shows a beard and eyebrows with impetuous vitality and wisdom. It is evident that he possesses his full powers, yet there is a hint of disappointment that lingers on the edge of cynicism. Tintoretto at age seventy shows despondency, exhaustion, and bewilderment. Rembrandt at age sixty-three appears proud, full, successful, and anticipatory. Titian at age eighty or ninety reflects a conventional solemn tranquility. Monet is the only one who is cheerful, even downright exuberant, with a clear complexion and bright, merry eyes at age seventy-seven. The *Triple Self-Portrait* by Norman Rockwell is a particularly delightful commentary on the self-image of an aging artist. In it an aged Rockwell paints himself as a much younger man as though that is how he sees himself in the mirror.

Among people affluent enough to have choices, the reaction to growing old often reflects an amplified version of their personality and values. Among writers, Walt Whitman maintained a cheerful optimism; Luigi Cornaro exhibited moderation and generosity; Goethe and Tolstoy addressed incessant struggles; and Ernest Hemingway never came to terms with his loss of vitality.

Illness is often more apparent to the person who endures it than it is to others. Aging, on the other hand, often is more apparent to others than it is to ourselves. As a defense, some old people prefer to think of themselves as unwell rather than as old. An eighty-year-old patient of mine said, "I feel just like a young person with a little something the matter with them." What seems to happen is that we grow old in other people's eyes, and slowly they convince us that we are old. How this influences a person's outlook, attitude, or expectations is highly individual. It is also something we have the power to control.

THE CHANGING PERCEPTION OF TIME

Remember the fifteen-minute recess in elementary school? Fifteen minutes! In that time we could choose sides and play a game of kickball or baseball. Time moved slowly, and Christmas never seemed to come. But as the years go by, time seems to move faster and faster. What causes this change in time perception?

In childhood, adults impose a structure on time: wake up, school, television or computer time, mealtimes, and bedtime. Days seem so long their end cannot be realized, and this provides the feeling of an eternity. An old person can grasp the future and the finiteness of life. The return trip of a journey usually seems to take less time than the initial leg of the trip because we have become familiar with the route and know what to anticipate. In addition, in childhood we have little life behind us, so proportionally years are longer. For example, as a six-year-old I had four years of memories going back to age two, and one year was 25 percent of my lifetime memories. Now at over age sixty, one-quarter of my memories cover more than fifteen years. So proportionally what I perceive in one year is roughly equivalent to what a six-year-old perceives in three and a half weeks.

The quality of our future changes over time from indefinite and infinite to more definitive and finite. As discussed in Chapter 12, habit accelerates time perception by making the future more predictable as one's schedule conforms to our prefabricated templates. Breaking habits and cultivating anticipation or small surprises can slow time perception. For example, traveling often creates memories that seem to play back in slow motion. Using mindfulness to counteract the natural speeding up of our life experience, it is possible to savor the time one has and live more fully in the moment.

LESSONS FROM PHILOSOPHY

We all must face the fact that aging will bring changes to our physical bodies and affect our relationships with ourselves and others. One major challenge is to identify what can make us truly happy during this transition, and how to square that with society's expectations of us. One philosophical view, espoused by Aristotle in his *Rhetoric*, is that we should resign ourselves to inevitable decline and loss and withdraw from relationships and contributory activities. Numerous other philosophers from ancient times to this day, however, have put forth counterarguments that are far more optimistic on the potential of aging people. In *On Old Age* (*De Senectute*), for example, Marcus Tullius Cicero raises and summarily discredits four negative views of aging: "First, that it withdraws us from active employments; second, that it enfeebles the body; third, that it deprives us of nearly all physical pleasures; fourth, that it is the next step to death." He posits that old people have much to offer in work and business. According to him, those who say otherwise "are like men who would say that a steersman does nothing in sailing a ship, because, while some of the crew are climbing the masts, others hurrying up and down the gangways, others pumping out the bilge water, he sits quietly in the stern holding the tiller. He does not do what young men do; nevertheless he does what is much more important and better." As for the decline in strength and ability, Cicero says, "You should use what you have, and whatever you may chance to be doing, do it with all your might." In his view, old people in fact possess greater capacity for virtue, reason, and prudence than the young.

Another perspective, perhaps best articulated by Plato, recognizes that old age brings qualitative differences in character and maturity that in fact bring benefits to society. Although aging does include some declines, they are offset by compensations and adaptations; there is no reason for older people to withdraw from the world, and they should remain an integral part of society.

Old age is no refuge from an empty life, and ultimately you are obliged to live in old age whether or not you have developed a satisfactory image of yourself. Accepting your limits and confronting your finite future are markers of maturity and not a matter of resignation or defeat. You have a choice in the attitude you take about aging.

■ WORK AND SATISFACTION

For many people, the satisfactions gained from work are central to self-definition, self-esteem, and social status. Yet in many ways modern society imposes views of meaningful contribution after retirement that are far too narrow. People who believe that they are valuable only as long as they are profitable deny *themselves* satisfaction in retirement and generate much future distress for themselves and others.

Reconsidering Retirement

Technology has a substantial influence on what retirement means. Before the Industrial Revolution, old people were valued for the useful information they held: it was the elders who remembered long-ago floods or understood long-term patterns such as the migrations of animals, for example. With the invention of the printing press, memories held by the individual became less important, as ideas could be written down and mass-produced. With the rise of industry, human value became measured by productivity and profit. Today the status of old people has become even more ambiguous with changes in the workplace. With the rapid and increasing pace of technological change, skills learned are soon outmoded. As personal examples, my former proficiency with Morse code, using a slide rule, or punching computer cards to run a statistics program on a mainframe computer are now obsolete. My children are not sure what a slide rule is or what it can do.

As the comic strip *Dilbert* reminds me daily, the workplace is not always fair. Job discrimination based on age is illegal, but business reorganizations with mergers, acquisitions, and downsizing seem to have a disproportionate effect on older workers. Should mandatory retirement ever be based on age? An irony is that in several instances older airline pilots just weeks before mandatory retirement have successfully avoided major disasters. Another irony is that a significant number of the most powerful people in the world, U.S. senators and representatives, Supreme Court justices, foreign heads of state, and military and religious leaders, are of such advanced age that they would be forced to retire from many U.S. corporations.

Professionals today are often treated with ambivalence after retirement. A retired physician may be well respected but is not asked his or her opinion on clinical matters. In a physically demanding job, such as athlete or performing artist, a person can be forced into retirement extremely early and swiftly. For example, women in their early twenties are considered already too old to compete realistically in some Olympic gymnastics exercises, though occasionally it is possible to shift from competitor to coach.

I would argue that older people have considerable contributions to make in the professional realm. With age comes the accumulation of knowledge, experience, perception, and even wisdom. There are plenty of examples of people doing their best work at an advanced age. Philosophy, for example, requires time to deepen, and generally philosophers' thoughts grow richer with age as they grasp more fully the implications of life's experience. Intellectuals, composers, and artists also tend to show greater depth in their work with age as they become conscious of the shortness of their future and the unique history of their experiences. Among composers, Bach, Beethoven, Monteverdi, Verdi, and Stravinsky, and among artists, Giovanni Bellini, Albrecht Dürer, Frans Hals, Auguste Renoir, Paul Cézanne, and Georgia O'Keeffe are notable examples whose style and accomplishment aged to perfection. Perhaps this derives from the complexity of music and art: they take time to master and require self-confidence to break free from established rules. Old age for politicians is a complex adventure. Old age itself and the experiences it harbors can in some ways allow one to "foresee the present," which is the task of statesmen, and indeed many politicians in the modern age have continued to serve in elected office well into the final decades of life. But retirement from politics can be a time of lost power and recognition for individuals who feel compelled to influence the direction of history.

These same patterns can, of course, be seen in a great diversity of occupations. A readjustment in our social consciousness is urgently needed as people spend more time in retirement than in childhood and adolescence—and sometimes are even retired for more years than they spent in the workforce. As we refine our abilities to split atoms and tinker with our stem cells and DNA, we need the voices of capable, experienced workers, leaders, and thinkers. Perhaps the aging workers of our society are not an expendable burden but a social necessity. And we simply cannot afford to squander such valuable human resources.

The Value of Meaningful Projects

Some older people keep right on working in a professional capacity as long as they are able, regardless of financial need, simply for the purpose and enjoyment they derive from their occupation. But most seek retirement from daily occupation in order to enjoy the idle pleasures denied to us by work. Too often, however, retirement marks the beginning of an empty future.

In many ways we understand the world and our place in it through our projects. It follows that if our projects diminish, the world for us grows poorer. Without projects to occupy our mind and channel our interests, our perceptions lose their sharpness. I have seen far too many older people reduced to a virtual intellectual and emotional standstill by the absence of meaningful engagement. The absence of projects kills the desire to know. Clinical depression further poisons motivation: "Why bother, what have I got to gain?" To desire nothing and to do nothing often mean condemning ourselves to a dark apathy; it is all too easy to fall into a vicious circle of indifference and inactivity.

People who cultivate many interests and meaningful activities seem to derive the greatest enjoyment from old age. This requires some flexibility: as Charles Darwin was said to have noted, "It is not the strongest of the species that survives nor the most intelligent, but the one most responsive to change." Freedom and mental clarity are useless without a goal, but they are of great value if one's mind is filled with projects. Age brings freedom and a questioning, challenging state of mind that can fuel problem solving and lead to deeper knowledge. The greatest good fortune in old age is to have a world filled with projects. When we are busy and useful, we can escape boredom and decay. As Aristotle reminds us, "Life resides in the moment" and "activity is necessary for happiness."

Our sense of the present depends on our past and the future. In nearly every field of endeavor, the relationships of elderly persons to the time in which they live change dramatically. Our sense of "our own time" is when we accomplish our projects. When projects cease, time closes around us. At this point time belongs to younger men and women to fulfill their goals. Older people seem left over from a former age and readily review their past, the time that belonged to them when they looked on themselves as whole and complete persons. Our vision of a meaningful involvement after retirement must be enlarged to include a wide variety of alternative occupations, personal projects, volunteer activities, and community contributions.

The Role of Money

Many older people face significant financial hardship; these concerns are real, have a substantial impact on quality of life, and must be addressed with compassion at the level of the society. But even for those individuals lucky enough to retire with sufficient savings to live comfortably, money can present other types of challenges. For some older people, especially those who have retired from daily occupation and are not engaged in meaningful projects, money and possessions can come to be falsely equated with their being. Money has obvious value: it represents insurance for the future and often is needed for our future care when we no longer earn a salary. But the importance of money can become overblown, and some people develop an inordinate fixation with it as they age. As a defense, affluent older people may assure themselves of their identity against those who may see them only as objects. This system of defense is vulnerable because the money may be lost. And when rich older people attempt to maintain control of their children by threatening to refuse to help them financially, the effort almost always backfires. Consciously maintaining a healthy and realistic perspective on money and its importance is a vital part of managing our emotions as we age.

■ FAMILY LIFE

The microcosm of our culture is the family, and the relationship between generations bears a powerful influence on our lives. In an ideal situation, older people receive support, care, respect, status, and a sense of purpose from the family and their role in it. In return they provide cultural meaning, stability, and continuity with the past. Interactions between grandparents and grandchildren often are characterized by playfulness, mutual affection, and the exchange of knowledge for respect and admiration. If we care for our children and they see us care for our parents, perhaps they will care for us.

A major fear in old age is being forced to move from responsible adulthood to being dependent upon help from others. Dependency puts us at the mercy of others, and this makes us feel uneasy. Many old people do not trust middle-aged people, perhaps as a reflection of our awareness of hypocrisy, insincerity, and double standards that may exist in others and ourselves. For example, I have seen some older people minimize or deny the development of an illness in an effort to head off the perceived (though not necessarily real) desire of family to institutionalize the aging person at the earliest opportunity. This tension is not limited to aging parents and their children. Married couples provide each other mutual care and support, but anxieties and uncertainties about the future merge and reinforce each other so each partner carries a double share.

Intergenerational Conflict

A Persian proverb states, "Children are the bridge to heaven," and the emotional equilibrium of older people often depends on the relationships with their children. In old age, we must rebuild and reinvent our relationships with our (now adult) children; our success in this can determine whether they feel affection, ambivalence, or hostility toward us. Mark Twain, in a quote attributed to him in the *Reader's Digest* in 1937 (but otherwise unverified), reportedly quipped, "When I was a boy of fourteen, my father was so ignorant I could hardly stand to have the old man around. But when I got to be twenty-one, I was astonished at how much he had learned in seven years." Some children may never overcome a youthful resentment of their parents. Parents who acutely feel their dependency and see themselves as a burden, as well as those who are overly demanding or distrustful, can exacerbate the emotional impact of such situations.

In literature through the ages we encounter many stereotypes of the relationships between parents and their children. Though these are often caricatures with faulty or outdated assumptions, it can be useful to be aware of them and how they align with your own life. Fathers and sons, for example, are often presented as butting heads in a struggle for authority or dominance. The relationship between fathers and daughters is often more tender. Greek playwright Euripides (480–406 B.C.) concluded, "To a father growing old nothing is dearer than a daughter." This relationship sometimes is marred by jealousy or an attitude of superiority on the part of the daughter after she marries. The relationship between mother and son is perhaps the least complicated, though often an aging mother is portrayed as bitter or jealous toward the woman her son marries. The mother-daughter relationship sometimes can become stuck in the adolescent struggle between conformity and rebellion, a sentiment humorously offered by writer Erma Bombeck: "My mother won't admit it, but I've always been a disappointment to her. Deep down inside, she'll never forgive herself for giving birth to a daughter who refuses to launder aluminum foil and use it over again." The mother also may feel threatened by her daughter's youth, and their relationship is strongly influenced by the way this is resolved.

Parables and fairy tales offer keen insights into the complexities of intergenerational relationships. One particularly poignant example is the Grimms' tale "The Old Man and His Grandson":

> There was once a very old man, whose eyes had become dim, his ears dull of hearing, his knees trembled, and when he sat at table he could hardly hold the spoon, and spilt the broth upon the

table-cloth or let it run out of his mouth. His son and his son's wife were disgusted at this, so the old grandfather at last had to sit in the corner behind the stove, and they gave him his food in an earthenware bowl, and not even enough of it. And he used to look towards the table with his eyes full of tears.

Once, too, his trembling hands could not hold the bowl, and it fell to the ground and broke. The young wife scolded him, but he said nothing and only sighed. Then they bought him a wooden bowl for a few half-pence, out of which he had to eat.

They were once sitting thus when the little grandson of four years old began to gather together some bits of wood upon the ground. What are you doing there, asked the father. I am making a little trough, answered the child, for father and mother to eat out of when I am big.

The man and his wife looked at each other for a while, and presently began to cry. Then they took the old grandfather to the table, and henceforth always let him eat with them, and likewise said nothing if he did spill a little of anything.

Intergenerational Love

Though they hold potential for strife, intergenerational relationships also are potent sources of love and support. These interactions are important for everyone. A quote I thought was attributed to Margaret Mead (but I cannot find the source) goes, "Old people can teach young people that it is OK to grow old. And young people can teach old people that it is OK to die." Perhaps the warmest and happiest feelings that old people experience are those sparked by interactions with their grandchildren. To quote the late columnist Abigail van Buren (Dear Abby), "I'm not a picture-toting grandma—but my grandsons . . . just happen to be the best-looking, smartest, best-mannered grandchildren in the continental United States—and you can throw in Canada and the Virgin Islands." Being a grandparent can bring great comfort when there are open lines of communication and mutual respect. Grandparents and grandchildren can love in a completely impartial and totally generous manner because they have neither rights nor significant responsibilities toward each other, and because they often have less of the emotional baggage parents and children have for each other. Grandparents do not usually have to rear the children, say "no," or sacrifice the present for the future. Grandchildren in turn can bring affection and take delightful refuge in their grandparents against their parents' rules.

Family structures and living arrangements have shifted markedly over the centuries. We see a tremendous diversity of arrangements in modern society as divorce, remarriage, and other shifts divide and mix families. In one blended family I know of, a young child has seven living grandmothers! The upside of this is that older people today often have a great diversity of people within their emotional sphere and can continue to build deep and enriching relationships throughout life. The meaning of "family" can extend far beyond the strictly biological.

In many cases, extended families are living farther apart than they ever have before in human history, yet technology offers us myriad forms of instant communication that can allow, for example, a grandmother in Japan to witness the first steps of her grandchild on a living room floor in Boston through the magic of video technology. Even as we become physically more distant, psychological and emotional closeness can continue to support and enrich these crucial intergenerational relationships.

The Power of Sexual Energy

People also derive great pleasure in old age from the emotional and psychological support of a loving partner. In learning to manage our emotions as we age, it is important to appreciate the nature and power of sexual energy. Gender is probably one of the first things we notice when seeing another person. This component of our lives often enters into much of what we do, especially in recreation. A desire for attention and an effort to achieve top records in sports or other activities may serve as part of our sexual identity rather than the simple pleasures of having fun and the desire to improve our physical and mental health. This circumstance creates significant opportunities for self-deception as we try to explain our participation by other motivations. However, sexual energy used for appropriate purposes such as within a happy shared relationship is not self-deception and is a potential source of vast realization.

Sexual energy reacts more strongly and more rapidly than other drives, passions, or energies. Normally we cannot destroy sexual energy—only illness does that—and it usually finds a method of expression. We can recognize this by an inordinate passion, fervor, or emotional intensity in a given situation coupled with a general ineffectiveness of the undertaking. Our exercise and recreation may become imbued with the desire for records, personal bests, and increased competition; our thinking and communications may become critical, aggressive, and argumentative; and our reactions to others may show vengeance, jealousy, or cruelty. The goal is not to repress sexual energy but to appreciate its power and potential.

Romantic Relationships

Widowhood and divorce leave many elderly people without a loving partner, and this can affect their sense of sexuality. This partner gap especially affects women because of their longer life-span, which not only increases the likelihood of widowhood but also reduces the number of available men. In addition, beginning a new relationship can raise complex emotions, such as guilt or disloyalty. Will I be attractive to my new partner? Will I be self-conscious showing my aging body? Will I be aroused and able to perform? It has been months (or years) since I had a sexual encounter, what should I do?

Some older couples stay happily together for decades. One key is that partners realize that they evolve over time, and they acknowledge and celebrate the changes. Disagreements still occur, but they are discussed honestly without anger or hostility. Successful couples also appreciate that aging involves increasing vulnerability to physical changes and possible dependency. But this appreciation does not have to produce anxiety. It can serve as a foundation of trust and support. Nonetheless, caregiving to an ailing spouse is one of the most stressful of life's circumstances. Conflicts that develop late in a long relationship can sometimes be a sign of cognitive impairment in one of the partners. Some of the early symptoms can be jealousy, suspicion, and delusions of infidelity. While a full discussion of this topic is beyond the scope of this book, the basic keys are to care for yourself and to reach out to your family, friends, primary physician, and other counselors.

Unless someone like you cares a whole lot,
nothing is going to get better. It's not.
— Dr. Seuss, *The Lorax*

All we have to decide is what to do with the
time that is given to us.
— J. R. R. Tolkien, *The Fellowship of the Ring*

Chapter 15 Specific Emotions and Ways to Manage Them

A Cherokee chief was sitting in front of the fire with his oldest son. The boy asked, "What bit of knowledge do you want me to remember?" The chief replied, "Always remember that inside us are two wolves that are continually at war with each other. One wolf is evil and tries to fill us with anger, greed, frustration, envy, hostility, and grief. The other is good and fills us with love, compassion, kindness, generosity, patience, self-discipline, and restraint." The son sat quietly for a long time in contemplation and then asked, "Which wolf ultimately wins the struggle?" "The one you feed," answered the chief.

Our emotions are an integral part of our operating equipment. They cannot be denied, and so we must rechannel, supervise, manage, and control them. We do not manage our emotions automatically; it can be done only as the result of a mindful struggle. Nature does not compel our inner personal growth in the same way that our genes compel our physical growth. Managing our emotions requires the elements of virtue: honesty, patience, self-discipline, and restraint. A framework, such as this book's analogy of the horse, carriage, driver, and master, can also help us see through the barriers.

We live simultaneously in two worlds: the inner personal world of thoughts and emotions and the outer physical world of the body and the society in which we live. The challenge is to attain a harmonious relationship between the two. We need to follow appropriate societal protocols, but we must not let society dictate how we think or live.

Problems occur when unguided emotions take over the work of the intellect. When the emotions direct the intellect, we may introduce impulsiveness, energy, speed, and urgency into situations where calm, objectivity, or reflection may be necessary. With these inefficiencies, we tend to run low on energy. Yet well-managed emotions and the intellect are tightly interwoven, and feelings are key to new knowledge, new understanding, and personal harmony. Archimedes's exclamation "Eureka!" on solving a complex problem (in his case, the question of whether or not a king's crown was made of pure gold) exemplifies the emotional reaction to appreciating new knowledge.

Disciplining our emotions is sometimes uncomfortable because there is a tension between work and comfort: productive inner work and perpetual peace tend to be incompatible. We do not sharpen a knife with a soft stick of butter. By becoming aware of the need for more emotional control, we can initiate the growth of our consciousness and begin to subordinate our mechanical, reflexive reactions. In our allegory, this is a key step toward bringing the driver out of the pub and preparing the horse and carriage for the journey.

One lesson I learned in childhood was to never, ever tell a lie. Putting all the religious and moral arguments aside, there is a very practical reason for this: if you are always truthful, you have much less to remember, because you do not have to keep conflicting stories straight. Later I learned that the truthful person is strengthened by the ability to face facts even if doing so may be unpleasant. We must strive to be completely honest with ourselves and our self-perceptions; only then can we be truly free.

■ DEALING WITH WORRY, ANXIETY, FEAR, AND FEELINGS OF INADEQUACY

Although worry, anxiety, fear, and feelings of inadequacy are common emotional afflictions in all stages of life, they often become more acute in old age. Worry is the incessant "what ifs" that plague us with potentially catastrophic consequences and overload our ability to appreciate the moment and the reality of the situation. "What if the airplane crashes?" "What if my business fails?" "What if my child gets an illness?"

Understanding the delicate distinction between worry and concern can help you illuminate your inner life and assist you in managing your emotions. Worry tends to be very "me" centered. Worry is something for which we feel unreasonable personal responsibility. We worry about things we have no control over, like the weather, or about outcomes beyond our control. Concern is more outward looking and is based on some reality that we may be able to control. For example, it is possible to be concerned for others without anxiety or loss of sleep. You can act on concerns by doing your best, fully and completely at each opportunity. When faced with overwhelming worry, you must learn to trust yourself. Find ways to transform worries into concerns that can be acted upon in a productive way and to let go of the things you cannot control.

Anxiety and fear are other emotions to watch for. Anxiety is the emotion you experience when you are not sure you can handle the future. As opposed to fear, anxiety is not a response to some immediate (perceived or real) external threat or danger. Fear may be expressed in restlessness, and boredom tends to bring us closer to fear. Some of the same things that reduce fear also reduce anxiety. True fearlessness is not the reduction of fear but is accepting and going beyond fear. Humility, empathy, and compassion can give birth to fearlessness. It comes from opening up without resistance or shyness to face the world and to share your heart with others. In embracing compassion, we open our hearts from self-interest to humanity—we are expressing love made visible. The essence of cowardice is not acknowledging the reality of fear.

Feelings of inadequacy stem from the fear that we cannot handle the demands of the world. Awakening yourself to the true reality of your situation helps to develop fearlessness and prepares you to respond appropriately to the outside world. This balanced awareness is dependent upon looking and seeing, listening and hearing, touching and feeling the reality of existence. Consider this Zen story titled "Without Fear":

> During the civil wars in feudal Japan an invading army would quickly sweep into a town and take control. In one particular village, everyone fled just before the army arrived—everyone except the Zen master. Curious about this old fellow, the general went to the temple to see for himself what kind of man this master was.

> When he wasn't treated with the deference and submissiveness to which he was accustomed, the general burst into anger. "You fool," he shouted as he reached for his sword, "don't you realize you are standing before a man who could run you through without blinking an eye!" But despite the threat, the master seemed unmoved. "And do you realize," the master replied calmly, "that you are standing before a man who can be run through without blinking an eye?"

When your mind and body are balanced and in harmony, then you have no need for doubt. The result is a gentleness that comes from honesty and a humble trust in yourself.

People tend to fear silence. Think of the diversions in modern life: we send a text message to a friend, turn on the television, or plug in to our personal jukebox with headphones. Our tendency to talk or fill the silence sometimes is based on a reluctance to see something or to confess something to ourselves, feelings we can avoid temporarily by these distractions. This tendency is virtually universal. Consider this Zen story called "Sounds of Silence" in which each monk breaks silence for a different reason:

> Four monks decided to meditate silently without speaking for two weeks. By nightfall on the first day, the candle began to flicker and then went out. The first monk said, "Oh, no! The candle is out." The second monk said, "Aren't we not supposed to talk?" The third monk said, "Why must you two break the silence?" The fourth monk laughed and said, "Ha! I'm the only one who didn't speak."

It is useful to become comfortable with silence and to cultivate the ability to dwell within your own mind. It is within this silence that we can find clarity and truth and overcome fear.

■ DEALING WITH STRESS

Stress is difficult to define, but we know it when we feel it. It involves a sense of being pushed to the limits of our coping ability in facing a predicament. We feel threatened by a situation and doubt our capability to deal with it successfully. The source of this stress can be physical, psychological, or psychosocial. An end result of severe stress is exhaustion and burnout. Burnout damages our psyche through the sense of disillusionment that underlies it. This can lead to a spiral in which we become cynical, embittered, and filled with negative emotions.

Our bodies are programmed to deal with immediate stressful situations through the "fight or flight" response. The adrenal glands pump out adrenaline and cortisol, the chemical messengers of stress. The thyroid gland accelerates metabolism to provide more energy to fight or run. Deep in the brain the hypothalamus releases endorphins, natural painkillers, in anticipation of trouble. Blood is diverted from the gastrointestinal tract to the muscles, and all of our senses become alert and vigilant.

In the short term these responses can be lifesaving, depending on the nature of the threat. But chronic stress can have a devastating impact on health. Too much adrenaline and cortisol compromise the immune system by reducing resistance to infections, malignancy, and illness. Excess thyroid hormone can produce insomnia and weight loss and can make you feel nervous and shaky. Depletion of endorphins can worsen arthritic aches and pains.

The key to reducing stress is to face it directly and develop an approach to deal with it. Denying stress or trying to avoid it altogether tends to backfire and only magnifies it. The best way to approach a stressful problem depends on the circumstances. If you have some control over your situation, you can actively reduce stress through effective time management, interacting with a person you like, and creating an inventory of your personal goals or a game plan for your career or recreations. If you are not empowered to change you situation, on the other hand, your efforts are best spent adjusting how you react to stressful circumstances. Attitude is critically important, and optimism will be much more effective than cynicism in dealing with stress. To me a law of the universe is that frustration equals expectations divided by reality. If you cannot change the reality, then you must modify your expectations.

Remembering the other four secrets of successful aging will bolster your ability to effectively cope with stress: appreciate your reality, challenge your body, stimulate your intellect, and nurture your spirit. General healthy behaviors also help: eat a healthy diet, avoid tobacco, get plenty of rest, take vacations, pay attention to your physical health, get a pet, and laugh every day. Ongoing stress management techniques include regular exercise, increasing your social network, meditation, self-hypnosis, and using positive imagery by remembering a joyful past circumstance or experience. As you can see, you can employ an enormous variety of techniques to reduce stress. As with physical activity, the most important (and most difficult) part is finding what works for you and sticking with it.

■ CONTROLLING ANGER AND AGGRESSION

In peace there's nothing so becomes a man,
As modest stillness and humility;
But when the blast of war blows in our ears,
Then imitate the action of the tiger:
Stiffen the sinews, summon up the blood,
Disguise fair nature with hard-favored rage,
Then lend the eye a terrible aspect;
. . .
Now set the teeth, and stretch the nostril wide,
Hold hard the breath, and bend up every spirit
To his full height! On, on, you noblest English.
—*Henry V*, act 3, scene 1

Anger is a symptom of unhappiness. The Buddha noted, "Holding on to anger is like grasping a hot coal with the intent of throwing it at someone else; you are the one who gets burned." Anger can span from frustration to rage and usually implies an unfulfilled expectation or need. Anger carries with it a desire for harm or revenge. Suppressed or unexpressed anger is a great accelerator of aging. As I mentioned earlier, it is like driving down the interstate with one foot slammed down on the gas pedal and the other foot pushing on the brake. You may be traveling close to the speed limit, but everything is working at cross-purposes. Unexpressed anger can be turned inward and cause physiological problems, such as hypertension, sleep disturbance, and heart disease, and psychological problems, such as passive-aggressive tendencies and depression.

According to legend, two monks were once traveling together down a muddy road. A heavy rain was falling. Coming around the bend, they met a lovely girl in a silk kimono and sash, unable to cross the intersection. "Come on, girl," said the first monk. Lifting her in his arms, he carried her over the mud. The second monk did not speak again until that night when they reached a lodging temple. Then he no longer could restrain himself. "We monks don't go near females," he said. "It is dangerous. Why did you do that?" "I left the girl there," the first monk said. "Are you still carrying her?"

Generally our choices for dealing with anger amount to expressing the anger or redirecting and rechanneling the energy it has aroused. If we can honestly express our feelings of anger in a manner that is both assertive and respectful, then the negative energy can dissipate. Another approach is to modify the response to an anger-provoking stimulus. Since anger is a form of emotional reflex, we need to recognize our need to turn it into a deliberate and thoughtful response rather than a destructive reaction. Mark Twain wrote in *Pudd'nhead Wilson*, "When angry, count four; when very angry, swear." Taking several slow deep breaths and using calming imagery or phrases can help. The goal is to avoid putting negative emotions into action.

Another antidote to anger is patience. Going back to the ancient formula that frustration is expectations divided by reality, we can appreciate that most of our emotional problems and negative emotions stem from our inability to accept things the way they are. In other words, we will never have all our expectations fully met, and we need constructive ways to address these disappointments. Patience is the ability to fully and openly accept whatever happens. The legendary UCLA basketball coach John Wooden noted, "Things turn out best for the people who make the best of the way things turn out." Most problems are inside your head, and cultivating patience opens the door to understanding and a heart of compassion. As the eighth-century Buddhist scholar Shantideva says in *The Guide to the Bodhisattva's Way of Life*, sometimes called *Entering the Path of Enlightenment*:

> If something can be remedied
> Why be unhappy about it?
> And if there is no remedy for it,
> There is still no point in being unhappy.

This approach does not imply weakness or passive inactivity. It means that we consciously address what we can remedy rather than reacting blindly through a rage of uncontrolled emotions.

■ UNDERSTANDING PRIDE AND VANITY

Ambition and the desire for recognition frequently infect successful and intelligent people. Although these are great drivers for human productivity, they can also present an emotional double-edged sword. Consider older people who believe strongly in the value of their work and closely associate it with their own personal worth. As they become aware of the limits of their available time, they may devolve into a state of anxiety over their lost potential, leading to a negative emotional state. On the flip side, an older person who no longer possesses interest, curiosity, or affection is ripe for empty ambition and its close associate, vanity. Vain people are less concerned with the future of their work than they are with the nature of their reputation.

Pride confers a feeling of satisfaction. Pride in the work one has done and how it has benefited others can be enriching in old age if it is not accompanied by vanity. But when accompanied by vanity or misplaced as a feeling of superiority to others (in a sense, a delusion of omnipotence), pride deprives us of humility, an attitude that gives us kinship and an understanding of others that is the essence of righteousness.

Vanity always requires an audience. It leads to self-justification, with our false personalities (who we think we are) trying to defend themselves as highly worthy. One of the first symptoms of vanity is that it blinds us to its presence. Another symptom is that it increases our awareness of vanity in others while providing us with a false and inflated sense of our own modesty and humility. It prompts much of what we talk about with others and directs many of our more excessive actions and activities. For some people, what they consider generosity may only be the vanity of giving, as real generosity does not expect repayment in any form, including recognition.

Pride and vanity can arise from many sources. People often feel elation at the sight of their possessions. Physical prowess or family ties cause some to look down on others. Those who cling too tightly to physical attractiveness often face a crisis in aging as their former youthful beauty morphs into an older variation. Religious devotion can produce admiration, praise, and a sense of increased respect, but if permitted this inner satisfaction can develop into a sense of superiority and being the favored one.

How do vanity and pride interact? Vanity deals with appearance, while pride can reflect reality. Aristotle uses the scales of worthiness to measure the two. If one is worthy, pride is appropriate, but prideful actions in an unworthy person reflect vanity. For example, when we are paid a compliment, our pride may make us feel awkward, but our vanity is delighted. We may be vain of what we do (or have) but proud of who we are.

Blows to our vanity make us angry, and often we are more offended than hurt. This point is made in the Zen story called "Egotism":

> The prime minister of the Tang dynasty was a national hero for his success as both a statesman and a military leader. But despite his fame, power, and wealth, he considered himself a humble and devout Buddhist. Often he visited his favorite Zen master to study under him, and they seemed to get along very well. The fact that he was prime minister apparently had no effect on their relationship, which seemed to be simply one of a revered master and respectful student. One day during his usual visit, the prime minister asked the master, "Your Reverence, what is egotism according to Buddhism?" The master's face turned red and in a very condescending and insulting tone of voice, he shot back, "What kind of stupid question is that!?" This unexpected response so shocked the prime minister that he became sullen and angry. The Zen master then smiled, and said, "THIS, Your Excellency, is egotism."

Blows to our pride hurt deeply and arouse instincts of self-preservation. When pride is directed outward, it can be an accomplice to vanity, and when pride is turned inward, it can lead to shame. Vanity is concerned with the more ephemeral things of life, while pride seems to belong to a more permanent and inner part of one's self, a part of our inner operating equipment. Pride often refuses to give in to laziness, while vanity often will arrange an approach to suit both laziness and pride.

We all have our own versions of pride and vanity, and we must observe them within ourselves. These internal self-observations can help in our emotional management and conscious development, as well as in our appreciation of the subtle interactions between these internal processes.

■ RECOGNIZING ATTENTION SEEKING

Human transactions always seem to have an attention factor. Can you think of any interpersonal interactions that do not in some way involve seeking and giving attention? Desire for attention begins in infancy and is linked to feeding, comfort, and protection. It usually remains a primitive desire throughout life and can go beyond mere satisfaction. The focus of attention can be a person, an item, or an idea. The hunger for attention may rise and fall and may be satisfied by friendly and welcoming attention or by that which is adverse and unpleasant. An individual following an authority figure is frequently either looking for attention from the authority (or others) or expressing a desire to give attention. An unexpected change in a person's opinion or attitude may reflect a change in one's source of attention. When a person deeply craves attention, he or she is extremely vulnerable to being influenced or manipulated by the source of attention. Raising the emotional pitch is one way to increase the regard for the attention source and may be a prelude to indoctrination or exploitation.

It is important for your emotional management and personal growth to appreciate your own attention seeking. Your motivation for gaining attention may not be evident to you, so you need self-observation. If your attention seeking is satisfied by such means as apparent generosity, false modesty, or self-deprecation, the result will be self-deception and a lower capacity for other productive inner activity. Too much or too little attention can be bad for you because of the inefficiency it creates for personal growth. On the other hand, it is possible (and useful) to learn how to examine your desire for attention and keep it under control. This learning requires sincerity, humility, effort, discipline, and common sense.

DEALING WITH CONFRONTATION

Confrontation, like domination or coercion, is an unnatural circumstance. It occurs occasionally but should not be a regular event. If you experience frequent confrontations, you need to take several steps back and view the situation from a detached perspective on the assumption that you might be wrong. Carefully examine your attitude, feelings, thoughts, motivation, and conditioning to see what is distorting your energy. This is not necessarily a mea culpa, admitting it is your fault. It is simply allowing for the possibility that you may be expressing lazy thinking, greed, arrogance, or other failings or weaknesses. Sometimes we try to push things too hard, and this leads to excess tension and pressure.

Suppose, for example, that you are seeking to criticize. The important first step is to examine your primary intention for confrontation. Is it a private, selfish, self-centered, egotistical motive, or an honest and objective attempt to make a positive useful step toward a better overall result? Remember one of Murphy's laws: if there is a possibility of doing something stupid, the likelihood is that one will do it at the most inopportune time. When things are not working, examine the situation dispassionately, objectively, and as gently as possible. Try to sense what is happening and reestablish your primary intention.

■ ACHIEVING HARMONY

Harmony means being in a position of compatibility, usefulness, and benefit to other things. Harmony is balanced understanding that cannot be forced, and it transmits greater harmony to others. Troubled minds, tensions, and frustrations are inharmonious, but they may yield to an effort to restore harmony. For example, a lullaby may calm a frightened child at bedtime.

Harmony works in concert with other inner activities that join with it, such as detached judgment, objectivity, clarity, and removal of layers of prior conditioning. Harmony slowly enters our awareness, and we can appreciate the resonance of harmony when it is present and feel the tension of disharmony as it departs. Harmony is necessary for productive inner development.

You can achieve inner harmony only through intention. Say to yourself what your intention is, and then concentrate on how to achieve it. If the intention, timing, and circumstance are appropriate, the necessary energy to gain harmony will become available. But the intention must be specific and not a vague "I want to be happy."

Harmonious influence is privately felt; it is not an attention-getting event. The intention is what makes it work. If you know what your intention is and can face and handle this, then your intention gives birth to the act. If the intention is not clear, you should be careful because the imagination with its numerous unexamined assumptions will tend to take over. This can lead to self-important, ego-centered, gratuitous disharmony.

The intention to use and implement harmony is a very careful and deliberate decision. Not everything needs to be harmonized, and you should not try to impose artificial harmony on a situation. Building up harmony is similar to learning how to relax: you cannot force it. You cannot harmonize with everything, because you may lack the knowledge and the necessary capacity.

■ CULTIVATING EMPATHY

Empathy is attuning yourself emotionally to other people to appreciate their feelings and see the world from their point of view. Like the American Indian analogy of walking a mile in another person's moccasins, empathy is an essential part of successful aging. We each experience lack of empathy almost every day as we interact with impersonal businesses that place their financial concerns ahead of our needs. Even hospitals are not always empathetic, and our health care system is just beginning to appreciate the critical importance of empathy in the quality of care. For most people the first questions asked when they enter a hospital involve their payment and insurance status and not the nature of their distress.

This empathic journey into another's heart is essentially a nonverbal process. It recognizes another person's emotional state as reflected through that person's facial expressions and body movements. Psychologist Paul Ekman showed in a number of studies over the last forty years that facial expressions are universal and are not culturally determined. For example, he showed photographs of facial expressions for various emotions such as anger or surprise to people from a great variety of cultures in Brazil, Japan, and the highlands of New Guinea, where tribal members had no contact with television, and discovered that all interpreted the same emotions from the expressions.

The better you understand your own emotions, the easier it becomes to increase your empathy for others. Through self-observation you can focus on those things that cause a change in your emotions, and this can help you understand the feelings of others. If you are at a restaurant or café where you hear a conversation near you, imagine the lives of the participants. How old are they? What do you think they look like? What are the style and color of their clothing? Then at a discreet moment turn around and compare your empathic imaginings with the actual people. While this exercise is more descriptive than emotional, it can help to develop your awareness and empathy. Another technique to increase empathy is to read fiction in addition to nonfiction, which can help you become more aware of others and their emotional states. Dale Carnegie's classic *How to Win Friends and Influence People* is filled with useful suggestions. Also make it a point to interact with many different types of people. Doing this will broaden your perspective and allow you to see things from many different points of view.

The opposite of empathy is indifference and being so selfish and self-centered that we fail to consider the needs of others. We all need to increase our ability to care for others. Practicing small acts of kindness without any desire for repayment or recognition can help us broaden our life by achieving meaningful empathy.

■ THINKING HOLISTICALLY

Your emotional state is part and parcel with the health of your body, the quality of your nutrition, the restfulness of your sleep, and the degree to which you stimulate your intellect. You cannot manage your emotions successfully or sustain a harmonious existence without also attending to these physical and mental needs. Have you ever noticed how much more quick-tempered you become after a sleepless night? Or how much more difficult it is to offer emotional support to someone else if you are feeling hungry or tired? Whether your primary challenge is anxiety about the future, fear of immediate threats, worry over things you cannot control, low self-esteem, feelings of inadequacy, anger at yourself or others, stress, or any other emotional pressure, it is crucial to take a holistic approach to set yourself up for successful personal growth. This means not only cultivating self-observation and awareness and welcoming harmony and empathy into your heart but also ensuring that your physical body and intellect are in a condition to sustain this inner work. A worn-out body, chronic sleep deprivation, or a stagnant intellect is not a suitable foundation for the emotional work that must be done. Remember the other four secrets and you will be well prepared to successfully manage your emotions.

We must become so alone, so utterly alone, that we withdraw into our innermost self. It is a way of bitter suffering. But then our solitude is overcome, we are no longer alone, for we find that our innermost self is the spirit, that it is God, the indivisible. And suddenly we find ourselves in the midst of the world, yet undisturbed by its multiplicity, for our innermost soul we know ourselves to be one with all being.
— Hermann Hesse

Live as if you were to die tomorrow. Learn as if you were to live forever.
— Mahatma Gandhi

Aging Secret 5 Nurture Your Spirit

Nurturing our spirit is the fifth and often most neglected aspect of aging well. The transition to a new perspective on aging will not be complete until you can fully appreciate the meaning and social importance of the last stage of life—the one that must end in our death. Appreciating old age means appreciating that much of life's meaning comes from the power of limits. Death is the ultimate limit; having it as our inevitable end is what gives life such power and potential. Within the limits of life there is almost infinite variety, as there is in the combinations of the twenty-six letters of our alphabet, the twelve chromatic intervals of music, and four base pairs of DNA. Life is never static, and even in old age we are engaged in a continual process of "becoming." The final decades of life are rich and varied years of continuing growth and change, a fact reinforced by recent studies in gerontology. Like a cathedral that is built, rebuilt, and adorned over many centuries, our personalities become more complex and multilayered through the years as our bodies become more unique and differentiated.

Maturity requires a sense of emotional stability and learning how to let go. For many of us the last part of our lives will ultimately require strong social support, whether in the form of financial support, help with daily needs, medical assistance, or emotional support. This support can come from family, cherished people, or the society at large. But all too often our culture does not adequately provide the support we need in old age. The other side of America's emphasis on youth is our insulation from death. We have become more comfortable isolating those for whom it is imminent. We urgently need a new social appreciation for death and for the role people of all ages play in supporting the older members of our society.

Each moment we live is precious and can never be reexperienced. Recognizing this, you can make your final years much more productive and continue your personal growth until the very end. In appreciating the vast spiritual potential of old age, it is vital to continue to pursue ends that give your existence meaning—devotion to individuals, groups, or causes or to social, political, intellectual, or creative work, for example. A lack of purpose, on the other hand, is a breeding ground for fear or depression. Our lives have meaning as long as we value and enhance the lives of others through love, friendship, and compassion.

With all living things we share a destiny of continual aging and ultimately death. Knowing our limits, we can make the most of the life we have and continue to be active participants in our own lives and in our society until the very end.

Will you still need me, will you still feed me, when I'm sixty-four?
—Paul McCartney

One of the oldest human needs is having someone to wonder where you are when you don't come home at night.
—Margaret Mead

Chapter 16 **Will Anybody Care?**

Sometime before death, usually near the very end of life, most of us will need help with our basic daily activities. Some of us will need financial support. We all will need emotional support. How will this support be provided? For many of us, considering this question triggers a fundamental uneasiness that can be even stronger than the fear of death: the fear of dependency.

Many people spend more time in retirement than in childhood and adolescence combined; some even spend more time in retirement than they did in the workforce. In middle age many of us contend with years, even decades of concern for how our parents (and their generation) will be supported and treated as their capabilities narrow. Then we grow older, and it is our own independence and that of our spouses and friends that gradually diminish.

The opposite of dependence is autonomy, the experience of authorship of our own standards of behavior. It is how you feel when you know you can make your own rules: when to get up in the morning, what to eat for breakfast, how to spend your time. The ultimate question you face is, how can I maximize my autonomy in the face of inevitable mortality and probable frailty? The answer is that, as individuals, within our families, and as a society, we must foster meaningful choices, reduce isolation, and allow people to preserve their personal value and self-identity. By focusing on these goals, we can create a social framework in which all of us can continue to contribute to society, find personal satisfaction, and nurture our spirits during our final years.

When age-associated declines begin too early, when these changes are rapid and painful, or when an older person is not adequately supported, society is partly at fault. Old age puts society to the test—in many ways it reveals how the society values life. How far will society go, and at what cost, for those who need care? Aging always takes place in the context of society, and the current societal status of elderly people must be improved in order to achieve a high quality of care for people across the diverse cultural spectrum in our country. It is crucial to recognize that *older people must be treated as people* and to reflect this commitment to human value in our social policies. As discussed in previous chapters, older people are not some distant group of "others" but our future selves. All of us suffer when society fails to care for older people.

■ LONG-TERM CARE: RETHINKING A BROKEN SYSTEM

Since the mid-1970s the number of long-term care beds has exceeded the number of acute hospital beds in America. Today more than 17,000 facilities are approved under Medicare or Medicaid for the chronic institutionalization of elderly people. This enterprise has molded a new social construction at the end of life: living behind walls in relative isolation. But it is a social construction built for a different era when the final transitions of life were significantly shorter and more narrow than they are today. A reliance on long-term care in its current form no longer works to the benefit of older people or society.

Most of us fear the possibility that we will be placed in a nursing home, and often with good reason. Personal, intimate care is often provided by nominally trained unskilled workers paid the minimum wage. Staff turnover in nursing homes is extremely high—there are examples in which 100 percent of the staff leaves and is replaced each year. The quality of care is sometimes less than optimal despite being highly regulated (only nuclear power plants have more regulations!). Occasional medical visits are sometimes superficial and perfunctory.

In addition to these deficiencies, the core of the problem with life in many nursing homes is that you are isolated and must sacrifice your autonomy. You are often afforded minimal privacy, with no lock on your door and no choice in roommate selection. You often must conform to the institutional schedule of meals, rest, and recreation. Even high-end care communities take away decisional control. For example, in one semiexclusive retirement community, residents living independently are asked not to call 911 if a person is found down; instead they should call the nurse on duty, who will make the 911 decision. It is a sad commentary that some elderly people would be better off committing a felony in order to earn themselves a ticket to jail: at least in prison your assets are preserved for your family, meals are guaranteed, and health care is scrupulously monitored and fully covered.

The deplorable way some elderly people are treated today unnecessarily deprives them of the opportunity to even live comfortably, affording little room for challenging the body, challenging the intellect, managing the emotions, and nourishing the spirit. These conditions are counteractive to the goals of aging well.

A REALISTIC LOOK AT THE "CONTINUUM OF CARE"

One modern American philosophy of assistance is that both quality and efficiency are best served if we move the individual to where the services are best provided. For example, it is more efficient to require people to visit a hospital or clinic to receive a CT scan than it would be to transport such equipment around to all the individuals who need it. You also can better control the conditions of treatment and ensure quality and safety by keeping such devices in a medical setting. But is this same principle truly effective and appropriate when applied to the daily care of individuals with dependency?

The notion of a "continuum of care" is essentially the application of this idea to the care of elderly people. In theory, a continuum of care represents a spectrum of community-supported services administered by various agencies to create a seamless patchwork of interrelated services for individuals requiring some extra assistance. People start out living independently, then move to an "assisted living" system, and then go to a nursing home as their dependency increases. While in theory the concept may be laudable, in practice it often unfortunately leads to a subtle reinforcement of dependency and unnecessary loss of autonomy. For some, the continuum is, in effect, a rapid one-way trip to a nursing home.

The continuum-of-care approach fosters a fragmented, compartmentalized care delivery system with well-defended turf boundaries. It is in fact highly disruptive to continuity as people bump along the continuum. Forcing people to physically move from living independently to an assisted living facility and then to a nursing home can be psychologically devastating as they change their living setting, proximity to friends, and location of care. The concept also encourages labeling people to conform to continuum criteria and needs. People's needs rarely fit perfectly within the often mutually exclusive boundaries.

Sterile definitions of service delivery in the continuum-of-care model mask the reality that functional impairment may compromise the most personal and ordinary functions. No checklist does justice to the intimacies of toileting, bathing, sexuality, and eating. Helpers become a part of one's personal space. Long-term care is necessarily intimate and personal care. Moreover, a narrow, literal approach to service delivery treats a bath or toileting as the *goal* without considering the *manner* and *timing* that shapes our very existence. As a result, in practice the continuum of care is often an example of autonomy overridden—either by family members or by well-meaning professionals who must operate within a "system" in which the needs of dozens or hundreds of people must be efficiently met.

The continuum of care and the continuum of aging in America have grown dissonant. Our current health care system is increasingly incompatible with the needs of our population, especially regarding chronic illness and long-term care. Despite their often marginal quality of care, nursing homes draw in enormous and increasing amounts of public money. Dissatisfaction is evident, but reforms are nowhere in sight. Why is this the case? The reluctance to confront the realities goes beyond simple denial. Failure to address long-term care reflects the societal belief that there is nothing that can be done. In this view, nursing homes can never break free of their strongly negative stereotypic image: smelly, dingy, disturbing.

We will not invest in achieving a high quality of care for our elderly members of society until we believe such care is worth investing in. We are much more willing to invest heavily in glitzy, high-tech medical procedures, despite the fact that these often carry a very low expectation of benefit. Until long-term care has a better image, few will advocate giving the industry more leeway to experiment with direly needed new forms of care delivery. Yet it is a chicken-and-egg problem, because without innovation the image of nursing home care—and hope for improvement—is unlikely to change.

One key to changing long-term care lies in changing our perceptions about whether people living in long-term care facilities would notice or would care if their situation were improved—of course they would! These currently forsaken patients are precisely the ones with the greatest potential to benefit. Good care makes a substantial difference.

Sweeping changes are needed, yet we can reap benefits from even tiny modifications. Scientific studies offer many examples of how even pathetically modest interventions—caring for a plant or keeping a pet, for example—can significantly improve the health and quality of life of people with dependency.

CONSIDERING A NEW APPROACH

Perhaps the opposite approach is the model employed in the Nordic countries, in which support services are transferred to the person, rather than transferring the person to (numerous, expensive, variable-quality) care facilities. There is great potential for better integration of social and medical care in the United States. The distinction between home and institutional care can be eliminated if services are separated from room and board. In addition, since chronic illness causes declines over time, we must reorient ourselves so that the goal becomes *slowing the rate of decline*, rather than some elusive cure.

What Needs to Be Done?

We must abandon the continuum-of-care concept and reorient our goals for the care of people who need help with daily activities. I would posit that these goals should be to provide a safe, comfortable environment; preserve the highest level of function; maintain individual autonomy; maximize quality of life; optimize care of medical conditions; and provide quality end-of-life care.

How can this be accomplished? One specific and urgent need is to reinforce the core values of medicine and strengthen the field of geriatric medicine. Historically, one of the core values of medicine has been compassion and caring for others. For a medical system to achieve this, the needs of the patient must be the primary concern. But since the 1980s, compassion and caring have been increasingly superseded by the values of the marketplace. When the value systems of medicine and economics are in conflict, it is the core values of medicine that appear to be at greatest risk of being compromised. Economic realities cannot be minimized, but they all too often serve as a convenient excuse for an insatiable desire to increase wealth at the expense of quality. Doctors and patients are aware of this conflict, and it has contributed to an erosion of trust in the doctor-patient relationship.

Excellent geriatric care emphasizes patience, honesty, compassion, and caring. Unfortunately, this standard becomes increasingly difficult to achieve for clinicians who face a daily onslaught of administrative complexity, demands for improved "productivity," and other pressures that get in the way of delivering the most effective and compassionate care to their patients. Caring for older patients takes time. Older people are incredibly biologically diverse and experience illness in ways different from those of younger people. Many have multiple chronic conditions and use multiple medications. These factors make clinical decision making more complex and time-consuming. In addition, many aged patients have impaired mobility, vision, or hearing and frequently need to involve family members and other surrogate decision makers in complex discussions of clinical care, further increasing the amount of time and attention needed to provide appropriate diagnosis and coordinate treatment.

We must revise the systems that determine the economic "value" of various forms of medical care so that we may better fulfill the core values of medicine. The relative values assigned to clinical services for purposes of reimbursement strongly affect the provision of services by creating incentives and disincentives. At present, the system tends to favor "high tech" over "high touch." However, increasing diagnostic capabilities or providing the most cutting-edge treatment technologies does not always equal improved care, particularly in the case of older patients. Geriatricians are among the lowest-paid medical specialists.

Another needed change is the more effective education of medical practitioners about geriatric care. Most physicians in practice, including recent graduates, have had no formal geriatric training. Although conscientious practitioners have learned some practical geriatrics by necessity, iatrogenesis (potential negative consequences of medical care, such as drug interactions or side effects) continues to be a considerable threat to elderly people. Geriatric continuing medical education is vital to bridge serious gaps of basic knowledge and to help clinicians keep up with advances and new information. We are learning more about the genetics of aging and chronic diseases, new medical and surgical technologies, better ways to palliate illness, and technological achievements that allow the rapid dissemination of new information.

Geriatric continuing education must emphasize that the increasing biological variability as we age challenges the algorithms, practice guidelines, and simplified decision trees so prevalent now in clinical practice. Because we become less like our peers as we age, geriatric care must be individualized, and a one-size-fits-all approach to medical care simply will not work. Continuing medical education in geriatrics is also necessary because the clinical perspective of geriatrics is fundamentally different from the perspective health care providers use when caring for adults and children. Unlike other life stages, old age is counterpoised against the certainty of death. The inevitability of death and the increasing burden of chronic illness and disability mean that, for many elderly patients, quality of life becomes more important than quantity. The target of prevention therefore must shift from enhancing longevity to promoting function and reducing disability. Practitioners treating elderly people must acknowledge this profound difference and emphasize strategies that maintain independence and quality of life.

To increase the quality of care for older people, we also must develop realistic and attractive career ladders for nursing home staff and especially for personal care assistants. We should link education and seniority to promotions and meaningful pay incentives. Interdisciplinary team models of nurses, physicians, pharmacists, and physical, occupational, and speech therapists (and many other disciplines) need to be expanded.

Nursing home policies need to be redefined to allow more autonomy and to reward successful efforts. We must create a policy environment that encourages the adoption of effective innovation. Risk aversion and punitive payment systems deter such action. Paying for *services* (which are all too often of questionable value or quality anyway) rather than paying for *results* reinforces the orthodoxies that drive our current decisions.

Old age is a time of life that is as fundamental to our personal evolution as any other. Aged people are integral to the complexion of our communities and to the cohesiveness of our social fabric. Marginalizing this time of life deprives our communities of this lifeblood and denies elderly individuals the sense of vitality that is the privilege of longevity. The remarkable demographic changes that have occurred in the twentieth century demand a new ethic regarding the care of elderly people. To marginalize elderly people today is to seal our own fate. Older people must be treated as people with a future, not just a past.

I am not proposing yet another government program populated by strangers and designed in the abstract. More than enough of society's resources are sequestered behind the walls of the existing institutions and government programs. Let's use our resources to foster intergenerational communities where elderly people live side-by-side with those who can benefit from their presence and experience over time: knowing them, living with them, and sharing life's challenges with them. And when it is time to die, it should be in our own bed, in our own neighborhood, with the full acknowledgment of our extended community. Ours should be communal memories. That is the higher calling.

Remember that you have only one soul; that you have only one death to die; that you have only one life. . . . If you do this, there will be many things about which you care nothing.
— St. Teresa of Avila

I am not afraid of dying. I just do not want to be there when it happens.
— Woody Allen

Chapter 17 **Resting in Peace**

Death is a necessary condition for our transcendence and the inevitable price we pay for our individuality. With conscious evolution comes the awareness that "I will die"; aging is therefore counterpoised against the certainty of our death. Most people require decades of maturation to outgrow the conviction that they are immune from death. First, you consider yourself too young for it. Then a fear of death awakens and the instinct for self-preservation kicks in. Sometimes this is replaced in later life by an acceptance of the inevitable. At the prospect of imminent death, the child may be overwhelmed but courageous. The young person loathes death but may give her life freely for some higher ideal. The adult often does not think of death because he is "too busy" but also avoids risks and begins to pay more attention to his health. For old people death is not an abstract fate; it is an event near at hand.

In truth, death does not draw closer with age; it is always inescapably near because there is no set moment for it to strike. The word "soon" remains as vague at eighty as at seventy. Sometimes death arrives unexpectedly. Orson Welles reportedly remarked, "It is like the child being sent to bed after being given some wonderful toys."

Fear of death is common, but it is not the reverse of a love of life. There are fates worse than death, such as extreme physical suffering or isolation. Death sometimes seems preferable when life has only suffering to offer. But even in a comfortable, joyful life the fear of death is unnecessary. The Roman philosopher Cicero posited that there is no reason to fear death because both the young and the old die but the old have had the joy of living: "Ah, but it is just there that he is in a better position than a young man, since what the latter only hopes he has obtained. The one wishes to live long; the other has lived long."

■ DEATH IN NATURE

We can die in youth, and old age is not a necessary end to human life. The real question is not why we age, but why we live as long as we do. Many creatures die shortly after reproduction. Death emerged long before humans, when cells started to specialize and organisms became complex. Cells needed to age and die to make way for other cells. For one-celled organisms, cell division isn't really death. In some worms death does not occur in all cells simultaneously but comes as a progression from highly metabolic areas to slowly metabolizing areas. It is like a creeping epidemic from cell to cell. Cellular immortality in higher creatures is not good for the organism. In modern terms we call immortal cells malignant because cancer cells have escaped the genetic controls of normal cellular aging.

Almost certainly there are death genes. Many cells contain enzymes that cause cells to digest and die at a genetically determined site. This is normal for many organisms, as occurs, for example, in the loss of the tadpole's tail. During the course of our lives our bodies are gradually sculpted as we shed millions of unneeded parts. For example, we shed our baby teeth to make room for permanent teeth; we deliberately kill off excess white blood cells after an infection has been successfully overcome.

As living things evolved, some members of species were ill equipped for living on the earth. Species that kept poorly adapted members were weakened, and death became a tool of change and progress in evolution. Multicelled creatures that neglected to adapt became extinct. Some species have advanced through the partial death of themselves. For example, the sap tubes that run up and down within the trunk of a tree die and thenceforth serve as life-sustaining water channels for the rest of the tree. There is the demise of the caterpillar after it spins a cocoon and fades away into a soupy disorganized mass, dead for all intents and purposes. Then the mass reorganizes into a totally different organism: a butterfly. Another example is the serpent repeatedly renewing itself by shedding its skin. Similarly, early myths and rites dramatize passage from one stage of life to another. In Greek mythology the princess Psyche was immortalized by Zeus as a personification of the soul and took the form of a butterfly. Everything that dies seems to be in trade for something that comes to life.

■ DEATH IN HUMAN HISTORY

One theme runs through all of human history: death is a mystery in which we are torn away from this world. It is clear that confronting death has been a human concern from the beginning, as archeologists have unearthed numerous sites of prehistoric ritual burial. The most ancient myths and religions attempt to make sense of death. In myths the theme of death typically is not a final act of annihilation but is part of a larger process. This view is shown in the sacred Hindu scripture Bhagavad Gita (ca. 500–200 B.C.), which makes death the province of Shiva, the god of dissolution, not of destruction. Lucretius, the first-century B.C. Roman poet and philosopher, wrote in his poem *De Rerum Natura* (*On the Nature of the Universe*) that death is not annihilation; rather, it breaks up connections and links them into new combinations.

Death in many cultures has been seen as part of the cycle of rebirth. Consider the myth of Demeter, goddess of the harvest. Demeter's only daughter, Persephone, was secretly carried off to Hades by Pluto, the lord of the underworld. No one would tell Demeter her daughter was in the land of the dead, and her grief was so great that nothing could grow over all the earth. Zeus saw he must save mankind from famine and struck a bargain with Pluto. Persephone would rejoin her mother on earth for eight months of every year but would descend to Hades for the rest of the year. Then every year fertility and abundance flourished when Persephone rose from the land of the dead, and the death of winter followed when she returned to the underworld. For two thousand years this myth was reenacted as part of the Eleusinian mysteries in Greece. The harvest celebration was held every five years for nine days in September and October. In addition to a cyclical focus, myths often view death as the necessary condition for the transcendence of one's own life, either in an experience of personal resurrection or in the onward march of future generations of one's descendants. Another variation derives from the early myths and rites that centered on passage into puberty, with death seen as a rite of passage into another mode of existence. The Roman Stoic philosopher Seneca the Younger (4 B.C.–A.D. 65) stated, "Anyone anytime can lose life—no one can lose his death."

The spread of agricultural societies revealed in new ways the necessity of death to ensure life. Among last year's dead stalks are the new shoots of spring flowers. Bloody sacrifices were undertaken to ensure fertility. Indeed, all life forms, plant and animal alike, survive and advance only through the death of others. For thousands of years this process has been part of many traditions. It also has been a metaphor for self-renewal in the spiritual or psychological sphere. A centerpiece of most religions and psychologies is that one's outmoded self must die in order to go forth and be transformed. In the words of Jesus, "Whosoever will save his life shall lose it; and whosoever will lose his life for my sake shall find it" (Matthew 16:25 and Luke 9:24). It also is arguable that death's inevitability is a great motivator in the pursuit of excellence and for living with seriousness or passion, as we may have so little time to achieve our goals. Zen master Yamamoto Gempo Roshi noted, "There is no murder worse than the killing of time." Paradoxically, death is a tool of change and progress and as essential to the continuation of living things as fire is to the forest.

Denying Death

Over the course of human historical experience we see a fascinating variety of attitudes toward death. To some the fear of death is fundamental; to others, death is not even considered inevitable. You might be wondering, how could rational people possibly deny death? In fact, there are many lines of thought and action that essentially boil down to ignoring or denying death.

In ancient Greece Epicurus said, "Death is nothing to us, since as long as we exist death is not with us, but when death comes, then we do not exist!" The hedonists of any time and place deny death by refusing to take it seriously. They look the other way and with extravagant intensity indulge themselves—eat, drink, and be merry—no matter the consequences. The Promethean attitude defies the gods and denies death by raging against its inevitability. "Do not go gentle into the good night," wrote Welsh poet Dylan Thomas. "Old age should burn and rave at close of day; / Rage, rage against the dying of the light." In such a view, death is not so much a natural and intrinsic part of the life cycle as an external enemy, an unbearable evil affront. Against it humans should wage unlimited struggle and spare no expense.

It is in this line of thought that we find the roots of the hubris of modern technology, with its exaggerated expectations of science and industry and its refusal to accommodate a tragic dimension in life. To technology, death is just another problem to be solved rather than a mystery that enlists all the spiritual understanding we can muster. Here we also find the modern nihilist angst, the anguish that accompanies the irreconcilable conflict between a human demand for life and rationality and a world that replies with what is seen as meaningless death. Very much a product of the modern technological age, this horror at sheer nothingness confronts many a twenty-first-century existentialist.

It is interesting to review how people have tried to escape the sentence of death in the past. When Ponce de León discovered Florida in 1513, he had been looking for three years for the Fountain of Youth. European alchemists during the Renaissance experimented endlessly to discover an elixir of immortality. In Egypt and South America, dead bodies were mummified, as though providing the physical stuff of life could somehow prolong life in some form. Perhaps the best known of these attempts to counteract death are the pyramids of Egypt. These were monuments to the memory of the pharaohs in which they were buried as mummies with paraphernalia to accompany them on their future journeys.

It is clear that the pyramid option was available only for the exceedingly rich and powerful. You are much more likely to get around the finality of death by winning fame and leaving a legacy of some kind. If you are talented and fortunate, then the memory of your life will be celebrated or memorialized. For thousands of years, though? It is, after all, a precarious immortality, and the wrong things may be remembered. Nonetheless, wanting to be remembered and leaving a legacy probably are close to universal.

Welcoming Death

Instead of trying to deny death, we can welcome it. Several cultures, religions, and philosophies treat death as a lesser evil than suffering in life. The author of the Old Testament book of Ecclesiastes welcomed "a time to die" in a mood of profound pessimism. This also is found in Buddhism: the Buddha's view was that life is essentially suffering, and desire is at the root of this suffering. Only the extinction of desire through strenuous spiritual exercises will stop the endless cycle of deaths and rebirths so that the blessed state of nirvana, or permanent extinction, can be attained.

In some cultures it has been respectable to seek death by suicide. During the migrations of a community of Australian food-gatherers, the aged sometimes would drop out to die voluntarily in order to relieve the group of maintaining them. Similarly, aged Eskimo women would go out to freeze on an ice floe after their husband died. Hindu widows would throw themselves on the funeral pyre of their husband in the Hindu practice of suttee. Suicide was acceptable in the ancient Greco-Roman world. It was practiced by a few philosophers (Democritus) and statesmen (the orator Demosthenes), but it was particularly Zeno and the Greek and Roman Stoic philosophers who justified the practice. Their phrase "living is not the good, but living well" has an uncannily modern ring. Much later Montaigne and the eighteenth-century Enlightenment philosophers, Montesquieu in France and Hume in England, all considered suicide a valid individual right. Today it is acceptable in much of the Far East, but generally Christians, unlike Buddhists, are not brought up to believe they have the right to decide for themselves to end their life.

Accepting Death

If neither denying nor welcoming death seems appealing to you, you have a lot of company. But there is another alternative: acceptance. Perhaps the ultimate dignity is in facing the inevitable nobly and courageously. In the seventeenth century, Edmund Waller, poet laureate of England, wrote,

> Stronger by weakness, wiser, men become
> as they draw near to their eternal home.
> Leaving the old, both worlds at once they view,
> That stand upon the threshold of the new.

Acceptance is often facilitated by identifying with something beyond yourself that will continue to exist after your death. Almost universal is the comforting idea that one lives on in one's children. God promised Abraham not personal immortality but multiplication of his seed. Some people expand their sense of identity beyond their immediate flesh and blood to their particular ethnic group or culture and even to humanity at large. We have seen how being human came to mean the activities of our symbolizing imagination, overcoming death through the continuity of the culture we create. Some people identify less with other individuals and instead with the cultural values on which they have founded their lives, such as freedom or justice, and for which they are willing to die. It is not as though this set of attitudes is foolproof. In modern society, with its built-in impetus for constant change, our children may disappoint us. On the other hand, sometimes a dying person attempts to control the next generation from beyond the grave by provisions in a last will and testament.

Some find acceptance of death by identifying with the ultimate reality of the universe. This is the aim of the ancient traditions of Hinduism and Buddhism. In both Eastern traditions the real problem is not death but endless rebirth into this world of illusion and suffering. Hinduism recognizes the identity of the individual human soul with the ultimate unconditional reality that lies behind the precarious flux and dualities of conditional human existence on earth. Our true selves, our souls, are all part of the same ultimate reality; hence, we are all related. The Sanskrit statement *tat tvam asi* translates as "that thou art." In human terms you are your brother. Realization of this will enable merging of the individual into ultimate reality. Buddhism, on the contrary, prescribes extinguishing the individual human soul by relinquishing desire and thus returning to ultimate reality. Somewhat akin is the modern secular scientist who accepts death as a merging into ultimate reality—physical reality rather than spiritual where, by disintegrating into the constituent particles, one's energy is subsumed into the whole wondrous potential of the universe.

Another manifestation of accepting death is the widespread belief in the personal immortality of the human soul. This belief often is combined with a belief that the destiny of your soul is determined by your conduct in life. If it was a badly lived life, you will be reborn as a lesser creature in Hinduism and Buddhism, or in Christianity and Islam you will be consigned to Hell for punishment. This way sin can become more terrifying than death.

The belief in a judgment of souls after death appeared first in Egypt in the third millennium B.C. and again in the area of Iran at the time of Zoroaster in the seventh and sixth centuries B.C. The Egyptian Book of the Dead furnished ritual guidance and practical instructions to help a dead person's soul find its way to the heavenly Kingdom of the West, as did the Greek Orphic tablets for the way to Elysium. Wall paintings in ancient Etruscan tombs were influenced by the Greek and Egyptian visions and show fearsome torments to be avoided. The Zoroastrian version influenced later Christian and Muslim ideas. In them the guidance offered to the soul became increasingly concerned with ethical behavior in life rather than with ritual after death.

A great comfort provided by the belief in personal immortality is the possibility that it opens up a reunion with one's loved ones. This concept points to a profound truth, even for those who do not believe in personal immortality, that a good death cannot be separated from a good life. The vision of a good old age and a good death is also the vision of a good life in a good society.

Tolstoy, in *The Death of Ivan Ilych*, portrayed a man who led a well-calculated, superficially correct, and successful life. When Ilych develops cancer, he goes through a living hell. Alternately suspecting and denying his condition, he both rages and despairs, but always to himself. Around him is a conspiracy of silence, falsity, insensitivity, and cold calculation. He is avoided and abandoned to his loneliness, no one tells him the truth, no one pities or comforts him except one servant. He agonizes over why he has to endure such horror because he led a correct life. But in reviewing that life, Ilych searches in vain for many happy memories. As he laments his present torment, he wonders if his whole life was really wrong. The realization grows that all he lived for was a terrible and huge deception. No, his life was not right, but then what is right? At this moment his son creeps in and kisses his hand, and Ilych has a revelation that he can still rectify his life. For the first time he feels compassion for his son and wife. He decides to release them from their distress and dies.

Though written more than a hundred years ago, this story has enduring significance. It faces the question of the good death in relationship to a good life. It is also a story of ultimate redemption: Ivan Ilych died to his former narrow self and was reborn at the last minute in a new understanding. Furthermore, the central new understanding was compassion, which is one of the ultimate human values in most of the world's great religions and philosophies. This story also is a brilliant portrayal of the psychology of a dying person and of the loneliness and falsity that may surround him. Talking about death has probably never been easy. Remember that in the Greek myth no one would tell Demeter that Persephone was in the land of the dead.

THE POWER OF SOCIAL CONTEXT

Social context powerfully influences our relationship with death. When aged people are treated as worthy at the time of death and are part of a culture that practices this treatment, they are more likely to have a strong sense of self-worth and satisfaction in the final years of their lives. In some societies, almost everyone dies with a greater acceptance because of poverty, extreme physical decay, or circumstances that destroy the desire to live. In these cases death is not much of a problem for anyone. Other societies surround death in old age with elaborate ritual. In traditional societies a sense of continuity may prevail and ease the loss of a loved one, and the work will be carried on by the next generation.

The age when decline begins always has depended largely on social class. Physical workers decline earlier because of the nature of their work, and their decline is more rapid. The body falls victim to exposure, disease, and infirmity. In old age lower classes often are condemned to extreme poverty, inconvenient and unsafe dwellings, loneliness, and a feeling of failure that they have not achieved what others have. Extended family ties can be particularly strong and supportive to help these people. In traditional societies where the cult of ancestors is strong, such as China and India, survivors may fear retribution from spirits beyond the grave, encouraging survivors to faithfully perform the traditional rites.

Until recent times, people grew up intimately acquainted with death because they had seen people of all ages die around them. Today adults and children have escaped this knowledge because of the dramatic success of public health in increasing life expectancy. What is new today is that most of the people dying are old, and many families are inexperienced and uncomfortable with their relatives' deaths. To the family a terminally ill person, even one who is much beloved, represents physical and emotional exhaustion, old family resentments unearthed, and possibly a drastic revision of customary relationships, especially when a grown child must assume the role of "parent" to the actual parent.

Throughout human history, and until very recently, most people died at home. In many cases in Western culture it was an occasion over which the dying individual would preside. The extended family and the community participated with visits, advice to the survivors, religious rituals, farewells, and blessings. It was a final affirmation of the person and his or her place in society. The moment has been captured in many paintings.

Art provides numerous examples of a more violent, disturbing transition into death. For example, the "dance of death" motif, depicting a frenzied dance performed with a corpse or skeleton, in which all people, regardless of status, were dragged to their death, haunted the Middle Ages.

In the fourteenth century, when the Black Death wiped out one-third of the population and the Renaissance redirected attention from heaven to the world of nature and humans, the predominant image of death became a hideous corpse rotting in nature. A whole new literature called the *ars moriendi*, or art of dying, sprang up. In Bruegel's paintings we see the fascination with natural rot and corruption.

In time, these fearsome depictions were replaced by the more benign image of death surrounded by one's family. Today most people die in institutions—in hospitals or nursing homes. Their care often is considered more a technical matter than one of moral concern. Too often in these institutions more attention is paid to diseases than to persons; there is more scientific curiosity about the machinery of the body than consideration of the human values that make a life worthwhile, and there is more focus on subspecialty technicalities and analgesic adjustments, with no one looking at the needs of the whole person. Being a patient alone in a hospital, subjected to multiple traumatic high-tech procedures and covered with tubes, has become a symbol of contemporary death. In these situations the very subject of death is carefully avoided: the patient, the family, the doctors, and the nurses sometimes engage in a mutual pretense that the dying patient is not dying but somehow is going to recover. Communication is unemotional and avoids all unpleasant topics. Meanwhile, the dying patient is isolated and deprived of his or her deepest needs for emotional support.

But it doesn't have to be this way. We can give ourselves and our loved ones the benefit of a peaceful, supported death that does justice to the life we live and the spirit within each of us.

■ THE PROCESS OF DYING

Dying is often one of the most peaceful events of life, except in those who steadfastly try to control the uncontrollable. We don't know exactly how the brain's biochemistry alters in dying, but we know it includes the release of endorphins, oxygen deficiency, sensory deprivation, and activation of the brain's right hemisphere. People appear to go through a succession of stages and become relaxed, then absent-minded, and then drowsy. They sleep and enter a hypnotic state, followed by coma and paralysis. Breathing slows and then stops, the heart and metabolism stop, and finally the blood congeals and rigor mortis sets in. Many physicians have noted in their experience a detached serenity in the dying person. In the sixteenth century the philosopher Montaigne wrote, "If you know not how to die, never trouble yourself; Nature will in a moment fully and sufficiently instruct you; she will exactly do that business for you; take you no care for it."

Sometimes there is even joy. Shakespeare wrote in Romeo and Juliet, "How oft when men are at the point of death have they been merry! Which their keepers call a lightening before death." The last words of the scientist Thomas Edison were "It's very beautiful over there." The philosopher William James said, "It's so good to get home." And Isapo-Muxika Crowfoot, a Blackfoot chief, said, "A little while and I will be gone—whither I cannot tell. From nowhere we come, into nowhere we go. What is life? It is the flash of the firefly in the night. It is the breath of a buffalo in the wintertime. It is the little shadow that runs across the grass and loses itself in the sunset."

Dying could be made a lot easier. The person near death in contemporary culture may experience anxieties about who or what finally they are now and will be in the future. We die only once, and there is no trial run: can we handle this great unknown? Our contemporary society to a large extent insulates death and dying from us and poses some important ethical questions by the ability of medical science to keep terminally ill people in "vegetative" states. Some doctors may regard death as their personal failure. Sometimes death may be more congenial at home than in an efficient and sterile health care system.

■ FUNERAL CUSTOMS AND RITUALS

Funeral rituals differ widely in various cultures in how they treat death as the culmination of life. Modern excavations have shown that funeral rites go back at least 300,000 years, when Neanderthals buried bodies covered with flowers. Fear of evil spirits prompted some ancient and even contemporary cultures such as the Zulu to burn the body in order to protect the living. Zoroastrians felt that fire was too sacred for body disposal and that burial would contaminate the earth, so they allowed the dead to decompose or be devoured by vultures. Cannibalism was another ritual that we will not dwell on.

In contemporary Christianity, the traditional custom includes three components: the visitation or wake, the memorial service or funeral, and the burial—committal to the ground. If the decedent served in the

U.S. Armed Forces, the casket may be draped with an American flag. Greek funerals allow the coffin to remain open during the entire ritual unless the body is not in a condition to be viewed. In Eastern Orthodox funerals the coffin is reopened just before burial.

Bereavement in Orthodox Judaism may include the custom of rending a piece of clothing when one hears news of the death. Jewish funerals occur soon after death and never display the body. Embalming or cremation is not allowed by Jewish law, and flowers are not appropriate to send to the family. Nothing of value is buried with the body.

In Islam the body is bathed and covered with a cotton or linen shroud. After the funeral prayers the burial takes place with the body placed in the ground without a casket and the head facing Mecca. Each person at the burial places three handfuls of dirt in the grave while reciting verse 20:55 from the Holy Qur'an: "We created you from it, and return you into it, and from it we will raise you a second time."

Buddhist tradition views death as a moment of transition within the cycle of rebirths. Cremation is a common practice, and some groups have practiced mummification. In Tibet, where the ground is not fit for burial and wood often is not available for cremation, the practice of "sky burial" or "alms to the birds" developed, which allows vultures to devour the body. In Japan nearly all bodies are cremated. After the cremation the relatives may pick the bones from the ashes using chopsticks and place them in an urn, beginning with the bones of the feet and moving up to the head. The urn may stay with the family or be taken to a graveyard, or the ashes are scattered.

■ SHIFTING YOUR PERSPECTIVE ON DEATH

It is the nature of things for death to be relatively invisible. So much dies around us that we do not see—ants and worms that die underground, the cellular structures that die, the creatures that die in the forest or in the ocean. We are sometimes disturbed to see a large dead animal beside the highway because we are not used to witnessing these deaths. A century ago, by age fifty a person often had experienced numerous losses: parents, aunts and uncles, brothers and sisters, and possibly a spouse and some children. Life then was a succession of funerals. People were born in the home, married in the home, and died in the home. Loss by death is less visible now and often takes place in a hospital or nursing home. This makes the process of dying seem more exceptional than it is. Think of the enormity of scale—there are now more than 7 billion people on earth, and in 120 years all 7 billion will be dead. Death is finality in their present form for all living things. Why do we hide it from our children and ourselves?

The emotions of a dying person are complex and contradictory. The Greek dramatist Euripides observed this five centuries before Christ. "God, these old men!" he wrote. "How they pray for death! How heavy they find this life in the slow drag of days! And yet, when Death comes near them, You will not find one who will rise and walk with him, not one whose years are still a burden to him." Is it the same today?

In the United States today the central anxiety is not as likely to be fear of either Hell or natural death or dread of some philosophical non-being as it is to be a visceral terror of a living catastrophe with bodily mutilation, including loss of mind, or emotional abandonment. Those who survive have choices about how they treat this dying person.

Some years ago psychiatrist Elisabeth Kübler-Ross published *On Death and Dying* and other books on various issues related to death. She identified a sequence of five emotions as stages of dying: denial, anger, bargaining, depression, and finally acceptance. Since then we have found that these emotions usually do not occur in this tidy order, and some may keep recurring or not occur at all. The important thing is to recognize and to respond to the dying person experiencing these emotions. Commonly, the closer people get to death, the less their fear of death and the greater their acceptance.

Hospice care is the process and philosophy of allowing a dying person to spend his or her last days in a dignified, peaceful way. Jeanne Garnier used the term "hospice" for the care of terminally ill people in Lyon, France, in 1842. When the end of life is inevitable, hospice care in a facility or in a person's home may provide relief of suffering, pain, and distress.

More likely than not, people will die in a manner characteristic of the way they lived, particularly as they lived in the most stressful times of their lives. Their previous coping mechanisms are a clue to the way they will react to terminal illness and approaching death. If they have coped effectively with earlier stresses, they are less likely to be depressed or anxious now.

One of the most pernicious misconceptions is that dying people do not want to know they are dying. Repeatedly, most patients say that they do want to know. When people learn they are terminal, they may intensely wish not for a whole new chance in life but for just a little more time to be with loved ones. As their activity is drastically reduced, they may grow into a calm and peaceful rest with heightened enjoyment of nature or of the simplest acts of kindness.

In the past when people died at home, it was considered a solemn duty to inform them they were dying so they could prepare for death in numerous practical and spiritual ways, as well as say farewell. Today there are still many such benefits of a preparation for death. A richly rewarding preparation for death sometimes is called anticipatory grieving or life review. The wisdom in this process is not new. In folklore the belief recurs that before one dies one must remember and relive one's whole personal history. To enable a terminal patient to share this is truly a gift of love. If you are the terminal person, you have the pleasure of recalling many life experiences. You also reinforce and leave behind memories of shared experiences by talking with family and friends. In this process, a final image of you as a person to be remembered is reconstructed. If you are not housebound, you might make final visits to places that were significant in your life. You can take care of unfinished business, straighten out old family quarrels, and structure your remaining future. You also can develop a picture of how the people close to you will go on without you. Not everyone can do all this because of pain or suffering from advanced dementia. But the potential comfort and psychic benefits to both the dying and the surviving are very great when the dying process is humane.

But the fruit of the Spirit is love, joy, peace, patience, kindness, goodness, faithfulness, gentleness and self-control. Against such things there is no law.
— Galatians 5:22–23

Stop acting so small. You are the universe in ecstatic motion.
— Rumi

Chapter 18 Specific Ways to Nurture Your Spirit

In our analogy of the horse, carriage, driver, and master, the culmination of life is when the master, seeing that the driver has at last emerged from the pub, repaired the carriage, and revived the horse, enters the carriage and begins his journey. This is the journey of the spirit toward personal growth and fulfillment.

Human beings have developed myriad religious and philosophical perspectives on the spirit over time. There are seemingly endless views on the spiritual journey: how best to cultivate an open heart, how to manage our relationships with others, the nature and role of the divine. A fulfilling aging experience depends on continued spiritual growth and nourishment. You must find your own way to appreciate your spirit and tap into that which is greater than yourself.

A Middle Eastern proverb relates that "the donkey that takes you to the door of your house is not the way you enter the house." There are various activities and experiences that can help you find the way to your spiritual house, but it is you alone who must enter it.

■ FIRST, DEFINE YOUR INTENTION

To open yourself up to the voice of your spirit, you must take time to define your intention. What is your heart's desire? Do you really want to feel more of a connection to your spirit? Some people find that meditating on self-improvement or a relationship with the infinite can help them find and articulate their intention. The ultimate aim of self-discovery is not ecstasy for yourself but the wisdom and power to serve others. Spend some sacred time every day to focus on your intention. Be still and quiet your mind, and you will find your path.

■ OPENING YOUR SPIRIT IN THE STILLNESS OF NIGHT

Conscious aging involves harmonizing your inner world with your outer experiences. Sleep and the still of the night play a key role in this. While your body and mind rest, your spirit grows, allowing you the potential to expand your inner consciousness. The inner world is the world of your energies, passions, and awareness. During the day you practice your skills and apply your knowledge to navigate the outer world. But in the still of night you navigate the landscape of the spirit: this is when your life's experiences reverberate through your inner being. You must find ways to cultivate balance between your inner and outer worlds so that they may grow together.

■ UNDERSTANDING THE GOLDEN RULE

One night when all was quiet, my spirit revealed to me that my perspective on love was far too narrow. My former view of love was as a golden cocoon enveloping two partners. In the dead of night my spirit taught me that love is all-encompassing, without desire, and that loving God with all my heart is to melt into an infinite space: with the expanse of the mountains and the depths of the oceans, a powerful storm and a summer's breeze, a blinding light and shining star, a vast tenderness and a generous dispensation.

How can you love your neighbor as yourself? Unexpectedly, while meditating on this, I found the answer in the poem "Perfection" by Kahlil Gibran. The first part of the poem describes what loving God is like, while the second part shows us our neighbors.

■ APPRECIATING SILENCE

An Arabian proverb states, "The fruit of silence is tranquility." Cultivating silence in your life is an essential part of nurturing your spirit. It is an active awareness, not simply the absence of noise or being alone in solitude. And it is not a mind fixed on emptiness. The sixth-century Buddhist mystic Huineng said, "The capacity of mind is broad and huge, like the vast sky. Do not sit with a mind fixed on emptiness. If you do, you will fall into a neutral kind of emptiness. Emptiness includes the sun, moon, stars and planets, the great earth, mountains and rivers, all trees and grasses, bad men and good men, bad things and good things, heaven and hell; they are all in the midst of emptiness. The emptiness of human nature is also like this."

Silence encourages us to appreciate what is happening around us, what is really here and now. Silence is an intentional activity that allows us to shift our awareness from sending to receiving. When I was in high school I was an amateur radio enthusiast. My simple apparatus was a transmitter and receiver for Morse code communications with others across the country. The process was to choose a radio frequency and then send out a message looking for a person to communicate with. Then the transmitter had to be shut off and the receiver was used to carefully listen for any responses. You could not perform both sending and receiving tasks at the same time. Many of us spend our time sending out messages and worries without listening intently for the replies. The Old Testament book Habakkuk, verse 2:20, reads, "The LORD is in his holy temple; let all the earth be silent before him." This statement is often said during morning prayer, and I used to think of it as an invocation that the service was about to begin and everyone should quiet down. Now I realize that it speaks to the value of silence. God is in our hearts, and we need to listen to his guidance, especially in the stillness of night.

■ CREATE A SANCTUARY

Create a small space or a room in your home, a sanctuary that brings you peace as soon as you are there. Use the time and space to activate the process, and carry the feeling with you all day and into the night. Do not intellectualize it; just watch the miracles unfold, however small they may be. Opportunities are always around us to guide us. For example, calmly watching our family cat wait silently for an extended time for a mouse to appear at the edge of a drain taught me an important lesson on the value of patience.

One approach to spiritual nourishment is to visit places that provide sanctuary and peace. You know them when you feel them. They are the landscape of the soul and have a presence and an awe-inspiring quality. The inner message is of a relationship of time to eternal powers that is experienced in that place. You can feel yourself expand into the space and become lighter as you do. Examples for me of places that are meaningful and provide me with openness and peace are cathedrals, old libraries, museums, natural wonders, and the ocean shore.

WALK IN A LABYRINTH

Another physical way to nurture your spirit and purify your experience is to walk in a labyrinth. A labyrinth differs from a maze by having only one long pathway that goes round and round in a geometric pattern. It is not designed as a puzzle to entrap as a maze does, with multiple choices and frequent dead ends. In a labyrinth there are no choices to make, just the commitment to go all the way from the beginning to the end. Labyrinths date to ancient times and have been used for personal meditation and group worship. Symbolism of the labyrinth may differ, but some religious interpretations are that the journey through the labyrinth is the journey of life. The beginning of the labyrinth is birth, and in the center is death. It can also be viewed as a journey within oneself and then a journey back out, into our awareness and back to the outside world. The various twists and turns in the labyrinth serve to disorient us and disconnect us from the outside world, allowing us to enter a more contemplative state.

If there is no labyrinth nearby and you are not familiar with their arrangement, you can find several images on the Internet. By focusing on an image of a labyrinth and following the route with your finger, you can experience a nurturing exercise for your spirit. Take your time and go at a comfortable speed.

OBSERVE YOUR THOUGHTS

Observing your own thoughts is another key to finding and nurturing your spirit. Worry, stress, fear, and criticism frequently get in the way and become disruptions because our intellect enjoys challenges and conflicts to solve. An intellect out of balance may actually create some of the conflicts to keep itself in control.

The illumination of the spirit is the recognition of the radiance of one eternity through all things. To do this you must release yourself completely from desiring worldly goods and fearing their loss. Your false personality—who you think you are, rather than the essence of who you really are—likes to think it is in charge and creates all kinds of diversions and distractions to stay in control. Negative thinking can easily become a habit. Spend time each day becoming more aware of your thoughts, reactions, and behaviors. Then expand the time until you are in a state of self-awareness. Quieting and neutralizing the false personality is the goal. Don't take the discovery of goodness too seriously. Rediscover that light touch of appreciation, a perfect and real sense of humor, and a manner of humility. Spirituality is not the same as religion. To me religion is doing. We do not think religion or feel it—we live it. Whether we like it or not, we show our attitude toward religion by our actions.

■ READ SACRED TEXTS

My definition of sacred is broad and includes holy scriptures such as the Bible, the Koran, the Torah, the Book of Mormon, the Upanishads, and some poetry. Samuel Taylor Coleridge summed up the value of poetry: "No man was ever yet a great poet, without being at the same time a profound philosopher. For poetry is the blossom and the fragrance of all human knowledge, human thoughts, human passions, emotions, language." Reading poetic works can give one a sense of peace and direction.

■ IDENTIFYING WITH THE LIGHT RATHER THAN THE BULB

Your spirit is within your heart and is ready to open and be shared. It is not in the things you own or the body you inhabit. Through love you can use your mind to create the bridge between your thoughts and your awareness of love. The American mythologist and author Joseph Campbell said that the challenge in middle age is to identify yourself not with your body, which is declining, but with the consciousness of which it is the medium. Am I the bulb that carries the light, or am I the light for which the bulb is a vehicle? Spiritual life is the flowering and fulfillment of a human life, not a supernatural virtue superimposed on it. The impulses of nature are what give authenticity to life, not the rules coming from a supernatural power.

Our main purpose as physical beings is to remember who we are, so that each of us can create our own unique purpose for being here. It's our choice. And if our intentions are lofty and focused on the heart and loving God and our neighbors, God will support us.

■ CULTIVATE A WILLINGNESS TO LET GO

In order to nurture your spirit, you must let go of fear, judgment, and self-doubt. True fearlessness is not the reduction of fear; it is accepting and going beyond fear. The essence of cowardice is not acknowledging the reality of your fear. Feelings of inadequacy come from the fear that you cannot handle the demands of the world. Relax and just let go. Reflect on "The Tale of the Sands" from *Tales of the Dervishes* by Idries Shah, an allegory of the journey through and beyond life that contains observations on death from several perspectives.

■ THE PURIFICATION OF EXPERIENCE

Trust the universe, trust God, and trust yourself. Know that everything is as it should be. Don't become attached to outcomes or have a lot of great expectations. This is not a passive stance. Another Middle Eastern proverb states, "Trust in God, but still tie your camel to the post."

Where are your blockages? If it's self-doubt, then embrace that emotion and reflect on it. Watch it melt away as your spirit replaces it with self-love. Daily affirmations and meditations will support you on this journey. Give yourself permission to feel joy, peace, love, and happiness. Maybe no one has ever told you that you can. Believe it is well-deserved and that you are worthy of the very best, and invite it into your heart.

We are here to help one another nurture our spirit and heal our heart. We learn best about our spirit and ourselves through our relationships. A good way to practice opening our heart is by being with others and honoring their existence just as we honor our own. We are living this human existence because that is what we chose. And everything about our life is what we created, but this isn't all there is. Go with it, accept it. Find humor in it. An old man in a rural community was asked how he was always able to be so serene and at peace. He said, "There is one thing that everyone must learn. There is only one center of the universe, and you are not it."

Gentleness comes from experiencing the absence of doubt and trusting our heart and in ourselves. When our mind, body, emotions, and spirit are balanced and in harmony, then we have no doubt. This balanced awareness is looking and seeing, listening and hearing, touching and feeling. Balancing our awareness develops fearlessness that allows us to respond accurately to the outside world. It is simply being accurate and absolutely direct in relating to the outer world by means of sensory perceptions, mental clarity, and a sense of vision. We can then appreciate the truth in the light of the moment.

Notes

Prologue

My first encounter with the ancient parable of the horse, carriage, driver, and master was in *Psychological Commentaries on the Teachings of Gurdjieff and Ouspensky* by Maurice Nicoll. Several discussions deal with various interpretations of this parable. The parable is ancient, and its source is not known to me.

Chapter 1

Demographic information is available from numerous sources. The statistics of increasing longevity from birth are taken from the National Institute on Aging's website (https://www.nia.nih.gov/research/publication/global-health-and-aging/living-longer).

For a cogent discussion of life course epidemiology and how it differs from proximate cause epidemiology, see *Worried Sick: A Prescription for Health in an Overtreated America*, by Nortin M. Hadler, M.D. By carefully reviewing the primary literature (or lack thereof), this book systematically exposes the excesses in the health care system, its underlying waste, and how treatments are often unnecessary and harmful. Another book by Hadler that deserves thoughtful reading is *The Last Well Person: How to Stay Well Despite the Health-Care System*. This book shows how much of what is recommended in health care is the result of skillful marketing, with very little meaningful benefit to the consumer.

Chapter 2

For more information on aging myths and stereotypes, consult *Breaking the Rules of Aging* by David A. Lipschitz, M.D., Ph.D. Here a scientist of stature and experience gives basic advice while debunking numerous myths. The reference to learn more about the Nun Study is *Annals of Internal Medicine* 139, no. 5, pt. 2 (September 2, 2003): 450–54.

Interesting studies on the relationship between dieting and mortality include M. Myrskyla and V. W. Chang, "Weight Change, Initial BMI, and Mortality among Middle- and Older-Aged Adults," *Epidemiology* 20, no. 6 (2009): 840–48, and D. D. Ingram and M. E. Mussolino, "Weight Loss from Maximum Body Weight and Mortality: The Third National Health and Nutrition Examination Survey Linked Mortality File," *International Journal of Obesity* 34, no. 6 (2009): 1044–50.

A concise review of the Swedish Twin Registry is P. Lichtenstein et al., "The Swedish Twin Registry: A Unique Resource for Clinical, Epidemiological and Genetic Studies," *Journal of Internal Medicine* 252, no. 3 (September 2002): 184–205. The major survey on sexuality in old age is S. T. Lindau et al., "A Study of Sexuality and Health among Older Adults in the United States," *New England Journal of Medicine* 357, no. 8 (2007): 762–74.

Chapter 3

Much of the material in this chapter comes from a paper Susan A. Gaylord and I published in the *Journal of the American Geriatrics Society* 42, no. 3 (March 1994): 335–40, titled "A Brief History of the Development of Geriatric Medicine." I first learned of the Egyptian hieroglyph for aging from F. D. Zeman, "Old Age in Ancient Egypt: Contribution to the History of Geriatrics," *Journal of the Mount Sinai Hospital* 8 (1942): 1161–65.

Chapter 4

For an overview on oxygen free radicals and superoxide dismutase, see J. McCord and I. Fridovich, "Superoxide Dismutase: The First Twenty Years (1968–1988)," *Free Radical Biology and Medicine* 5, nos. 5–6 (1988): 363–69. Another good source of understandable aging biochemistry for the nonscientist is *You Staying Young: The Owner's Manual for Extending Your Warranty*, by Michael F. Roizen and Mehmet C. Oz.

Modern theories of aging are reviewed comprehensively in the *Handbook of Theories of Aging*, 2nd ed. (2009), edited by Vern L. Bengtson, Daphna Gans, Norella M. Putney, and Merril Silverstein. A more condensed source is *Wikipedia*'s page on senescence (http://en.wikipedia.org/wiki/Senescence). Joshua Mitteldorf's demography theory of aging based on population dynamics can also be reviewed at *Wikipedia* (http://en.wikipedia.org/wiki/User:Mitteldorf/Evolution_of_aging).

Chapter 5

Much of the material in this chapter comes from my book *The American Geriatrics Society's Complete Guide to Aging and Health*.

Chapter 6

A good readable source of useful information on the biochemistry of exercise and how to get and stay fit is *Younger Next Year: Live Strong, Fit, and Sexy—until You're 80 and Beyond*, 2nd ed. (2007), by Chris Crowley and Henry S. Lodge.

Two articles that set the stage for the role of interleukin-6 are B. K. Pederson and M. Febbraio, "Muscle-Derived Interleukin-6—a Possible Link between Skeletal Muscle, Adipose Tissue, Liver, and Brain," *Brain, Behavior, and Immunity* 19, no. 5 (2005): 371–76, and A. M. Petersen and B. K. Pederson, "The Anti-inflammatory Effect of Exercise," *Journal of Applied Physiology* 98, no. 4 (2005): 1154–62.

A good overview of evolutionary biology is *Human Evolutionary Biology: Human Anatomy and Physiology from an Evolutionary Perspective*, by Arndt von Hippel. The graph of organ system function over time (ill. 5) and the discussion come from an article I published in the *American Journal of Medicine* 76, no. 6 (1984): 1049–54, titled "Clinical Implications of Aging Physiology."

Chapter 7

An excellent resource for nutrition information is the *Nutrition Action Healthletter* from the Center for Science in the Public Interest (https://www.cspinet.org/nah/). Another commendable publication is the *Health and Nutrition Letter* from Tufts University's Friedman School of Nutrition Science and Policy (http://www.nutritionletter.tufts.edu/). *Younger Next Year: Live Strong, Fit, and Sexy—until You're 80 and Beyond*, 2nd ed. (2007), by Chris Crowley and Henry S. Lodge, also contains excellent nutritional advice, as well as an in-depth discussion of the interactions between diet and exercise. The Harvard Pyramid is discussed in *Food Pyramids and Plates: What Should You Really Eat?* at Harvard's Nutrition Source website (www.hsph.harvard.edu/nutritionsource/what-should-you-eat/pyramid).

Chapter 8

A good review of the dopamine reward system is Ó. Arias-Carrión and E. Pöppel, "Dopamine, Learning and Reward-Seeking Behavior," *Acta Neurobiologiae Experimentalis* 67, no. 4 (2007): 481–88 (in English, available free online at http://www.ane.pl/linkout.php?vol=67&no=4&fpp=481). The reference for the Harvard Alumni Health study is I.-M. Lee, C. Hsieh, and R. S. Paffenbarger Jr., "Exercise Intensity and Longevity in Men: The Harvard Alumni Health Study," *Journal of the American Medical Association* 273, no. 15 (1995): 1179–84. *Younger Next Year: Live Strong, Fit, and Sexy—until You're 80 and Beyond*, 2nd ed. (2007), by Chris Crowley and Henry S. Lodge, mentioned in the notes for Chapters 6 and 7, also contains specific advice on exercise and motivation.

Chapter 9

Much of the material in this chapter and subsequent chapters was stimulated by *The Coming of Age*, by Simone de Beauvoir. This tour de force examines aging from numerous perspectives and contains many provocative insights. Alan D. Baddeley has several good articles and books on the psychology of memory; a useful review of his is "The Psychology of Memory" (chapter 1 of *The Essential Handbook of Memory Disorders for Clinicians*, edited by A. D. Baddeley, M. D. Kopelman, and B. A. Wilson), available online at http://media.johnwiley.com.au/product_data/excerpt/1X/04700914/047009141X.pdf. Another resource is *The Right Mind: Making Sense of the Hemispheres*, by Robert Ornstein.

A good technical overview of the evolution of memory is S. B. Klein, L. Cosmides, J. Tooby, and S. Chance, "Decisions and the Evolution of Memory: Multiple Systems, Multiple Functions," *Psychological Review* 109, no. 2 (2002): 306–29. An amazing book that shaped my thinking on how we think is *The Evolution of Consciousness: The Origins of the Way We Think*, by Robert Ornstein. His basic message is that the world we have adapted to has changed, and we need to change from our tribal way of thinking to a new cognitive approach.

A valuable reference for thinking about your future self is *A Whole New Mind: Why Right-Brainers Will Rule the Future*, by Daniel H. Pink. In essence Pink argues persuasively that linear, left-brain thinkers are outmoded because of abundance of food and resources, inexpensive labor in Asia and other places, and automation that can perform most sequential left-brain tasks faster and more accurately than we can. He proposes six senses to help expand our right-brain activity: design, story, symphony, empathy, play, and meaning.

Chapter 10

An excellent book on the continuing artistic creativity with aging is *The Crown of Life: Artistic Creativity in Old Age*, by Hugo Munsterberg. This work develops the theme that there is a distinct style in older artists. It introduced me to the German term *Altersstil* to describe the development of a distinctive style in old age. The two examples of sculptures when Michelangelo was young and old were taken from that book.

Chapter 11

A comprehensive source for background information on memory and the interrelationship between memory and sleep is the website Super Memory: Forget about Forgetting (http://www.supermemo.com). A useful resource for information on aging and sleep is the "Sleep and Aging" page by the National Institutes of Health (http://nihseniorhealth.gov/sleepandaging/aboutsleep/01.html). Another helpful summary is M. V. Vitielo, "Sleep in Normal Aging," *Sleep Medicine Clinics* 1, no. 2 (2006): 171–76. A comprehensive review of circadian rhythms and sleep is C. A. Czeisler and J. J. Gooley, "Sleep and Circadian Rhythms in Humans," *Cold Spring Harbor Symposia on Quantitative Biology* 72 (2007): 579–97.

Chapter 12

The reference for the Mayo Clinic memory study is G. E. Smith et al., "A Cognitive Training Program Based on Principles of Brain Plasticity: Results from the Improvement in Memory with Plasticity-Based Adaptive Cognitive Training (IMPACT) Study," *Journal of the American Geriatrics Society* 57, no. 4 (2009): 594–603. Additional memory-enhancement strategies are found in *Successful Aging*, by John W. Rowe and Robert L. Kahn.

Chapter 13

Simone de Beauvoir's *The Coming of Age* provided me with much useful information for this chapter. Medieval iconography is comprehensively reviewed in M. Didron's *Christian Iconography; or, The History of Christian Art in the Middle Ages* (translated from the French by E. J. Millington) and in George Ferguson's

Signs and Symbols in Christian Art: With Illustrations from Paintings from the Renaissance. A more specific reference to the depiction of old people in classical art is *The Art of Aging: A Celebration of Old Age in Western Art*, by Patrick L. McKee and Heta Kauppinen.

The iconography of the De Lisle Psalter, "Wheel of the Ten Ages of Man" (ca. 1340), reflects the point that wherever you are in the circle of life you are equidistant from the center. It can be viewed at *Wikipedia* (https://commons.wikimedia.org/wiki/File:De_Lisle_Psalter_Rad_des_Lebens_stages_of_life_British_Library.jpg). The "Stages of a Woman's Life Cycle from Cradle to Grave" (ca. 1840) represents the linear iconography of the nineteenth century. It can also be viewed at *Wikipedia* (https://commons.wikimedia.org/wiki/File:11-stages-womanhood-1840s.jpg). Notice its linear, stair-step iconography, with middle age as the peak of life, in contrast to the iconography of the De Lisle Psalter above.

Chapter 14

A helpful online review of self-portraiture with excellent examples and discussions is *Wikipedia*'s "Self-Portrait" page (http://en.wikipedia.org/wiki/Self-portrait). The experiential impacts on time perception are reviewed in J. M. Tien and J. P. Burnes, "On the Perception of Time: Experiential Impact," *IEEE Transactions on Systems, Man and Cybernetics, Part A: Systems and Humans* 32, no. 6 (2002): 768–73. A very useful summary of philosophical views on aging is Patrick L. McKee's *Philosophical Foundations of Gerontology*.

A comprehensive review of the effects and impacts of interpersonal relationships is *Mind, Body, Health: The Effects of Attitudes, Emotions, and Relationships*, by Keith J. Karren, N. Lee Smith, and Kathryn J. Gordon. It details how strong, stable relationships protect our health and promote our well-being. The Mark Twain quote comes from "Old Times on the Mississippi," published in the *Atlantic Monthly* in 1874. An interesting and informative review of aging lessons in fairy tales is Allan B. Chinen's *In the Ever After: Fairy Tales and the Second Half of Life*.

George E. Vaillant shares excellent information on interpersonal relationships and creative retirement in *Aging Well: Surprising Guideposts to a Happier Life from the Landmark Harvard Study of Adult Development*. It covers scientific evidence on what successful aging is and how we can achieve it. The strong influence of Simone de Beauvoir's *Coming of Age* also is evident in this chapter.

Chapter 15

Practical resources on dealing with stress and anxiety are in *Minding the Body, Mending the Mind*, by Joan Borysenko, and *How to De-stress Your Life*, by Gregory L. Jantz. Each book contains suggestions for dealing with a variety of negative inner states from anxiety to burnout. The Zen stories can be found at the website Zen Stories to Tell Your Neighbors (http://truecenterpublishing.com/zenstory/zenstory.html). Thoughtful observations on achieving harmony can be found in

The Course of the Seeker, by Omar Ali-Shah, a series of edited transcripts of a Sufi teacher. Paul Ekman's books that informed me on the emotional basis of facial expression are *Emotions Revealed: Recognizing Faces and Feelings to Improve Communication and Emotional Life*, by Paul Ekman, and *Unmasking the Face: A Guide to Recognizing Emotions from Facial Expressions*, by Paul Ekman and Wallace V. Friesen. Daniel H. Pink's *A Whole New Mind: Why Right-Brainers Will Rule the Future* shared several ways to increase empathy.

Chapter 16

My thinking about long-term care has evolved over the past thirty years, strongly influenced by firsthand experience. Robert L. Kane has been a visionary in this area, and much of this chapter draws from his works. An example is *It Shouldn't Be This Way: The Failure of Long-Term Care*, by Kane and Joan C. West, available online at http://muse.jhu.edu/books/9780826591944. In addition, the chapter contains insights from "Mainstreaming Elderly People," an entry that Nortin M. Hadler and I wrote for Maggie Majar's *Health Beat* blog (http://www.healthbeatblog.com/2010/07/mainstreaming-elderly-people/), and from a paper I coauthored with Jonathan Evans titled "Caring for Our Future Selves," published in the *American Journal of Medicine* 117, no. 7 (2004): 537–40).

Chapter 17

Death and transcendence are principal themes in the works of mythologist Joseph Campbell. I have been inspired by his books *The Hero with a Thousand Faces*, *The Masks of God*, *Transformations of Myth through Time*, and, with television journalist Bill Moyers, *The Power of Myth*. The conversation between Moyers and Campbell captured in the 1988 video series *The Power of Myth* on the Public Broadcasting System was for me a major personal epiphany.

Wikipedia provides a useful summary of apoptosis and programmed cell death (http://en.wikipedia.org/wiki/Apoptosis) and an online summary of funeral customs among religious and ethnic groups (http://en.wikipedia.org/wiki/Funeral). The landmark works by Elisabeth Kübler-Ross are *On Death and Dying: What the Dying Have to Teach Doctors, Nurses, Clergy and Their Own Families* and *Questions and Answers on Death and Dying*.

Chapter 18

The website Gibran (http://leb.net/gibran) provides an archive of the works of Kahlil Gibran. The Middle Eastern proverb comes from the works of Idries Shah (see http://idriesshahfoundation.org/).

Index